My Sea
is
Wide

Rowland Evans

But I, being poor, have only my dreams;
I have spread my dreams under your feet;
Tread softly for you tread on my dreams.

'He Wishes for the Cloths of Heaven' – W.B. Yeats

Sunpenny Publishing

My Sea is Wide

This book is based on the author's own experiences, some elements of stories that he has borrowed from others, and documented legends. Some characters and events are composites, rather than being founded on any one person or incident. Names, dates and certain identifying characteristics, such as dialogue and details, have been changed, reconstructed or omitted, except when explicity stated, to protect the privacy of individuals.

Sunpenny Publishing
United Kingdom
www.sunpenny.com

Text copyright © 2009 by Rowland Evans
Cover illustration © 2009 by Alex Pribnow
Cover design © 2009 by Sunpenny Publishing

All rights reserved

ISBN 978-0-9555283-4-7

FIRST EDITION: 2009
Printed in the United Kingdom

Other books by Rowland Evans:
45 Minutes in China

Endorsements for "My Sea Is Wide"

Rowland Evans portrays, with bardic skill, the journey into meaning that we all face. He combines the earthiness of his soldier background with the vision of a poet. His unrelenting honesty is tempered by the beauty he sees in the forms and faces in his homeland Wales, and in the mystery yet humanity he explores in little known stretches of China and Tibet. The contemplative steps of the inner journey weave a rich tapestry around a fascinating travelogue. He points to landmarks in our humanity, and, though we may have seen them on many occasions, we gasp at what they now reveal. Rowland allows us to come with him into his new beginning. His gentle humour often probes the meaning behind the bizarre. He has the ability to see beyond the overwhelming, to the individual, interpreting to us the value of each life. He writes of layers of realities, often provoking more questions than answers. Through his search, his excitement, his pain, and ultimately his faith in the One who will allow him to be totally who he is, we are strengthened a little to face our own new beginnings.

—*Gail Dixon*, *Director, Nations Trust*

It is a rare privilege to be allowed into the inner workings of an artist's soul. No less expressive than the delicately crafted Chinese characters that he describes ... this glimpse into how faith and dreams combine with weakness and vulnerability to build history. Drink deeply – Rowland's honest account of his relentless pursuit of God's purposes in this world will surely inspire and challenge you to find and navigate your own "Wide Sea".

—*Neil Rees*, *International Director, World Horizons*

I believe that there is no great man of God, there is just a man who walks with a GREAT GOD. Praise our God who lives in this ordinary man. You can sense his humble and wise attitude from the very first page of this book. Rowland is a living example who has a passion for God and compassion for the nations. If you were looking for a mentor or model for your life as a missionary, this is IT!

—*Maria Jin*, *Journalist*, New Wine Magazine, *South Korea*

Rowland Evans is a man of character and wide experience who has sought to put pen to paper and record one challenging year of his life – his seventieth. The story is fascinating, full of the unexpected and at times unbelievable events that happen to any person who places their life's destiny into the hands of the One-True Living God. Rowland, with the spirit of a true Welshman, has done just that, and given back to the world some of the gift of life he has received. The story makes compelling reading for those who love something different, and is full of the beauty of a special place (Wales) that exists in the nations of the world.

—*Dr Kevin Dyson, President of New Covenant International University and Seminary, Lake Worth, USA*

Rowland's book is imaginative, poetic and descriptive. It falls between several genres: travel book, spiritual guide and autobiography. I felt as though I was walking the streets of China and Wales with him. Most of all I found it deeply challenging, as Rowland unfolds the story of the destiny of a nation and his part in it. A must-read for all those who feel they have come to the end of the road. There is more!

—*Gareth Jones, UK Director, World Horizons*

Very powerful, and the power accumulates as it progresses, which is as it should be.

—*Bill Davis, author*

The writing stimulated my imagination and your allegorical, symbolic and indirect description impressed me like poetry. You tried not to confront but indirectly corrected the reader's understanding. I was able to read in you a blend between Hudson Taylor's aggressive spirit and Henry Nouwen's contemplative spirit.

—*Miss Jong Sook Ahn, Editor of Plus Life, published by David Yonggi Cho of Yoido Full Gospel Church, Korea*

Contents

Foreword

Rowland Evans was born into a steelworker's family in the small South Wales town of Morriston in 1936. He left school at thirteen, more or less abandoned educationally because of his dyslexia, a condition of which little was known in those days. He first found employment as a milk-roundsman's helper, moving on to do a similar job for a local baker, before going to work in the poisonous atmosphere of the tin house in the tin works. He then entered an apprenticeship as a motor mechanic but left after three years to join the regular army and immediately began to thrive within its austere framework.

Rowland saw service in Malaysia during the troubles and suffered badly from malaria following a mosquito bite. It was during this time that he began to experience a profound personal transformation and change in outlook. It was only much later, with the help of a military medical orderly, that he came to recognise this as an experience of personal faith.

On his return to Britain, he left active service but continued as a Reservist. He was grateful to the army for imbuing him with a sense of self-worth, for discipline and for the comfort and camaraderie of his fellow soldiers. As a soldier, he regarded himself as a peacemaker and not as a killing machine. All these factors were to play an important part in his later life.

He returned to his home town, but deeply felt the loss of army life. Within two years he left Wales to take up a position with a full-time Christian organisation, and for the following fourteen years he regarded this as a time of education and missionary preparation. Wales beckoned again, this time to the town of Llanelli where around him gathered a group of younger people who shared his missionary interests. This group proved to be the nucleus of what became a world wide mission known as *World Horizons* with himself as director. He was rather bemused by being recognised as the head of the organisation because, although he had his dyslexia under control by this time, he was now surrounded by many professional people and more academically-gifted supporters. It was a mark of the respect in which he was held that such people should insist that he was the man to lead the movement.

To accommodate students for training as missionaries, Rowland bought up several buildings in the seaside area of Llanelli which were left empty when the town lost its heavy industries. Thousands of students from all parts of the world have passed through their portals and many have achieved high honours on the mission fields of their choice.

In later years he came to realise that in spite of its continuing success in the mission field, *World Horizons* might not be able to fulfill the furthest reach of his vision since it was European-based and multi-national in its outlook and structure. He went on to found a second missionary group called *Nations*. This sister move-ment is based on the work of indigenous people who know exactly what is required in each particular area. Rowland gave up the leadership of *World Horizons* when he founded *Nations* fifteen years ago.

Now, in his early seventies, having gained several degrees and a doctorate despite his dyslexia, he has somewhat curtailed his travels around the world but has reserved to himself his favourite territories, which were one of his earliest childhood dreams; China, Tibet and Central Asia. He has already completed nearly twenty years of missionary development there. It is China which occupies most of this book, though there are references to other parts of the world, and China with its obvious dangers and its serious problems of homelessness, especially among the young and aged, is of great concern to Rowland. Many hundreds of Christians languish in jails and, though he would never admit it, Rowland can sometimes take his life into his hands when he is there.

I first came to know Rowland in 1994 when he joined the Llanelli Writers' Circle, of which I have the honour to be President. He came over as a shy, almost diffident person but I soon realised that he was a man possessed of a tremendous depth of feeling. He had published no writing by this time but, within a year, his book *45 Minutes in China* had appeared and we suddenly knew a lot more about him. In *My Sea is Wide*, which covers a much wider canvas, he expresses his love for Wales and shows how its history and its landscape have shaped his perception of life. This leads us on to accompany him on his journey of self-discovery in which his incredible adventures are often tinged with his consciousness of Welshness which is so important to him. He is proud of the fact that Llanelli has adopted him and he has a real affection for the town and its people.

It is difficult to place the book in any particular genre in the same way that it is impossible to place Rowland in any particular pigeon-hole. He himself describes the book as a journey of self-discovery. That journey is described in detail which is minutely observed with a poet's eye. Take, for instance, his description of a tiny Welsh lake: *'Tall reeds grow where an underground spring chuckles out its fresh water'*, or *'the nightly celebration of swallows that skimmed low over the water'*. This is not just poetic prose; this is pure poetry.

He also has a flair for narrative and where this is found, it always rings true. Rowland's philosophy is unique. In a meeting with an allotment holder, he says: *'Wil knew the value of silence. He knew that deep things are seldom shared by words but lie in the silence between them or even in silence itself.'* His concept of Dream appears to allow him to inhabit a parallel existence and takes him close to an existentialist position, as in: *'It raised a question I had already answered but was yet to find the courage to ask.'*

This is a remarkable book which I would urge you to read and ponder. It is totally inspiring – like Rowland himself.

—*John Edwards M Ed; BA (Hons):* Historian, Lecturer, Broadcaster, Editor, Author, Honorary President of the National Eisteddfod 2000, and Founding President of the Llanelli Writers' Circle.

Introduction
by Gail Dixon, Director, Nations Trust

Every individual's journey is unique, and yet there are landmarks we all recognise. Rowland Evans is now in his seventies, and still relishes the adventure of launching into the unknown. This book is a small part of his own journey. The contemplative steps of the inner journey weave a rich tapestry around a fascinating travelogue. Even in the far flung corners of the globe, he points to landmarks in our humanity, and, though we may have seen them on many occasions, we gasp at what they now reveal.

Rowland has always had the ability to do that for me. I met him first when I was a student. He was running expeditions to North Africa, at least that is what I thought. For him, he was opening a doorway for each student to embark on a lifelong adventure. His own passion to beat a lonely trail of discovery, and perhaps especially self-discovery, has been contagious to generations of young people, not just from the UK, but from Korea, China, Africa, and elsewhere.

Some of his sayings have stuck with me over the years, and helped to form the way I now think. I know I am not alone in this. Maybe if I share some with you, you will catch what I mean.

'Impossible is just an opinion'

'Pray outrageous prayers, because God is bigger than our wildest imagination'

'If you like it, it's a bonus'

'Live by dying'

'Listen to what is being said between the words'

'Prayer is answer'

'Find the paving stone where God is and stand there with him'

'Ask God, "What's the greatest thing I can do for you today?"'

Perhaps you can hear the army background, but also the poet and the dreamer? The mechanic and the man of faith?

He is the founder of two movements, both out-workings of his longing to express what he has discovered as true LIFE. *World Horizons* and *Nations* are registered charities in Britain. The former is a multinational mission movement with over 500 workers around the world, enhancing the lives and well-being of thousands of others; the latter, a small group who are nurturing and enabling young mission movements in Asia and Africa to develop according to the dreams they find unfolding in their own hearts.

This book is not an account of his life and achievements; maybe someone else will write that. It is an honest continuation of his search for full meaning. Rowland allows us to come with him into what is for him a new beginning. In his search, his excitement, his pain, we recognise the landmarks, and are a little strengthened to face our own new beginnings.

He reminisces too, and invites us into his recent journeys. It is at times uncomfortable, and definitely not a page turner. However, if you will read with your heart, and let the spaces between the words find expression, maybe a revelation of meaning will come to you.

Rowland pointed out to us that another translation of the first verse of the gospel of John could read, *'In the beginning was the meaning'*.

Maybe all our searching will bring us back to our beginning, and this time we will understand it.

Dedicated
to those
who have
weathered many years
and who ask the question
"Is there anything left
... to Dream?"

Dream is the miracle
All else is just making it happen

A Note from the Author

I love Wales. I have not found it difficult to overhear the song of its earth and to veer away from discordant notes. I am a product of its history, and the energy that simmers in its landscape has shaped my perception of life. Its vibrancy I owe to the many before me who faithfully made their way to destiny's moments and fully occupied them. They have added a rich quality of humanity to our nation's wealth. In my ripening years I wish my writings to honour the land that has borne me and to return a little of what it has unstintingly shared with me. I would like to show how its hidden vitality has enriched other nations; sometimes as crisp fresh springs amongst rocks and stones; at other times through streams that run slowly in deep channels, carrying heavy cargoes that have helped to sustain the courage of many. Without hint of triumphalism it has taken pride in its anonymity: to be unseen and unknown is its virtue.

My pencil seems to have travelled miles across paper through endless revision while writing this book, yet it has been a discipline I have learnt to love. I have waded across literary rivers strange to me and found them to be six inches higher than my wellington boots. I have often lamented the quality of my courage to tear away the insulating layers of dishonesty that cocoon my human heart. For the mayfly brevity of life has seemed too short to allow a leisurely search for the purity of writing I long for.

So this account of my personal reconciliation to life beyond my seventieth year is unlikely to fit easily into a recognised genre. Yet I would be honoured to have your company on this journey of self-discovery that most of us will need to make. Then, perhaps for the first time, we shall understand that learning about ourselves is the forgotten reason for our being here.

Acknowledgements

To Steve and Kathy   whose seamless hours
of typing, correcting, encouraging,
advising and editing
glow with deep devotion to Another
far greater than myself

To Gail   whose patient tuition
has helped me change
the nuts and bolts
of rusty words
into the timeless music of poetry

To Meri   whose ability to see in Welsh
has enriched with Celtic colour
my pale landscape

To Bill   whose prolific writing skills
have taught me how to tame
the wild stallions among my images
and to present them with the manners
of refined English

To John Edwards &
Carole Smith   whose selfless encouragement
through the Writers' Circle
has opened doors
to the literary world

To Maria

A Korean writer and friend
who taught me how to transform
the discipline of writing
into a love of the finished work

To my many
Chinese friends

whose smiles
welcome me to 'Shen Zhou'
their ancient Land of God
that I am hungry to explore

To Anne

for nearly fifty years
my wife, whose quiet faith
has tracked my steps
to help bring the impossible
within reach

And I ...

as willing apprentice
work to learn their skills
and with fumbling hands
and unsteady eye
attempt to chisel words
from uncut stone

Thank you – Rowland

PROLOGUE
- The Poet -

In time's frame of earth and sky, the Poet dreamed a garden, a riot of colour that flamed with light. From its humble soil we came and, in the rhythm of his poem's lines, we have lived and loved and searched its deeper meanings.

Without life, death has no existence; so, from among the many worlds, it chose ours to make its home and, in the shadows that surrounded our births, prepared its bloodied altar.

So life has become a tension between beginning and ending, living and dying, its nature forever changed.

So the Poet wrote himself into his lines and, in the language of love understood by every human race, laid himself upon that altar taking our place.

So our story is no longer written on flat slate. Life has brought height, death has given depth and dream transcends beginning and ending.

His poem reunites us with ourselves and with his dream. In the wildness of life, with shalom restored, among the possibilities that wait our exploration, is an end to the greatest tragedy to wound our favoured earth ... a life that is unlived.

Among the lame I follow the procession. Without hiding place I wait at judgement's gate where you have stood and watched.

Will you tell me if my Wild Goose flies, and where I may find my Wide Sea?

Shalom Restored

WHEN SKIES SWIM GOLD
- When Dreams End -

At an age when young men become restless and their explorations into life are confusing, I began a courtship with the army. After Japanese forces surrendered the Malay Peninsula, Communist guerrillas flowed into the vacuum. National wounds were reopened. I entered the conflict and grew up.

One among hundreds of raw soldiers, I learned to believe in my role. It gave me purpose. I enjoyed the pride of belonging to a regiment and the camaraderie of dedicated men. I glowed with admiration at the veterans of the Korean War. I understood the morality of military presence. We were not a killing machine, but an international police force.

As belief in myself grew, unexpectedly a personal faith grew comfortably alongside it, and years later I came to know Malaysia well, and experienced the dramatic changes their freedom bought.

So I am a Welshman who at eighteen became a soldier and who, without intention, then became a missionary. The uncompromising military environment gave me stability, motivation; and its discipline provided a vehicle for my beliefs.

I followed my passion and I closed my eyes to all else.
When I opened them, fifty years had stormed into history.

For five decades of hammer-on-rock existence I pursued an ideal that placed a force of many hundreds of men and women of many nationalities in some of the most unlikely parts of the world, there to carve out a future. Their quiet presence is helping to build a positive history.

Yet as I wake to my seventieth year, the past seems to be adrift from its moorings. I am a breath of time almost over. Friends talk avoiding my eyes, and choose words as if I am not there. Friendly small talk becomes filled with airy, conversational nothingness. I occupy a space but have no value.

The little boy in me sits in the centre of an empty room and cries bitterly, abandoned, not knowing why or where he is. He still longs to pursue his dream, yet age has become the barrier to its fulfilment.

I reel under the shock of my seventy years. A chasm yawns between myself and the younger men and women I have lived to love. They are excited, at the dawn of their personal futures as they explore among the fragile mists that drift over faith's pathway; but I am tired in the evening of my long day.

My grandchildren become distant as they mature into individuals. We reverse roles, and I am the infant in their worlds. I build a defence. I quieten my thoughts so that new realities do not add to my hurt. I learn to use my eyes to distance myself, while I slide beneath the familiar soil of questioning.

As a personal celebration of reaching seventy, I make a lone ascent of South Wales' highest mountain. I am comfortable on the roof of my world. Here, horizons are further out. There is space to think, and to escape the expectation of my culture that subtly feeds me with thoughts of uselessness: sunshine holidays, slippers and endless cups of tea; an illusion of life, abandoned by progress. My shell may be present, but inwardly I am absent.

Under this arch of cold sky and steaming breath, memories flood warm ... an attic room in a house I was attempting to buy, its scant furniture no more than a small table, a hard chair, some etchings of chained African slaves and an atmosphere of sadness. It was the study of John Newton, the slave trader who became a priest. It was in this room that he enshrined his experience by writing the words of the hymn, *Amazing Grace*.

It was not his passion for the abolition of the slave trade that moved me, but a strong sense of his unfinished prayer for African destiny. In thick silence and with wet eyes, I knelt and added my name to those who would attempt to stand in the space he had vacated, and to bring his passion to a conclusion.

The little boy in me continues to cry. Perhaps there is a parallel. In the wide space of the mountain I want to commit myself to the unfulfilled dream of my younger self that lies beyond the chasm my advanced age has opened. The Welsh language has a beautiful description of the seventieth year – *oes yr addewid*, which can be translated 'the age of promise'.

During the turbulent year that follows, I discover that circumstances are no kinder to me than they have been. In fact, I find many new challenges that need to be painfully borne. The emotional and physical struggle to bring to completion a half century of intense building, and to forge a new beginning, has been extremely harsh, leaving me feeling raw and unprotected.

The Chinese language has delicately crafted characters that describe every human emotion, among them an ancient character called *tun*, that accurately describes my own. Its written form shows a fragile shoot breaking through crusty earth. It would not survive except for a strong supporting root that lies hidden below the ground. Not surprisingly, the character means 'a new beginning'. The root that remains out of sight is the scene of intense activity. A single plant can produce a million or more microscopic hair roots, which thrive in the darkness and guarantee the growth of the shoot. Just as all life follows nature's season of rest and growth, I want to stay connected to the root embedded in eternal purpose along which the future unfolds.

As my exploration has practical and spiritual elements, I hold conversations within myself and sometimes refer to the other part of myself as 'you'. So 'you' and 'I' travel through my troubled inner geography, while outwardly exploring a variety of landscapes and mingling with many different races.

I could not have predicted how, in a few months, the concept of the future being as open and wide as the sea would become obvious to me.

MY SEA IS WIDE
- The Atlantic -

I feel at ease with old things that do not threaten me with new technologies. My car fits easily into this category. It is not yet a classic car, but polishes to a head-turning shine and is slow, comfortable and reliable. When I have the opportunity for a holiday, my pleasures are equally simple. If I am unable to borrow a friend's cottage in the remoteness of an Aegean island, then I love to visit France; not the end-to-end concrete strip that edges the Mediterranean, but the quiet inland regions of mountains, valleys, rivers and lakes. The brassy hotels with sun-cream swimming pools and plastic chairs have no appeal to me either, but relatively unvisited municipal campsites. Here the scent of grass, wet with dew, mingles with a hint of garlic from open-air cooking, and the music of the French language, the comedy of old men at boules, and a daily charge that does not make me want to cry, bring indescribable warmth into my soul.

It was at the close of a visit to the Dordogne that my faithful Rover became ill. It had burnt both exhaust valves in an overheating cylinder. Local agents chuckled among themselves when, in clumsy French, I asked if they had replacements. There was no alternative but to pay the high season price of a car ferry from Caen to Portsmouth. The remaining three cylinders functioned well enough to enable me to drive back to Wales. Beyond this, however, was the trace of a stray thought: that my old friend, Rover, was an accomplice in an episode I would not have planned, for I would never have been able to foresee the outcome ...

I feel a chill in the air. I move towards one of the funnels that tower above the open deck, and stand with my back to a ventilation grill. Rising with the heat are the sounds and smells of the diesel engines, the throbbing heart of the ship some twelve decks below. The sweating, half-stripped firemen with blackened faces shovelling Welsh coal into the boiler furnaces are just nostalgic notions now.

I am alone, the sea is wide ... an uncluttered space where horizon melts into the sky. The sky and the sea are two sisters. Whatever colour the sky wears, the sea follows. Today the colour is blue and the far edges are lightened by a touch of white mist.

Though the large propellers lever us through the solid water at twenty knots, the space occupied by the ship does not elongate. As the horizon opens before us it closes behind us, giving the impression that we are standing still. We too move through time, always occupying the same amount of space, though time's horizons are far closer in and as we enter one moment another closes, and its possibilities vanish. Nothing stands still.

It is the long wake that runs out behind the ship that gives it its sense of movement: two humps of violently-thrashed water with a foaming valley between. They flatten out to the width of the hull and taper into the distance until reclaimed by the saw-edged waves.

This stream of fractured water marks our progress. It is able to reflect light in a profusion of directions. It can be reassuring or condemning, as it accurately records before the witness of the sky every command from the bridge and every deviation by the helmsman.

If I am not careful I shall do what all old men are good at. They stand, stare and reminisce. It is as if I have been asleep and my past, like an Australian dreamtime, almost does not exist. But the water my life has troubled carries the wake of my history, its progress and deviations, from the horizon over which I appeared.

Now that I have been shocked into action by young voices that call me 'grandfather', my quest is to know how to take advantage of the years left to me. I am a privileged guest into this favoured world, yet this fact also reminds me that at some point I need to leave my space here to another. So to unlock my remaining years and to live in them with the dignity of a lifetime's preparation is important to me.

This wide sea is restful but it is not bland. Its surface has a unique texture. It is patterned by wavelets. They may be just inches high, and their swirls and eddies serve only the whims of the wind. Yet each wave's short life has a wake that records its history and a translucent crest that emits light. When the sun is low behind them a unique transformation takes place, for each one disappears into its own shadow yet, in the same instance, diffuses the sun's rays into a million points of light which intensify the beam that fingers towards me. I am staggered by how intricately hints of the spiritual are woven into nature.

It is then I notice that, regardless of the passage of the ship and the direction of the wind, below the disturbance of the wavelets there are watery hills in the sea that seem to march in ranks with military precision and purpose, as if following some predetermined route towards a distant shore. The lesser wavelets do no more than to pattern their surface with the texture of the sea.

Yet there is power in their purpose. As the hundreds of tonnes of water displaced by our ship's hull move outwards, they form their own watery hills which impact the marching ranks with the fury of attacking forces. Neither giving place to the other, they volcano upwards, scattering the sea to the wind. Without the caging effect of land, the sea has room for wildness.

Suddenly we are not alone in our space. A large black-hulled vessel is approaching diagonally. If it stays on course it will pass under our stern. The identifying name of *Hanjin* is painted in large letters along its sides. Its decks are stacked five high with shipping containers, its bridge scarcely higher. As it ploughs through our wake there is a clash of histories ... and ours is destroyed. Something of value has disappeared forever.

When we are uncertain of where we have come from we drift, for we become unsure of who we are and so have no 'inner knowing' of where we should be heading.

When the cooling embers in the sky die and there is neither moon nor stars, the sea becomes black. Only the throb of the diesel engines tells me that we are still underway, but just to be going somewhere does not necessarily mean progress. Tomorrow morning the sky will light again and, though it may still be an angry red, the sun will be in a different place. If we do not realise this and treat all things as they were when we entered our night, then we will be travelling a pathway back down through our own history.

So this is a personal story of a search for a way through the labyrinth of ordinary life. In particular it is a search for the purpose which wisdom has withheld from me until I trust the validity of my inner life, and age has distanced me from the erratic path of youthful ideals.

The demons I face are not the insidious visitors from another dark world, but those conjured by the set of my own mind. My culture has created a negative hierarchy of things I cannot do and goals I cannot achieve. The temptation has been to put these things first, and everything else nowhere. They are like brain implants with a circuitry wired to trick me into believing that decline is the only aspect of change open to me. Any thought to the contrary would be a violation of the privilege of living and an unforgivable act of overcompensation for my age.

Today the doors I try to open are stiff through lack of use, yet behind them waits my wide space, and perhaps the most fulfilling period of my life. I have no wish to remain just a disturbance on the surface of the water, while at another level purpose marches on to its proper conclusion.

Most of all, I do not want to lose my sense of personal history to the intrusion of the Western cultural concept of mature years, for which there is no real answer apart from a seat on the bus and a subtle return to childhood in everything but appearance.

My history has helped form my identity. Whether acceptable or not, it is a record of what I am and is the only starting point to what I can be. So from here I take the first steps into my biggest challenge yet ...

WHERE REALITIES MERGE
- Reflections on Llanelli Shore -

Llanelli is the small town which has adopted me. Although just twelve miles distant from where I was born, the cultural difference and the local Welsh accent made me and everyone else I knew believe that the Llanelli community was 'different' in an uncomplimentary way. It was rumoured that hidden among its decaying megaliths of exhausted copper, tin and ironworks, coal pits and potteries, there was a market that sold cockles, laverbread (boiled seaweed), and red rugby shirts which boys wore on their initiation into manhood. Black suits mourned Sundays and ladies dusted respectable hats. Children were locked in parlours and gazed hungrily through the windows at empty park swings. Strangest of all, men sang a local anthem to a small saucepan!

Clearing the industrial legacy of its Tinopolis years and recovering its beautiful coastline is evidence of the town's brave new face. To keep alive its eccentric heritage, developers have covered its waterfront greenery with exquisite imitations of communist bloc flats. These have at least inspired work-clothed, flat-capped pensioners to reminisce of war years' barrack rooms or allotment sheds, while visitors look on in silent embarrassment ... or is it disbelief?

After forty years of loving and despairing over this anomalous town, I have grown to accept its place and character as an essential part of the wider South Wales heritage. It is as if this land has sought to keep alive the memory of its people's search for a spiritual and practical significance, however diversely this has been expressed.

The history of the hills, valleys and coast are like a series of overlaid maps that chart our quest for an answer to our sense of alienation, through megalithic monuments, bronze- and iron-age forts; through the monasteries of the Middle Ages, church spires, lonely chapels; and through revival years. Above all else for my modest ambitions, this small, untidy town has been the gateway to a land willing to yield up its secrets to those who search for truth.

I screw my eyes against the light, and search the horizon. I am rewarded. Where a desert of sand runs to meet the bottom of the sky, a crisp white line of tide holds both apart. Rippling and pulsating with energy, it thrashes the ancient glacial debris at the limit of its retreat into the Irish Sea.

From the crescent above the earth, the signal for the invasion of this seemingly endless field of sand is given. In hours the tide's shock waves will reach inland along a river that flows light through the lonely hills of Pontarddulais. Meanwhile the occupying flood will wash against the defending sea walls.

I have a great fondness for this estuary. It is not a harsh, dry Gobi, for the clear waters of the river Loughor spread across it thinly on its way to the sea. I walk on the wet sand to meet it, and I see another wonder: the shallow, moving water is reflecting the sky. I can walk in the river and walk in the sky. Both are real, but one is a reflection of the other; yet the reflection itself is also real.

From the sand I put one foot into the clear, cool water. The blue sky closes around my ankle and fluffy white clouds move against the current. The sun radiates back itself. It is not a trillion miles away, but just ten centimetres from my foot. In cupped hands I scoop up the sun, yet it also remains in the water. Without growing less, it seems eager to give itself away, but slowly in tear-drops it leaks back. Like borrowed memories, they are restored to their place.

The sky is disturbed by the tears; it ripples blue, flashes light, and the sun trembles. So many complementary realities coexist in one moment of time. The river is running to the sea, the sea steps out in response, and I walk in the sky.

Across this silvered ribbon and sand, a horizon of low hills that frame the estuary finger towards the encroaching, foaming tide.

When Atlantic mists fill this watery space the hills look detached from the land. Today it is clear.

I look up at movement in the sky. Two large birds are hugging the contours of the land and sea. They flow through the saddle in the hills; their turbines whine, their propellers bend the air. The Herculean lords of technical progress are on their regular surveillance training flights. They fly low over the stones that stand in nature's symmetry, tall with the ambitions of prehistoric pride. Undaunted by ten thousand storms, older than Egypt's pyramids, they stridently reach towards the 'planes. Each a monument to human instinct thrusting hard against the limits of their knowledge, each forced apart by the extreme ends of time; yet together they lie silent in the water.

The sea wall invites me; a place to sit and let imagination soar. Heavy timbers crafted by the weather; their feel, their scent in the salt air, work to their designer's dream. They raise thoughts of tall-masted, wooden-hulled schooners moving through the harbour mouth.

I try to close down my inner senses to the sounds of the rolling mill and iron works that a century ago boiled the sea with their waste, to the smoke stacks that killed the air, to the rumble of coal drams in the forgotten network of mine shafts under land and sea which, since Roman times, slowly rise to the surface. The blackened ruins of the former glory of Tinopolis have given way to the clear air and green, flowing landscape. Yet in defiant disregard of time, both powerful images overlap ... if only in me. The heavy bench seat welcomes me, the strong beams at my back inspire security. In the warm sun images of multi-tiered realities, separated by thousands of years and thousands of miles, swim together in a molten sky and sea.

Once, above red dust where the air was crisp and thin, the source of the great River Nile trickled through a rock and chimed through my hands. It reflected a different sky. History and future spun together in a fine thread of water. How long will it take the droplets my hands have touched to reach the sea ... and to return?

Amid this ambience of created wonder where my tomorrows may be easily counted, I must find meaning for my years or become marooned somewhere in an experiment called time.

Enthusiastic hope raises many fanciful routes to the future. I am fortunate; there seems to be a route that I think has chosen me. The horizon appears to be open; there is uncluttered space to follow my dream.

Yet I am troubled. At times, life has been unkind and I have felt splintered on its sharp edges. It is as if I need to come home to myself and to reunite with my young years, and perhaps step closer to the recovery of personal wholeness.

I reach into my rucksack for my notepad, and from memory borrow a fragment of ancient wisdom and quote from its widest meaning:

Yn dechreuad roedd y ... Freuddwyd.
In the beginning was ... the Dream

FIGURE ON THE BROW
- Clasemont -

Dream has gentle restorative power. It can bring the quiet strength of wholeness into a fragmented existence. It is able to interpret strands from the past that stabilise the present, and to be the architect of the future.

Portrait of an Old Man

I enter the veiled corridor of the past, to where memories of the dawn of my childhood days are framed, for I wish to be reunited with my young self and to rediscover the honesty of a simple desire to live once more in the purity of youthful dreams, and uncomplicated hope.

If I can do this, then I think that I will satisfy *hiraeth*, the longing which my advancing years has awakened, and will reignite the dying embers of my inner fire. Indelible in my memory of Wales are its gentle hills, just high enough to make secret the many tiny lakes they shelter and nourish.

Today I stand at memory's shrine and recall the past through the uninhibited flair of young eyes. So, among the images of a youthful imagination, I look across the wave-bounced sunlight of a lake which, below a gentle hillside, has scoured for itself a home.

My eyes follow the shoreline. Its banks are firm, like miniature cliffs surrounding a Lilliput sea. Tall reeds grow where an underground spring chuckles out its fresh water.

I have been here before, I muse; *many times before.*

The crunch of pebbles beneath my feet regenerates thoughts of the end-to-end sunshine of childhood days. As the wavelets splash against the stones, I can feel the water teasing my young feet. I cup the water in my hands; it is flecked with the green algae I have disturbed. I once more enjoy the sensation of it running between my fingers.

I choose a grassy knoll as a seat. I breathe deeply the spiced offering released by my footprints on the grass, and enjoy its crisp feel under my hands. I reach out to a weather-bared stone. Its texture speaks its history to my fingers. It was here before I was born; it has witnessed my every visit; it has seen me grow old. It has heard every song sung by the wild wind to the water. I look at the artistry of the sun, the rain and the frost that have coloured and moulded its shape. It may have been rolled by the currents along some forgotten seabed. If this silent witness could speak of the centuries that have poured over it, I wonder which of its myriad stories it would choose to tell.

The small lake is known to the locals as the 'fish-pond', and for as long as any one remembers it has held carp in abundance. Today water birds dance to the rhythm of its waves. Others bob and dip on its pebbled beaches, drinking and splashing.

Through the diffused images of age my eyes struggle to focus on the brow of the hill. I am not going to be disappointed. My inner sense is alerting me to be patient and wait; for out of sight a small boy's journey has begun ...

Portrait of a Young Boy
Restlessness gripped his wiry figure. His tender years, just seven or eight. His short trousers, so long they covered his knees. His ill-fitting jumper, knitted from the unravelled yarn of an older garment. His socks, that wouldn't stay up, concertinaed above a pair of shoes resoled by his father and already grown old on someone else's feet. His untidy fair hair, bearing the scars of home haircuts. For these were the years of Europe's sorrow, and although the bared steel of the battle lines of war lay in France, the stress of need had awakened a home-grown courage which attempted skills that were dormant in less demanding times.

The boy could sense a new adventure, and was impatient to get on with it. From a secret hiding place in his bedroom he slid a small, flat package into his pocket. Carefree, he jogged and skipped down the hill, turning at his grandfather's house into the stony lane that ran between open fields with high hedges. Unconsciously his eyes searched for the views through the gaps; once he had spotted a dead aeroplane crashed in the field.

He walked past the freshwater spring where the local farmer washed his milk churns, where his family and neighbours drew water when the frost spiked their windows, and when the water pipes were smashed as German bombers roared from shell-pocked barrage-ballooned skies on their devastating attempts to destroy the town of Swansea.

The lane led on to a disused cottage, once a home to forgotten generations, its mossy-green walls crumbling, no longer supporting the decaying remains of its thatched crown. Its vegetable beds had surrendered to a tall weed known locally as 'Sally Rhubarb.' These broad-leafed canes grew taller than the boy. Among them, he and his friends made winding passages leading to dens where they could be alone to talk secret things, and to hide the green apples the abandoned trees still produced. As an act of initiation they would strip the skin off the fresh green Sally Rhubarb shoots, and eat them, never daring to admit defeat, or the extent of their revulsion.

Now the boy searched for last year's growth, fallen and hidden in the grasses. These dry canes were woody in colour, strong and light with bamboo-like segments. Back in the lane he squeezed through a hole in the maythorn hedge, into the buttercupped and purple-clovered field. He thrilled to the sound of the grass squeaking under his feet, and the scent of ripening earth.

From his pocket he began to unwrap his secret: a traditional single-edged razor blade. It had been discarded by his father, but he had salvaged it from the waste bin and carefully packaged it into the cardboard wrapping of the new blade. This was the tool that would help him transform his imagination into a present reality.

The wide open space and fresh wind in his hair fuelled the excitement as he carved one segment of the cane into the hull of a sail boat. Soon, with Skipper Jack at the helm, it would sail into a wild, wide ocean. It would have the freedom of the wind to carry it wherever it should go ...

I felt happy in my green sanctuary, surrounded by memories which opened before me like the pages of a much-loved book. I knew by heart the detail of what was happening, though I was in awe of the young boy's intuitive understanding of hull design and control of a model sail boat. I knew that the pointed corner of the razor blade would nick a tiny hole in the foredeck, and of his diversion to visit the stunted hawthorn tree to find feathers preened by roosting birds. One of these would match the hull size, fit into the notch on the foredeck, and become the sail. I knew that he would slot the razor blade into the hull's underside. It would be keel and rudder in one. By altering its angle slightly, the model would sail across the wind, and even in a large circle ... bringing it back to the point from which it was launched. I knew that he would need to view the craft on the water so that he could adjust its trim. Its bows needed to be slightly higher than the stern, to compensate for the wind's down-thrust on the sail.

The boy's work completed, he ran the final distance to the fish-pond. The sight of it, and the smell of cattle that watered there each evening, made him breathless. He thought it a fragment of paradise carved by nature's hand, a free inheritance to which his young soul had bonded.

At the water's edge he arranged the pebbles until they quickly became a harbour. With the trim adjusted, the keel angled, the naming ceremony over and the launch completed, he watched the sail gather the wind as the *Destiny* nudged into the swell at the harbour mouth.

The tiny vessel rolled in the confused water of the bay, then gathered speed as she headed into the crested, sunlit, dancing sea beyond ...

Portrait of a Mariner
Skipper Jack stood in the window of his cottage overlooking the bay. Unthinkingly, he caressed the binoculars that lay ready on the table. They had accompanied him through all his seafaring years and, like old friends, they were never far apart.

Jack Solomon Davies had been born into the poverty of a coal barge on the Vale of Neath canal, the home and workplace of the

Davies family. The harsh grip of the industrialists' iron hand lay firmly across the Welsh valleys. In the daily struggle for existence, the family had lost out to the advance of steam and iron rail, and coal barges became redundant.

His father, Llew Davies, had been forced to leave his family in the vain hope that the deep sea would provide for them. He did not return from the second voyage. At fourteen, young Jack took his place at sea.

In retirement, Jack's bearing of quiet authority reflected not just the discipline of the waves, but his early years of commitment to his dependant mother and siblings, alone in the biting, stark poverty of life in the Welsh valleys.

His white-washed stone cottage had been hewn out of the hillside many years before. He had to stoop to enter through the low front door into the stone slab-floored living room. His garden was a rockery of randomly collected, yet thoughtfully placed, stones. Between these, lavenders and heathers moved with the breath of the wind and fragranced the air. A hand-crafted driftwood fence, bleached white, with a gate just high enough to deter wandering sheep, enclosed the whole.

Jack pined for the sea. He missed the feel of the hull alive under his feet, and the thrill of bringing his vessel into a harmony with the energy of the wind and the restless movement of the swell. He thought he recognised the music that the sea was playing today.

A stone harbour nestled within the bay, and his gaze rested on its quiet water. In winter it was a defence against the remorseless westerlies that carved the coastline. Today, the water mirrored the sky which had closed around the clean lines of a wooden-hulled sail boat – his own vessel, lying at her moorings against the outer wall. She too was eager for the open sea, where she would be at home in the confused water of opposing currents and wave patterns.

We both need a troubled sea to reach our potential, thought the mariner. *Neither of us cares to be tied up too long.*

From the round table by his window he reached for his binoculars. The weak morning sunshine spliced through the rigging. The sight awoke in him the passion of an art lover. Captured in the water's reflected light, the gold leaf-embossed, carved bows flashed a single word ... *Destiny*.

An old wireless set behind him boomed out the shipping forecast. It seemed reluctant to give him the unqualified "okay" he had hoped for, yet still it signalled him to go. In the corner of the room his long-time sailing companion, instinctively aware of his mood, uncurled from the basket and whimpered softly at the door. His terrier, Mate, intuitively sensed when a voyage was about to begin.

He pulled the door closed and turned the key, gazing at it in his hand before pushing it deep into his sea bag, which he slung across his shoulder. Closing the front gate, he again looked back at his cottage, words coming easily into the silence.

"There is something different about our leaving this time, Mate."

Turning slowly, he followed Mate, who had scampered down the path to the harbour. Overhead the gulls complained loudly as they soared and wheeled. Like his sail boat, they too used currents of invisible air. The roar and sigh of the waves on the pebble beach, and the scent of drying kelp discarded by the tide, filled a space within his soul that had seemingly been created for them. Yet his love for the sea arose from something much deeper. The sea was where he found his personal meaning.

To his way of thinking, the voyage had already begun. He loved the lines of the craft that rose and fell on the gentle swell. For almost a hundred years its timbers had withstood the wash of the sea; a tribute to the keen eyes and deft hands of age-old craftsmen. He admired the sleek, Bermudan-rigged, slippery-hulled yachts that visited the bay during the summer months, but felt more at home with the sloop's oak timbers shaped by a carpenter's adze. He liked the bowsprit that reached for'ard enabling the large foresail to draw energy from the softest breeze. He felt confidence in the gaff-rigged mainsail that was not designed for speed, but had empowered heavy coastal traders for centuries. The only modern addition he had allowed himself was the small inboard diesel engine that helped him manoeuvre in port.

He busied himself with the ship's trim, its sails and mooring lines. *I'm not putting out for the cod*, he thought, *nor the bass, nor even the willing mackerel.* The conger eels among the deep-water wrecks were not his motivation either. *I am putting out to sea because I want to.*

His mind had begun to plot itself a course, and Mate's stumpy tail flagged his understanding of the skipper's decision.

The Squall

A trace of blue smoke escaped from the stern quarter as the single-cylinder diesel engine bumped into life and settled into its rhythmic, steady knock. The bows of the *Destiny* nudged into the swell at the harbour mouth. The playful breezes that followed the contours of the grey limestone headland fluffed out the sail enough to steady the roll. A confused sea began to tantalize the hull, and the old mariner interpreted its meaning through his feet. The swell, the wind, and the opposing tidal currents caused a build-up of turbulent water in the only navigable channel. Gusts teased the foresail, and he juggled the sheets. He had to keep it powering strongly if he were to hold his course through the choppy waters. There was little room for error.

The opaque water of the bay lay to the lee of the towering headland. He stalled the engine and hoisted a partially reefed mainsail. Ahead, an angry line of dark water etched the horizon. The strong offshore squall challenged an incoming swell from a distant Atlantic storm. Tremors in the masthead warned that the craft was rapidly approaching the turbulence. Astern, darkening the sky, a brooding cloud rose from behind the headland. Thunder rolled boulders over its roof. Lightning rippled in its dark belly. It seemed to be gnawing on the available light as it advanced.

Across the bows, the battle lines were drawn. The wind howled at the threatening swell. With flying spume from hooves that scalloped the water, a thousand wild-eyed wave stallions, breath steaming the air, galloped towards the ranks of the advancing green mountains. Flared nostrils snorting their defiance, terrifying in their purpose, the incoming waves broke under the weight of their charge.

Seizing the opportunity, the sloop heeled steeply as he brought her around and made for the gap. The heavy boom swung to port. The mainsail cracked open, rigid before the force of the following wind. As the bows plunged, a foaming torrent angled across the foredeck. The hull shuddered. In the cockpit well Jack felt its distress, and wrestled with the helm to avoid a broadside. Slowly the vessel rose as the water spilled from its decks. They were through the turbulence.

Around him the wind ripped streamers from the crests of the hysterical sea. He was making too much speed. The bows plunged once more, submerged under an unbroken sheet of green water as they surfed a following sea. The scuppers were insufficient to clear it. Swirling water reached his knees.

Too much canvas, he thought.

Roping the helm and clipping himself to a safety line, he moved forward to the mast. Braced against the pitching hull and the gusting wind, he let out the mainsail halyard and it ripped through his wet hands. He recoiled at the rope burn, and amid the wildly flapping canvas the gaff crashed against the low cabin roof. To run before the wind on the foresail seemed the best course, in the hope that the squall would abate with the same speed with which it had struck. He paid out spare mooring lines over the transom to act as sea anchors to slow him down and give some directional stability. Once out in quieter water, he would attempt to change course.

He had weathered many an Atlantic storm. This one, however, was different. It had risen unannounced from the north-east, a force eight maybe, with an icy Arctic feel to it. His hands had become numb, and the furious, spray-laced wind cut into his weathered face. Instinctively he turned around as, above the wind, he could hear the hiss of the next wave bearing down on him. He drew his head deeper into his storm hood. Tons of water cascaded over the stern. Shaking herself free, the stern began to rise and, as if tossed by some giant bull, the *Destiny* slid stern first down the back of the onrushing mountain before wallowing in the following trough.

Evening began to overtake the afternoon, and his hope rose as the sky lightened and visibility increased. He knew that he was miles off course, and his mind raced over the charts stored in his memory as he worked to fix his position. The waves had lost some of their disordered formation. Urged on by the wind, they were like serried ranks of a victorious army of giants marching on to the shore.

As visibility increased he expected a frost-crisp line of surf to come into view; yet more immediate, his seafaring instincts were alerting him to another danger. Above the shriek of the wind in the rigging and the hiss of the waves bearing down on him, his hands as they gripped the helm, his sodden feet in the deck well, and the bulkhead against which he steadied himself, were all signalling a message they demanded be heard:

There is insufficient depth of water beneath the keel to allow the rise and fall of a swell this tall.

His senses snapped into a single focus. He was aware of the offshore rocky shoals, but had been slow to recognise that he was now blown near them. The changing sound of the sea and the increasing height of the driving waves confirmed his fears.

A sudden jolt took the bows down sharply as the keel slammed into rock. He glanced behind him in the hope of finding precious seconds in which to attempt a manoeuvre, but what riveted his gaze was a threatening green wall descending on him with awesome purpose. As the stern began to lift, the keel stuck firmly in the hidden rock gully. With no forward progress possible, the pent-up power of the towering sea released its fury against the hull, flicking the stern around like a piece of driftwood. The *Destiny* lay full broadside to the wind and sea. Heeling over, her heavy keel lay horizontal across an ancient undersea peak. Her mast crashed into the boiling, foaming water, her foresail sodden, her stretched rigging hanging limply.

The next wave thundered in, raising the half submerged vessel. This time the hull timbers would take the full force of the rocks as she slid down into the next trough. The cockpit was awash with freezing water which tore through his clothing, wrapping icy fingers around his body.

Dazed, Jack had not fully realised the extent of the pain that stabbed at his chest. Automatically his hand grasped for his heart ... losing his hold on the helm. He thought he heard Mate whimpering below deck. He reached for the hatch as the next wave hit, but it wrenched itself from his grasp.

Water swirled into the cabin below.

The old mariner had often wondered how he would go. The sea had always been there to animate even his earliest memories. He had been indebted to it for his livelihood all his long and eventful life. Several times it had surged towards him as if jealous that his life could be shared with the land. Each time it had receded ... but now?

If it were calling for him, he would have no regrets. He had enjoyed the freedom of its deserted space and learned to live with its wild moods, each one filling him with excited wonderment, each voyage an adventure into the unknown. He had discovered himself as he explored the sea. It seemed as if they were twins in the same womb. He had never been parted from the sea and had always hoped that it would be in its company that he would make his final journey.

He did not call himself a religious man. He had tried the recognised forms of religion, but compared to the wildness of the sea, they seemed always to make him a captive. He found that his personal holy moments lay outside them. He had spoken his secrets to the wind, the sea, the land, and even to the rock beneath his keel. To his own satisfaction, his harmony with creation had led him into harmony with the Creator. In his simply-expressed, profound faith, he said that he had a heavenly father the moment he committed himself to him as a son. For him, eternity's endless present held no fears.

The pain returned. He struggled for breath. His eyes were wide, but their blinds were slowly being drawn. A very wet friend pressed comfort into him as Mate snuggled his nose into his hands; somehow, against all odds, the dog had reached his master!

The *Destiny* shuddered at the impact of the next wave and sluggishly began to rise. As the foaming, breaking crest rushed past, the hull seemed doomed to founder on the rocks of the watery valley ... but didn't. Instead, it shook itself free from the sea, rising higher and higher.

The mariner was not aware of the shadow that fell across him, nor the movement that came from somewhere above the waves, heading directly for the *Destiny*. The storm had been but the creative dream of a young boy ...

The Reunion

I had sat and in the wonder of imagination watched the boy follow the progress of his model boat. By walking and running around the pond's edge, he was living every metre of its voyage. The pond was his sea. It held impossible dangers and notorious currents.

The wind had proved too strong for the amount of deflection he had calculated into the angle of the keel and the set he had given the sail. The *Destiny* was way off course. He had watched as the keel struck submerged stones, the hull broadside. A knock-down was inevitable. In a surge of energy, he leapt onto the slippery green pebbles and, with one sleeve of his jumper pulled back, he reached forward as the next wave lifted her clear, extending his fingers to coax the fragile hull gently into his hand. Lifting it from the water, he clutched it to his chest, turned, and took a few short steps to the safety of the bank. He sat on the grass, the sail boat held out in front of him. With its voyage completed, its worth was infinitely more than before. This treasured thought filled him with a silent awe.

I mused on the truth of the words: *The imagination of a little boy absorbed in play is perhaps the nearest thing to being fully alive.*

The warm afterglow of the sun, which had begun its retreat towards the western ridge, lit up the pleasure on the boy's young face. The wind had dropped, the sky had cleared, the nightly celebration of swallows that skimmed low over the water had begun. He loved these moments of stillness when sky and water held each other in the day's final embrace. Reluctant to break the spell, he knew he should start his journey homeward. He would not be lonely when such presence surrounded him.

I also rose to say my farewell to the scene. I wanted to call out to the boy, "May God go with you, little man. Watch out for the hidden rocks on your journey!" – but I knew this would be futile. I would meet with the little fellow again, but never exactly in the same place or the same way. Soon a part of myself would be disappearing into the encroaching shadow of the hill.

Home for the boy lay in the direction of the cooling sun, and he began to follow it. Unexpectedly he stopped, looked lovingly once more at the *Destiny*, then turned his gaze to the far bank and my stooping figure. He ran and leapt over the uneven ground to stand in front of me. My age-lined hand spontaneously reached out to tousle his fair hair, but it made no contact.

It was then I noticed that his blue eyes, though sparkling with the enjoyment of life, looked at me with a mixture of belonging and a questioning of something yet to be understood. A response of love stirred deeply in me. It seemed to rise from where spoken language had never been heard. Then his serious expression gave way to a relaxed smile, as he sensed that some things are best shared without words.

Through his eyes I had followed the epic voyage of the *Destiny*. I had watched myself build the boat and launch it on its maiden voyage. I had re-entered my youthful dream world of the fish-pond, and beyond. Of the high Himalayas. Of the Tibetan plateau. Of monasteries and lamas. Of the mighty Sahara. Of blue-robed Tuareg tribesmen. Of goats, camels, and sweet water oases. All shone with meaning in the boy's mind.

It was then I thought ... what if the reverse were true, and my young self were able to see through my eyes – what would he see?

Someone old and tired, for I have lived through a winter of the undreamed ideas of others, a desert of dead words, where hollow echoes have decided the outcome of my years: an empty offering, rather than what could be.

A signal flashed from blue-eyed innocence, and with it a sense of purpose, older than time, had reached its appointed hour. Two small hands reached out to me, and in them the *Destiny*, his most precious gift. Unsure of myself, I responded hesitantly, and for a moment our hands met around the sail boat.

It was as if eternity shone through a translucent moment of time. Inextricably we had become joined through a small sail boat. In another reality, I realised that I had become re-united with myself. I could once again be the man I longed to be, for I was rediscovering the power to dream.

The boy released the boat. His arms hung loosely and his fingers moved nervously. With his head to one side, he looked towards me expectantly. I wept, and through the veil of tears looked into my hands, but the boat was not there. It was only through my inner eyes, undimmed by age and tears, that I could see the curved hull and the gold-leaf emblazoned word ... *Destiny.*

A soft voice sounded. It could have been the mariner's voice or my own: *We need never search for destiny, for destiny is forever searching for us ... but, like a figure in the mist, we seldom recognise it when it appears.*

The boy, the mariner and I had voyaged together on the water and in the sky.

The young boy turned to leave. I followed a little way, then watched while he ran and skipped up the gentle hillside. The lengthening shadow was drawing together the colours of the day. He turned, waved, and was gone. My gaze returned to the fish-pond, now bathed in subdued hues, reflecting the sun's benediction. Carp nosed the surface, causing painted ripples of sky to move slowly to the pebbled shore.

It was also time for me to leave, yet an inner presence was calling for the completion of something that had not ended with the fading light. The grass bank felt inviting as the land returned the warmth of the day and the night sang to the staring moon and waking stars. This was the hour for my soul to awake. I took the invitation that beckoned me from the mirror of my mind. It led me back through the fields of rich memory.

Opening the Russian Doll

I pondered over the events which, like the traditional Russian doll, enclosed each other, and began to dismantle the overlaying images. My years had taught me not to raise questions needlessly. I had learned to make room for mystery, as the human spirit has the capacity to receive mystery without devaluing it by reducing it to the level of the understanding.

I had visited the lake on a journey of spiritual pilgrimage and eavesdropped on the voices of my childhood. My purpose had been to see if the ambience of pleasant memory might hold a key that would unlock my autumn years.

I had felt concerned that my sense of personal value was weakening before the irreversible advance of age. I was also discovering that meaning and direction are close relatives to a sense of worth. I did not savour the feelings of being adrift and dependant, accruing a debt of kindness my diminishing years would not allow me to repay.

Set amid the tranquil green, an azure sky and drifting cloud lay unrolled over the water, as I had remembered it. The lush bank had invited me, and the soothing sounds of wavelets at play on the pebbled shores had awoken in me a memory of a childhood day – one that evoked a forgotten sense of belonging to a past age – and so assisted my escape from time.

Just as I had looked on at myself as a boy, so I began to relive the carefree enjoyment of the exploration of the childhood world.

I watched myself produce value from the valueless, while at the same time enjoying my forgotten feelings of achievement. A dead cane. A razor, blunted by a workman's stubble. A feather unable to soar. Put together in the right order ... priceless!

My young self had dreamed to sail the storm-savaged, wildest, widest ocean on earth. The voyage was completed, the dream fulfilled, and so the value of the *Destiny* increased a million times. The pebbled harbour, the bows nudging the swell, and the voyage across water and sky had begun. The sudden squall, the near shipwreck ... The boy had dashed, I had cheered ...

The storm had not wrecked our *Destiny*. When all looked lost, we had won!

The voice of the mariner deep inside me said, *Old man, do not let your dream die either!*

And on the periphery of my consciousness I wondered whether we might be the characters within a greater dream. A true dream is a share of a greater dream, entrusted to us to live out in time. In the free air of dream we find direction, and personal worth is restored.

During my tender years, my simple beliefs did not embarrass me. I seemed to live in the smile of the One whose name I did not know, but whose presence I took for granted. He did not appear to me to be an austere, judgemental figure, but a watchful friend, responsible for the world he had created, and for inspiring and shaping my dreams.

"Yes," I spoke to the air, gazing fix-eyed into the past; "I enjoyed his presence. I was as unfettered as the wind as I followed my dreams, and I found meaning."

On this reality I had also based my adult years, until age brought uncertainty. It was at that moment of meeting again with my young self, where our hands joined around the home-made sail boat named the *Destiny* and together made it an offering, that I felt I had crossed an invisible threshold back into a world where I belonged. Both the boy and the boat had disappeared, but what remained was the permission I had given myself to become again the person I was really meant to be. I had readopted my simple, boyish approach to life. To dream again wild dreams. To be blown to the furthest reaches of the wildness of the wind. Young and old could be spun together into the fine thread of meaning that would carry the sky and water on an uninterrupted journey to the sea.

Inwardly aglow, I sang a hymn to the warm private evening.

In the Day's Final Benediction
As the day slipped silently into its final hours, the fish-pond melted into shadow. Among the thoughts of the day, one lingered which I was reluctant to own. It raised a question I had already answered but was yet to find the courage to ask. The small lake was now no more than an echo in the darkness. Would darkness ever hand it back?

The answer I found hard to accept was that the lake had not existed outside of my dream.

Oh, it had existed before the ditching machines had drained the land; before the fish huddled together in the wet mud; before the unrelenting sun's gaze had blistered their scales; before black-headed gulls had feasted on their unprotected eyes.

But gone is the ancient spring, its sweet water now moving waste along a drainage system. Gone are the skylarked fields of yellow stars in the waving green, where their song rose to the morning; where a patient shire-horse neighed to passing children.

All sacrificed to the lava flow of ... progress?

Anonymous cement-laced grey building blocks have trespassed the green. Rows of identical houses with staring windows follow washboard concrete roads. Uncut grass, weed and uncultured shrubs in a despair of neglect struggle over their low front walls. Oh, occasionally there are houses that look lived in and cared for, lightening the effects of misuse and decay. Others, abused by their tenants, are boarded up, hiding together in frightened huddles.

A grey-laced curtain moves fractionally, just enough to catch the eye. An uneasy Asian refugee, her children clinging to her sari, peers into the garish yellow street lighting. She is looking for signs of a non-threatening pavement.

Bare but for the litter of an abandoned car, the road rises to the brow of the hill. It also happens to be my way out of this housing estate. Confidence has returned, and injected a new certainty into my gait. I remember that I am an old soldier – and I march towards my dream.

Destiny awaits, and I hear again the familiar sound of meaning. I walk on until I am no more than a silhouette on the brow of the hill. Haloed by the day's afterglow, I tear off my coat and dance as if no one is watching.

DISGWYLFAN
- A hill of expectant hope where vision is unrestricted -

To be without dream is to be lost to ourselves. We become hermits among the rocks of un-knowing. Confused, we stand in our own way.

To dream is to enter into harmony with eternity's perspective; to look back at the past and the present and, for the first time, understand that the stars which hang in our personal universe are the possibilities designed to shape our future.

Yet dreams bring their own discipline. If we speak them out where they cannot be received, we expose ourselves to personal discouragement and to unpredictable consequences. (Remember Joseph?)

A mentor is a rare figure that may not often appear during a lifetime. He understands how to receive another's dream without weakening it, for he knows the vulnerability of honest openness. He holds the person and the dream as treasures in his trust. His presence is usually sufficient to be a sounding board for reality. The disciple quickly recognises when he is misinterpreting or is astray without the mentor's comments. When he does speak his words are usually few, but they offer support.

One of the greatest gifts to me has been the support of a mentor at critical periods of my life.

Between the sky and earth I live and walk, a minute measure of the sea amid the humanity of every ocean combined, a transfigured random droplet steamed into transparent vapour. As I climb my beloved hill to Disgwylfan, *Abraham's stars of promise seem closer to me.*

The cottage faced south and seemed to be forever in the sun. It was not hard to imagine it being the home of an unusual man. It seemed to exude integrity of purpose. The quarried stone walls and low slate roof brought strength into its harmony. Two thick-stemmed roses outlined the front door. Bloom clusters nodded red, and lightly fragranced the air.

Inside the sunlight splayed through the small windows, and dawned into being the solitary presence of Dan.

He usually sat at a polished oak table whose surface and corners bounced the sunlight around the room, striking the bookshelves against the far wall. The books seemed exceptionally large, with plain bindings. When Dan expected a visitor, he sat side-on to the table with his right arm extended along its edge. At the faintest rattle of the door, a deep melodious Welsh voice would call out, *"Dewch mewn.* Come in."

He would offer you a chair, which you were expected to pull from under your end of the table. Only when he sensed you were settled would he invite your conversation. Time ambled in Dan's presence, for it was not measured by the rise and fall of the sun. It had been healed by the sounds of his own inner timeless ocean. This allowed you to look around the room and let the cold nose of his welcoming Labrador snuggle into your hand.

If you had not already known it, you would then realise that this poet, philosopher and historian of extraordinary calibre – was blind. His voice always sounded from his darkness, yet it was like energy within a thunder cloud, alive and resonating with light.

"I want to dream."

"Then dream on, *'machgen i,*" says the voice from his dark. "There is a wide sky waiting for you and you stand on a lonely planet. There is room for your dream, *bach.* Go to the furthest pavilions, to wherever your dream makes room for you. You will find that 'out there' holds the deepest secrets of 'here'."

"I am too frightened, for the dream is causing me pain."

"*Pa boen, bach?* What pain do you feel?"

"The pain of uncertainty, of the dream not being mine."

There is a smooth silence, gentle in its flow. Not ugly nor empty, but with warm encouragement it encloses me. Once more the voice breaks softly through his darkness.

"*Dy freuddwyd di yw hi, 'machgen i* ... it is *your* dream. Dream it while it is your day. If you sleep it will pass into yesterday. You have your own unique world within you, so your dream will be like no other. There is room for it in our universe, for this is where you belong, and belonging has room. Your future lies in the space 'belonging' has reserved for you. It is yours to fill. You must find the courage to be as wild as your dream."

"But as I reach for it, it is always just beyond me, and slips away."

"Ah then, you have not yet met your dream, you have only seen it in the distance."

"Then how do I meet my dream? Where does it wait for me?"

"Come now, *bach*, you have been this way before, many times. Dream needs its own space in you. It needs to find its home in you. No, more than its home, its *aelwyd*, the hearth of your home, the cradle of your belonging. Where the warmth of the glowing coals reaches the heart. The inner place where you come home to yourself; where you enjoy unconditional security; from where you will not want to wander. Where there is eternity in the presence of the belonging that surrounds you. Yes, you need to find the *aelwyd*, '*machgen i.* The *aelwyd* is your birthright. It is not something to create. When you were born, the *aelwyd* extended to receive you. *Hawdd cynnau tân ar hen aelwyd.* Lighting a fire on an old hearth is easy ... the embers are ready to ignite fresh flames."

"I think I may be too frightened, for my soul rooms are haunted rooms. They hold memories that terrify me. Because they are closed, I too may be closed."

"It is at your *aelwyd* that the parts of yourself will find a loving warmth for each other. They will graciously fall into their own order. Let them shed their unhelpful names, then you will no longer need hammer blows to shape your identity to fulfil the expectations of others. Let your bad memories, like good friends, become your faithful counsellors. Let your *aelwyd* hearth become the place where you connect with who you really are."

"Perhaps I am just too frightened to dream. I am a civil war of opposing selves. A battleground between the raging and skulking parts of me. I have an identity which is inhospitable to reality, ever-changing, unreliable and weak."

Quietly the voice says, *"Gwir dy eiriau.* Your words are true. Dream breaks the predictable frame of experience. Dream itself can be forbiddingly dark before it becomes like the free air that is wild with light. It can lead to a new and disturbing direction that will bring to the surface even more of your hidden vulnerability, and expose you to loss and emptiness. It will attack and destroy your old complacency. Even so, the dream calls you to embrace it, and not to fear it. The deepest longing in you is the voice of your dream. Your dream alone is aware of where its trail leads. When you hear its voice, you simply have to follow. It is calling you to courage and humility. To renege means sowing disappointment and regret."

This time I stretch out the silence. Like a thick rug, it absorbs the stray sounds. I am drawing the moments on, to my side. Each seems a year long. It allows me to capture the words that ring in the air about me. I am losing the edge of panic, my thoughts are slowing down.

"Have you visited the *aelwyd?*" I ask.

The dark answers with words that sound relieved at my willingness to progress.

"Yes, many times, *bach.*"

"Then you know the way?"

"I know my way, *bach,* but not your way."

"How will I find my way?"

"It's not difficult. Let 'hiraeth', your soul longing, be your guide. Continue to climb to your *Disgwylfan,* for providence waits to meet you there. *Cofia 'machgen i,* some prayers are born with us and are waiting their hour to be prayed. Make room for your inner silence, for it is there you will overhear them. *Rho eiriau iddynt* ... then put words to their echoes."

I had said goodbye to Dan and was about to close the front door when a voice from his dark rang out again.

"You want to find the space where you can explore your dream's wildness, don't you, *bach*? When you understand it, I'll be waiting!"

Here among my familiar and much loved landmarks of Wales, my journey to my unexplored *Disgwylfan* was about to begin. I took my place of inner belonging with me, for my *aelwyd* had no walls. I became a rucksack man for, apart from a few present necessities, I wanted to meet life afresh and carry nothing of yesterday's world.

However, there was yet one more thing I needed to do.

BORROWED EARTH
- Llangyfelach -

I knew where to find Wil 'Lotment ... behind the parish hall, in Drew's field.

John Drew had once farmed the land on the east of the village. At the breakup of the farm, his sons had bequeathed the field to the village allotments. Wil 'Lotment rented one for a few pounds a year.

Growing vegetables was his first love. His second was giving his vegetables away, and accompanying them with a visit. This could be to the elderly, though often no older than himself, or someone widowed, or a family with a sick child. The allotment gave Wil his own value among the community. In spite of his work clothes, he radiated dignity.

I did not feel awkward walking to Wil's allotment with a plastic sack rolled under my arm. Of all people, I knew that he would understand my request.

"Hello, Wil."

"'ello, old fella," was his response.

"Onions looking good," I commented.

"Aye, not bad, *bychan*, better after some rain though. See you got a bag. Come for some veg, have you?"

"No, Wil, not veg. You see, I wondered if you could spare me some of your soil?"

"'Course you can. Have some, you don't need me to be here for that. You come and help yourself any time – but it's a bit late for chrysanths, mind."

I shook open my plastic sack and sat on a low stone. With my hand I began to guide some of his freshly-worked soil through its opening.

"No, not from there, *bychan, fan hyn,* come over by here."

Wil stepped over a parade ground of equally-spaced onions, picked up his spade, and made for the compost heap. Before I could say that ordinary soil would do, he was standing there with his spade loaded with rich loam.

"This will make 'em grow, whatever they are."

A second and third spade followed.

"I'm not sure yet what I'm going to grow, Wil. I've just been thinking."

"Ah," interrupted Wil with a smile, "been thinking have you? Thought as much. Don't tell me now, or I'll 'ave another 'eadache. Let me dig this compost in and I'll call round later."

He stepped across to me and placed his rough hand over mine. Looking intently at me, he spoke with a voice that overflowed with knowing.

"If you are on another journey, *bach,* you will do well to remember that everything you see about you is on loan from the soil. All of us start and end here, and we are on a short leash."

Holding out a handful of compost, he said: "We are all borrowed earth. We try to educate ourselves without knowing who we are. Some of the most significant mysteries within us are explained by the earth ...

"Here, have these onions to go with you."

His jacket was worn. His pullover was unravelling at the neck. His shirt was without a collar. Having a charity shop as his personal outfitter naturally fitted his lifestyle. That his clothes did not match was of no concern to him. He would say that a few days in the allotment and all his clothes would match! He was different, in a pleasant sort of way. That was how I knew he would understand my request for a little of his earth.

With the sack and the onions across my shoulder, I left Wil to the tall elms, to the chapel-black, cawing jackdaws, to his preparations for spring, and the fragrance of fresh lettuce. I left Wil to his thoughts and his love of life. In the stillness of myself, I stepped out to the slow rhythm of my thinking. The close bramble-tangled lane, berried red, was scented with invitation.

As my seventy years of life have unrolled, time has appeared to circle back through a number of stages, each stage ending where it began but in a different time and in changed circumstances.

The overlap of endings and beginnings have a familiar feel. What makes my present beginning different is that, though there is a sense of loss at the passing of the old, there is a reminder that I have not been here before, so I cannot take for granted the certainty of the new. Who can tell me if I am about to reach the unravelled end of the thread of my existence? Am I like the presumptuous climber who has misjudged the length of his abseil rope, and discovers this when already part-way down the cliff face?

It is as if I need to rediscover the source of vision and inspiration that brings with it the assurance of a full new day. It is not surprising, perhaps, that this age-old quest to discover the womb from which the pattern of life has emerged should lead back to one of the most ancient of traditions ... the timeless creation story.

In the conscious stillness of eternity, a dream overflowed into the evening and morning of an earth day. An act of creation had begun. Nature's day truly begins in the relaxed hush of an evening. Then, in the unconscious life of sleep, regeneration takes place, and the revitalised soul rises in a kind of resurrection to a creative new day.

I think that this happens because we carry within us a signature of the Creator. The sanctuary of sleep is full of meaning, for below the landscape of life lies the eternal dark cradle of all origin. Out of that darkness the creative gift of wild divinity within finds its place – the exception being that the seventh day follows another pattern. It is as if the rest of the friendly darkness overflows into the following day ... where there is no evening.

During my early years, when pressing hard against the frontiers of my personal experience, protection did not consider me a good investment. In the pressured ranks of military life, I succumbed to the unfriendly fire of an enemy whose ammunition took a microscope to detect: I became an inglorious war casualty to a solitary mosquito.

Later, in Asia's tangled jungles and Africa's tall rainforests, I fought with similar scourges and was sometimes overcome – with unpleasant results. Yet it was the original encounter with this malaria-carrying parasite that triggered my first conscious thoughts of a journey into faith's unknown reaches.

More than a lifetime's unhelpful events have continued to compete in me for space. Often the scales of favour have not leaned towards my recovery. Today, I look out at the world through emotional and physical scars I do not proudly bear; yet amid the fog of my inner wars there seems to be emerging the embryonic shape of purpose.

If another uncertain day is advancing towards me in time, then it is fitting that I relax into an evening of reflection, and a night of regeneration.

From the open sack I lifted a few handfuls of moist, crumbling soil. It looked common and valueless, yet the weight of aeons through which the earth has passed guarantees its ability to incubate and nurture life. Being created from humble earth assures the miracle of our ability to host the germination and nurture of new life. Even though our lives in time are as if they are lived out in the reflected light of the moon, they are a parable of the invisible, where the eternally sunlit reality continues.

It was late afternoon before a familiar tap on the window announced Wil's arrival. Pointing to his work boots, he signalled that he would come through the side gate.

In an age of mechanical diggers, I had always thought Wil's boots to be special. They represented a primal contact with earth and were an essential part of him. If I were to choose something of his to treasure, it would be his boots. I would polish them and turn them into objects of meaningful art.

We sat on a hardwood bench seat, with two mugs of tea on the low table before us. The sun had mellowed and released the fragrance of the garden. Elegant black bamboos, restless in the slightest breeze, whispered tall over us. Shades of yellow, orange, purple and pink followed the sun amid the green textures. I watched Wil's eyes rest on a bed prepared for young tomato plants, and saw his unconscious nod of approval. Behind us, gulls complained bitterly at the quiet sea.

It was the nod of approval that I valued in Wil. It was not so much what he would say, as how he would listen. I knew that he would never be in a hurry to respond. Just speaking out my thoughts in his presence would help me choose my words carefully so that they would be reshaped, reformed, and transfigured. Wil knew the value of silence. He knew that deep things are seldom shared by words but lie in the silence between them, or even in silence itself. For what is understood in the depths of inner solitude cannot easily be communicated in an environment of noise that has little meaning.

He seemed unbothered by the superficial chatter which played on the surface of the mind. Friendship, he believed, lay in the silence between two people, and their desire to hear each other. Strikingly absent in him was a rush to respond with personal experience, or second-hand remedies for this or that, or problem-solving techniques which are dismissive and repetitive.

In Wil's presence I felt that it was silence that most accurately mirrored faith.

The warm tea was having its effect. Slowly I said, "Wil, thank you for coming. I think I need your help."

"The sack of earth is to grow something new then, is it?"

He was not really asking me a question, but affirming me and giving me permission to speak on.

"You know, Wil, I have reached seventy, normally the time when the baton must be passed on, but I have an unrest. I think that I may have another season to run, and this is my difficulty. At no other of life's stages has popular opinion so vigorously defined my value and lifestyle. I am an enigma. I am a dead man still alive. My culture has separated me from myself. My wish to be taken seriously is itself a joke. I am an outgrown parent, so I am called grandfather and reduced to being a plaything of children – and so I lose my appreciation of them.

"I am locked inside the image my age presents. I am thought to enjoy looking after things that are of little importance, without having the authority to change them. Acts of intended kindness no doubt, but each inflicting a pain. If I don't go along with this I am odd, unhelpful and stupid. The space allocated to me is like a rocking chair which gives an impression of movement, but without progress. A shelf on which I gather dust, a wardrobe in which I hang, a small dark room where I cannot stretch ... condemned to minding the neighbour's cat. Few realise that behind the façade of age, there is something deeper going on."

Wil nodded slowly, with growing understanding.

"Will you listen to my story, Wil? Will you come with me to where the road ends and the trail of hard-packed earth and stone continues? Will you pass under the archway that, in bold Chinese characters, proudly carries the name of the village?

"It is quiet there, with a silence that invigorates the senses. There is the cooing of the rooftop mating doves who see the entire village, and the low grunting of pigs that see and know nothing beyond the four walls of their pens. There is also the call of the blind man. He is dressed in brown, with a cloth bag that crosses his shoulder. He walks confidently between the rows of homes, his long pole testing the ground. These are peasant-farmers, forcibly relocated onto the site of an older village. I have not asked what happened to the previous villagers. Each arrival had to build his own home – all identical, in long straight rows. The homes are one-room open living areas. To the front there are heavy wooden gates, which are closed at night, and the back opens onto the pig pens, chained dogs, a goat or a cow, and chickens. Sleeping areas are curtained off in the open living area. They have open toilets, no sewer, no drains and no heating. When water is available, it may be only for two hours each day.

"I sit hunched on a low wooden chair outside the front of the house. It is a cold day, but the sun warms me. The second household dog, an unchained, small-bodied Alsatian look-alike, has made a friend of me. His name in the local dialect means 'mouth'. Whenever the word 'mouth' is mentioned, this dog comes running. It means acceptance, and he performs tricks for food.

"Wil, when 'old man' is called, I feel like that dog. I am tempted to run, as that way I gain acceptance. However, there is something far more humiliating.

"When I think of 'old', it is 'old' that keeps running to *me*. It is always the same 'old' that demands my attention. I feel trapped. If I want to be accepted I must respond to the expectations of others, and 'old' is the name our culture has given me.

"Sometimes I am afraid to face the complexity of myself. It seems easier to beat the wild hopes of my interior life with the stick of other people's second-hand thoughts and drummed-up permissions. To cease to be a presence. To become an angry old man, shaking a fistful of sand at time itself, while the grains trickle remorselessly through my fingers, and the neighbour's sleek, fat cat purrs coaxingly around my feet!"

I felt bad at my outburst, but Wil remained unruffled. He was still among the peasant farmers in the remoteness of a Chinese village; he was present with me in the garden; he was lost within his own deep solitude, and the palm of his hand held the soft earth as if it could explain everything.

In his unhurried way, he said, "You know, 'machgen i, all of us have borrowed our earth. The ones in the village, and us here in Llanelli. We will have to give it back at our nightfall. Whatever we think of ourselves, nothing changes. Look at this now ..."

He sprinkled the earth over the small table and placed a white pebble in the middle.

"Look," he said again: "we think that our outer life is like the earth and our inner life like the pebble."

He then moved the pebble to the outer edge of the table.

"No. Our inner invisible life is like the earth, and our outer life, the pebble. What you call by name, like the old dog, will always come running to you. When you listen to dead words spoken to you and think dead thoughts, don't be surprised when a dead 'old you' comes running to yourself. You have a vast continent of inner life to live in, but you stay at the one point that gives you pain."

His simple words had the raw edge of accuracy.

"What can I do?" I asked.

"Call the dog by another name, bach, and see what comes running! Change the name from 'old and 'useless' to 'experienced', or 'freedom', or 'greatest time of your life'. Or, if you are really dancing, try shalom. Baptise your old self-image in a new name, then go and live in it."

"*Shalom* means more than peace," I said.

"Yes, it is more than the absence of war. It is the active commitment of divinity's total goodness."

"Wil, I want to exorcise from myself every name I have taken to fulfil another's expectation that has never fully described myself. Dead names for the things I have thought myself to be. Dead titles that have come with every job I have done. Titles which, in reality, I could never have fulfilled, as each brought its own restrictive forms. Strong voices I have followed which have sought to shape me into what I am not. There is a wheelbarrow full of dead names around me. Will you take them?"

"'Old' does not describe the vibrancy of inner life, *'machgen annwyl i.* You can be as silent, as free and as full as a reflection of *shalom*. A continent of possibilities is yours to live in. Peg out your claim, set your own boundaries. And mind, *bach*, if I take your dead names, they are not going on my compost tip!"

"What do you mean, Wil?" I enquired earnestly.

"When you are stronger in your freedom, you will find a new way of understanding them. When you avoid them, they remain locked up inside you. When you learn to call them by other names, they will become friends of your destiny. Learn to be a good parent to your delinquent selves, for you have many of them. Renamed negativity will point to new possibilities of progress. Jesus' words, 'Love your adversaries', are a signpost to an infinitely richer landscape."

"Ah, I think I know what to grow in my borrowed earth now."

Wil said nothing, but the regular nodding of his head said everything. Empty mug in hand, he stood up to leave.

"Use the soil to make a memorial plot, and be sure you plant it right out to its edges." Then, with a wry smile, he said, "and don't make it a rockery!"

He passed through the side gate back into his own world ... or did he? For he turned and said, "Before you leave, call in to see Dan and me. He knows you're going, too!"

I had not said anything to Wil nor Dan about leaving. How could they know? ... Wil 'Lotment, in his elemental wisdom, had neither recommended to me, nor asked me, what I would grow in my borrowed earth. I think this was because we shared an unspoken understanding that we should venture only where the dream should carry us. For it is by accepting the validity of dream that we inhabit the mystery of divine intention.

IMPOSSIBLE IS JUST AN OPINION
- Llanelli Shore: The Beginning Ends -

The last of my characters has disappeared, but my bench remains comfortable. It is the hushed sounds of evening that stir me. The distinctive scent of a full tide clings to the air. The mackerelled waves that flash silver are well into retreat, and excitement at the salt-crisp water's edge has quietened. Along the sea-walled promenade the few tide-watching, pointing figures grow indistinct as the ebb tide of daylight also steals away.

I am filled with the wonder of living in two realities. I have been by the sea while I have been at the fish-pond. I have been with the mariner and the boy whilst also being with the figures on the edge of the dark. I have been with both Dan and Wil, yet I have been alone with the salt, the wood, and my thoughts.

Across the purpled sky of the bird-winged bay, a gull flies perilously close to the low suspended sun. It is unharmed, and I take courage.

I fly in the face of my fear. I look into myself, and I find no consistent form. What I see does not describe what I long to be. I see myself only as a wisp and curl of steam from a boiling kettle. Were I to frame its shape, moments later the frame would be empty.

Before me, clouds are strung across the horizon. They too are flying close to the sun. As they enter its glowing sphere, portraits appear in the sky. First an old man's face, which in moments changes into that of a child at play. These drift and flow their forms into hundreds of differing portraits. They float across the deepening red, driven by the invisible air stream. Through their short day they constantly transfigure their shape. I cannot name a single one and say that this is the form of my inner life, for when I attempt this, I imprison myself into a single representation.

I have no desire to become predictable when the reality I yearn for lies in the ever-changing wildness beyond predictability. I do not want to be driven by the compulsion to name the inner things that flow into me. I do not want to be that which fulfils another's expectation, but to which I am a stranger. Without language it is hard to imagine how life would continue, for it is the currency of communication. Yet I have a fear of words, for in their multiplicity, *meaning*, the very stuff of existence, can be lost.

As I watch the clouds, I think I am the sum total of all the changing shapes that drift across the sun's diffused globe. I know I will feel comfortable in this wide space that defies the restriction of a name. Inwardly, I crave to lose definition; to be able to wander the full extent of this wildness, and to be ... whatever life makes me. Like the river that rose in Eden, I too can be content in the knowledge that I carry no name.

For a second time my footprints indent the wet sand as I make my way to the shallow river. From the sky's darkening dome I see evening's offering appear. I scoop the cold water into my hands, and hold it before me. I have captured handfuls of stars, a celebration of promise.

Filled with an emotion that silence alone could interpret, I enter again my timbered temple. The sound of the retiring sea and the chorus of roosting gulls do not disturb the solemn hush of dusk. Africa's most ancient people, the Kalahari bushmen, say that at such times they hear the stars sing. I am not surprised.

The glowing sun now fuses with a retreating magenta sea. Its reflection reaches from the earth's western rim. Its colours touch the river, the pools left by the tide, the wet sand, and touch me.

From my rucksack, I take my notepad. The sheet has no more written on it than the line scribbled this morning:

'In the beginning was ... the Dream.'

From the same source of ancient wisdom I add a companion line: 'and old men shall ... dream dreams.'

Yn dechreuad roedd y ... Freuddwyd. a bydd eich hynafgwyr yn gweld ... breuddwydion.

I feel warmth on the inside. My inner voice, gentle with faith's fresh innocence, calls to me: 'Impossible ... is just an opinion.'

And I listen, for I have walked in the water and in the sky.

Shalom Tested

FAREWELL TO A FAIR LAND
- Wales -

So often in our transitional stages, it is by an act of self-redemption that we make progress. We make deliberate choices based on the inner promptings that we have judged to be right for us and then follow our decisions. In other words, we ask ourselves the question: 'What would I attempt to do if I knew that I would not fail?'

Wales and its characters, the Wils and the Dans, who like diamonds hold memories of the sun, have played my host and mentors. Their words hover silently around me. They are the treasures I have collected while beachcombing time.

The gentle landscape is itself a poem written to the sky. Its rivers and sea transpose it into music. There are valleys among the hills where the sun hesitates before disturbing their primal peace. The rocks that dwarf us in size and time remain as they have been over thousands of years. These valleys are like worlds within a world, where innocence seems to reign and where man, like Adam, could step into existence at any moment of time.

It was to such a valley that I brought my brother's remains. Eight years younger than me, we had walked and climbed in these mountains. The powerful effects of nature scaled to size our personal sadness, and the free wind would fill us over again with life's elixir, until a greater sadness overtook us and someone else's smoke stole away his days.

It seemed right for him, and to me, as I poured his ashes at the base of a timeless rock, that he should disappear back into a valley he had loved. Here, unheard, the mountain stream plays its tribute to the moss-greened stones, the heather, royal-purpled, and the gold gorse flaming among the shale.

I have found inspiration in this womb of solitude, and an energy in its stillness, and have been able to overhear the echoes of purpose. I have found courage re-birthed during the evenings and mornings of change. My country has received me twice ... by second birth, perhaps, but on a long and wayward leash.

There are none so lonely as those who hide a secret. Yet to the mountains I have emptied my feelings, sometimes shouting loudly when no one was near, at other times with inner voice and a tear. Today it is as if the land is honouring my longings and encouraging me back to where Asia's vast plains and wide deserts speed outward. To where the sky bends to meet earth's distant horizon and the mountains crunch with brittle blue ice. To where the silent dark of village life births hope, and faith breaks through the crumbling crust of communist ideology that projects man to be the centre of all, and their leaders ... gods. To where this new season brings forgotten purpose into its springtime, its sanctity restoring inner peace. To where spiritual instincts alone can guide.

China will distance me from Wales and provide the context in which my dream may be proved. For I will need to search among the stones of China's millions if I am to discover the space that providence has arranged for me. It is to this wide expanse of the unknown, and perhaps unknowable, where the romance of an ancient civilisation retreats before the advance of anonymous concrete and unbreathable sulphuric air, that I want to make an offering of my unspent years. From me, it will be a life. From Wales, a gift from the gentle hill and the small lake where I found the confidence to dream again.

If we make this journey together, you and I, we will be far from the brassy trails where the tourists, with loud shirts and voices, waddle behind guide-waving flags, having 'done China'. We will be insignificant among the most numerous and historically-rich peoples. We will be separated by experience as well as by culture and language, for no wars of our past century have equalled the suffering and death that their trusted leaders have inflicted upon them. Long memories and suppressed energies foster the unpredictable as China's economy soars, distancing the few from the nightmare of the powerless poor.

So there, between China's earth and sky, we will be in their story – but we can never be a part. We may become dislocated from our world and theirs, non-citizens in our universe, but perhaps with the courage to follow freedom, and – who knows? – bring healing to their house and ours. At this threshold of expectant unknowing ... we wait.

CHINA
~ An Introduction or What? ~

From whatever perspective we may perceive China, it is a slow-burn explosion that spreads outwards in all directions at once. Hungry to empower its future, it is on-line to open five hundred more coal-fuelled power stations in the next decade – that is, roughly one each week.

This massive appetite for coal will by the year 2009 push China past America as the world's biggest polluter, as its colossal greenhouse gas emissions affect the world. The throes of China's traumatic transition inflame the sensitivities and confuse the mind. If China's 1.3 billion reach the lifestyle of the USA, then it will consume something like the total world food production.

In Beijing the new wealthy can dine in restaurants on servings of animal genitals, while many of China's rural population are destitute. The three million cars that gridlock the capital produce enough toxic chemicals for the inhabitants and visitors to inhale the equivalent of seventy cigarettes each day – comically called 'The Great Pall of China'.

Of even less comfort to its 17 million residents is that spring winds can storm more than 300,000 tonnes of Gobi sand onto the city, heralding the advance of the Gobi Desert's thirty-metre dunes at a rate of two kilometres each year. Hopes to slow the process lie in a ring of trees some 5,700 kilometres long, longer than the Great Wall, that farmers are being encouraged to plant – but with 200 square kilometres of China becoming desert each month, perhaps the aspiration flies a little too high.

Ask any package tourist who has sped through heritage sites and glamorous cities with the strange feeling of being an 'air-con' sardine, and they will confirm that China sucks up half the world's concrete production, and walks over laminate floors that absorb half the world's hardwood production. Its hunger, consuming a third of the world's steel output, fuels the fastest-growing crime rate in the developed world as thieves steal everything from manhole covers and copper wire to railway tracks, and ship them to China.

Similarly, Shanghai fragments the sky with twice the number of skyscrapers as New York ... and is still growing. Sadly, as your climbing plane stirs the yellow toxic sky, what tarnishes the dazzle is the information on the seat-back computer, which coolly states that four million tonnes of sewage and industrial waste pour into the Huangpu River daily ... not a great deal of comfort when you realise that your morning wake-up cup of coffee could have come from the same river.

The sleeping dragon of Napoleon's nightmare has awoken, and is breathing fire.

Yet as China slides away westward like a nine million square kilometre lake running from the wind, its antiquity and mystery still linger, an eternal mist. Within its borders are the highest mountains in the world, and its deserts are among the hottest. Its climate varies from the sub-Arctic north to the tropical rainforests of the south. From the high plains of Tibet rise two of the world's greatest rivers: the Yangtze and the Yellow carve their courses through the harrowed landscape. Apart from the scattered minority groups, the weight of China's billion is grouped around cities; two-thirds of the landmass is inhospitable, and not able to be cultivated.

Even so, it is the staggeringly high mountains, the peaks of frozen snow, the unforgiving deserts and plains that sweep to the sky, that are all part of the China I love.

Then what of the people, with their seemingly differing versions of Mandarin and the multitudes of local dialects that appear to rival their 15,000 characters (although they tell me I would just need to recognise four thousand characters if I would like to read the daily tabloid)? – They are among the dearest friends I have.

FIRE STORM
- The Ancient Land whose Name is Shen Zhou:
the Land of God -

I have begun the climb to my *Disgwylfan.*

Is it what you expected?

Not exactly. I seem to have two dreams, one within the other. Yet one has already faded. This troubles me, because I know that it is an important part of the whole. What I am seeing is quite unpleasant. It is a dancing figure. It is an ugly, angular and angry dance. It is bumbling and ungainly, yet it has a coordinated insensitivity. It is as if the crude clumping and stamping has a purpose.

Since life is seldom as it appears to be, it is important to follow dream closely, for unlike fantasy, it brims with insight that shines deeply.

There is a clarinet playing, sweetly swinging high and low, softly imitating the human voice. It seems to be calling all other sounds into itself. Silence is building as breath caresses each note. Quieter, quieter, the senses calm under its stillness, and silence becomes pregnant with the sound of meaning and of the sight of things that cannot be seen ... then sounds like gunfire break out, coming from all directions simultaneously. It is deafening.

There is a battle beginning. Maybe two, three or more battles raging at the same time.

Exploding rockets blast against the windows, even though I am eleven storeys high. The deep drum tone of an exploding mine. The thud of artillery. The shrill whine of incoming shells. The chatter of machine-gun fire. A blaze of automatic assault rifles as battle groups engage.

Ground fire I cannot identify seems to be heading upward towards me, but it falls short. Shells are star-bursting overhead; shards of shrapnel flail down with terrifying force. If it were not for their thunderous explosions that strike white light through the windows and reverberate between the blocks of flats, they would be spectacular.

A tank has dug in nearby. There is no hint of panic in its powerful gun. It is getting its shells away with laser precision and unhurried regularity.

I hear building alarms sounding. A loud cry just a few metres below me is drowned in a purge of fire. In the distance to my right something large and inflammable is alight. A fountain of flames, red with highlights of white and yellow, leap against the black sky. Molten missiles streak out at all angles, fading as they cool.

Flares now hover over the tallest buildings, reflecting off glass, tile and dull concrete, bathing the battle site in white light. A fury of automatic fire sweeps the ground as the cover of darkness is lost. The flares stop ... perhaps a direct hit on their launch site?

I can feel the vibrations of the explosion through my feet. Pressure changes deafen me. White light angles through the windows, disorientating my senses until tower blocks lean this way and that.

Tracer shells arc steadily over the dark outline of tombstone rooftops, stopping and starting in a sadistic code. *Death-death-death!* they write in the sky.

A searing, blistering shriek of raw power, terrifying as a thundering fighter jet, flings fear as its presence rips apart the sky and shreds earth's dust into a burning wake. It is on a horizontal flight path. I cower beneath my raised arms and turn away. It howls by; we are not hit – its flight duration has been calculated; it plummets downwards.

Assault rifles crack again. They have a hollow, echoing tone. There is no return fire, for they are now within range of a tank. To a computer controlled turret they are a well-defined target. Carefully, the ammunition is chosen. The main gun recoils; the shell explodes. The shrill whizz of shrapnel, the roar of a carpet of flame, become lost in the lake of battlefield clamour.

The tank has now become the target.

The rasping hiss of the hand-held missile launcher, the sledge-hammer ring of steel against steel. A hole burns through the turret wall. A muffled implosion; its belly of steel plates rips open – its burnt crew no more than a statistic.

The advancing battle group greets the death of the tank with a silent cheer. Well, a sort of cheer, for at least they are not pinned down. They will now advance against a hail of steel as they move forward to establish a new front-line. Some make it; others stagger drunkenly in the smoke, not knowing in which direction safety lies.

The artillery move up, punching holes in the thick air, their shells devastating the ground ahead of the advancing infantry. The thud of the guns and the report of the exploding shells became one long sound. The fury of the assault rifle fire is like a storm of volcanic fallout on a tin roof.

Behind the shock troops, the second wave of occupation troops are forming. They move forward and hold ground that has been taken. They will deal with sniper fire and round up dispirited prisoners.

Unhindered by incoming fire, the artillery are registering their targets with pin-sharp accuracy. The advance is gaining momentum, and the victory sweep across enemy positions is now under way.

The battle has been twelve months in preparation, its ammunition carefully tailored to the predicted conditions. The soldiers have rehearsed the battle plan and trained for fitness. The first barrage sounded at 1800 hrs, the final rounds at midnight.

The firecracker celebration is over, and the old year brought to a fitting close. The hush of the New Year has begun.

The Chinese Year of the Dog has arrived!

In the damp grey of a cold morning, families count their change from what has been the most expensive night in the Chinese New Year celebration. Below my window a small car is parked, its nose tight against the wall. It is an ugly car, tall and narrow, like an upturned box on ugly miniature wheels. It looks terrified by the sounds and smoke of the night. All four indicators are flashing; the alarm is more of a whimper. I feel I can identify with the car.

Women street sweepers appear. The fluorescent strips upon their jackets reflect the weak dawn light. They look like matchstick figures. Their palm-frond brushes recirculate dust into the air, and the battle debris into heaps. Their handcarts will soon be filled with shreds of exploded cardboard cartridge cases.

In villages, towns and cities old traditions have been honoured, new fantasies explored, and the population has found release through nationwide celebration. According to Chinese folklore, strings of rapidly-exploding firecrackers, like ancient Egyptian sitrum rattles, drive away bad spirits from houses, shops and streets while at the same time investing in good luck and prosperity for the coming year. The newly-wealthy entertain guests with a cacophony of noise and fire. Village families pool their resources for a display.

Where are the spirits driven to?

Who knows? Perhaps to faraway hills, demon-infested lairs; to palaces of demon kings.

Will they swoop down and invade the streets again?

No two people give the same answer. The strangest suggestion I have heard came from a Korean clergyman who said that the home of these spirits was the mountains of Wales!

But perhaps it is human beings who have demonstrated the meanest spirits to haunt China. It is well-documented that the most severe famine in history was fuelled by Mao's plan of self-promotion to communist world leadership. It is said that his favour-gaining sprees of aiding communist uprisings with money, food and arms accounted for more than twenty-two million deaths from starvation in 1960 alone. His supporters sacrificed others to make room for themselves. They indoctrinated the population to believe that denouncing a relative or neighbour to imprisonment or death was a patriotic virtue. Like a perverse sainthood, this would earn them a favoured position in the poverty-enforced rivalry among villagers.

In their millions, the Chinese labour force is still recruited from the rural poor. Their energies are poured into building mega cities, or harvesting crops for very little return. The nation has been here before; Chinese poetry has so eloquently captured the suffering of the powerless poor during the years of building the Great Wall.

Like a confused sea, conflicting realities collide in an explosion of sound and energy. I can accept that what I imagine to be the emotions that rise from the heaving depths are beyond my experience. I have not suffered the pain that could cradle the quality of compassionate understanding.

It is not surprising, then, that through a myriad of different jarring, frightening sounds, households and streets rain a fire storm against the unseen hierarchy of terrifying beings that invade our world and inhabit the people. Angers and frustrations are dispersed into a wild freedom, and feelings of power re-established in the hands of the powerless.

Does this firecracker war work for the nation?

It does if China continues to make economic progress. If its cheap exports continue to find ready international markets. If they strike new energy deals. If Middle-Eastern wars continue to weaken an already fragile USA. If their long-term strategists are making correct assumptions and China soon becomes the new world-dominating superpower.

An emerging world power cannot possibly believe in idol shelves, in spirit-reflecting mirrors, in Feng Shui, in firecracker wars.

I don't think it needs to. Many things they do not have to believe in, but simply leave them in place and allow them to work. There are wars within wars, both to preserve the beliefs of an ancient nation and to engage effectively with the wider world. Perhaps it's easier to talk of China's inner wars than our own. I am tempted to hide my personal wars behind a mask of what others of my immediate culture find acceptable. My inner wars determine my views of others, so truthfulness takes a step back and I add to the illusion I call life.

If we live in silent agreement with an illusion, where can we find the authentic and true?

The issue is not finding the authentic, but what to do with it when it is found. To live on its base line could write us out of this story. We may become non-citizens of an illusionary world. We may be called mad. We would need to hide behind closed doors and, like Egypt's Desert Fathers, listen only to what the walls of our cell could teach us. Perhaps there is no other place for the non-citizen, and death the only redemptive power.

Perhaps we should be prepared to live within the illusion, and to paint pictures of the life from which we are adrift?

Then our brush strokes would need to be discoveries of a new originality, and our words would need to be overheard in silence, then arranged to describe the reality. Our search for the authentic so often ends at a cliché which recycles us to nowhere. Language can be hollow at its core, empty of meaning. I am not sure how much reality we can hear. Unreality is our pressure-release valve.

Through the years of my emerging spiritual awareness, I pictured divinity as a far-off mountain cloaked in threatening cloud, lit by lightning – frightening, but inviting.

Deep in the hold of a ship in the Indian Ocean, I caught sight of a booklet. Being an unlikely find in such a place, I began to read. It was a Gospel of John. It seemed to be written for someone like myself, and painted miniatures of divinity that I could handle. Judgement ceased to be a threat, became more of a releasing process. I found the confidence to tease out the thinking of others on these matters, yet the conversation turned to the relative value of the picture frames, rather than the reality the canvas portrayed.

So, perhaps, even word pictures of divinity can become clichéd and meaningless gods of our imagination; hollow ghosts that hang in the corridors of our history ... and we will still need a place to hide.

As a small boy looking through an uncle's geographical magazine, China etched itself indelibly on my young soul. Determined to learn more, I asked my mother to register me as a member (possibly the youngest) of 'The Wide World Brotherhood'. Later, when, during my army years among Chinese people, faith unexpectedly entered my equation and a dimension outside of myself came into being, I began to see the possibility of where I might fit as one person among China's millions. I moved towards the confidence to believe that, in some way, I would count.

As I re-enter China I am aware of some of its internal conflicts. When I take sides, it is as if my emotions become deeply-torn flesh. This is also the environment where my personal hurts resurface. I have collected many wounds from my inner wars. Taken together, they may prove too strong for me and I will begin to skate across the surface of life. My judgement of others will be affected, and I will become an embittered old man. I have everything to prove. Faith is the star I hope to steer by in my seventy-plus years, but it brings its own costs. Its purity adds to the pain of my poor judgements and damaged friendships.

DRAGON KING
- Ningxia Province -

Chinese story tellers are popular, so Chinese authors are master story tellers. I would like to tell you one story in as far as I can recall reading it.

It was during the years of Mao's 'Oppose Spiritual Pollution' campaign. On hearing a rumour that he was about to be sent to a notorious prison farm, a celebrated author escaped Beijing and wandered the length of the Yangtze river, from its source through the Three Gorges eastward.

He told the story of a spring festival held in a small town whose name I have forgotten. I have added to the remnant of his story brush strokes of my own experience in similar large villages at similar seasons.

The main street of the town had been built along a river bank. At one end there remained the ruined site of the Dragon King Temple, possibly destroyed during the Cultural Revolution. The eaves of the houses that lined the narrow streets almost touched. They had upswept corners, with an array of small creatures mounted on the tile crests.

During the day there had been a procession through the lanes. There were girls marching four deep, dressed in red, the front row each carrying a large sheet of red card on which a single Chinese character had been brushed. Behind them came a succession of small three- and four-wheeled trucks. The trucks carried mainly men with enormous cymbals strapped to each hand. Some cymbals were plain, some adorned with long white tassels. The men were dressed in everyday village clothes and had deeply-lined weathered faces, missing teeth, untidy straw bales of black hair, and large calloused hands; they crashed their instruments together in a crazed rhythm understood only by themselves.

Low wires and roofs periodically brought the parade to a halt while they were negotiated. Thunder bangers thrown from the trucks exploded near to people not paying proper attention. Strings of firecrackers welcomed them into the streets. Outside the Catholic church a table had been set, offering packets of cigarettes, bottles of rice liquor, flasks of green tea.

As the convoy of revellers cymballed and crackered their way past the church, only the flasks of tea and a lone figure remained, watching and listening until a corner and a new street muffled the hub-bub-bub of the single cylinder diesel engines and hid the black smoke plume.

When the noise had died away, older ladies in white jumpers cycled past. Death had not respected the festival. These were professional mourners. Soon their cries would join the village sounds.

Towards evening, crowds began to gather at the ruin of the Dragon King temple. Along the street that lined the river, shops had hung small red packets from bamboo poles; it was not so much that each shop was giving away money, but rather that each was investing in their own good fortune for the coming year. The culmination was the rice shop opposite the temple, which had strings of firecrackers that hung from the upstairs windows – but the little red packet that hung from a bamboo pole was the real prize for the night.

Sprinkled among the crowd were the red, black, white and yellow turbaned heads of the performers of the night's highlight: the Dance of the Dragons. Four dragon teams of thirty or so young men from villages along the river donned the colour of the dragon with which they would perform; they were to compete for the packet at the rice shop.

The drums and the gongs began to sound, and heads among the throng started moving to their rhythm. In a sea of light and to the roar of the firecrackers, the performers demonstrated their skills, each one wheeling and somersaulting in turn. The most skilled and demanding work was displayed by those manipulating the dragon's head and a round embroidered ball.

It became the turn of the final two performing dragons, Black from the small town where the event was being held, and Red beginning its advance from the far end of the street. The Blacks were led by the home town's hero, and the young girls called out to him, offering him drinks, while the young men cheered him on.

Dripping with perspiration, the hero unbuttoned his shirt and threw it to someone in the crowd. He had a large black dragon tattooed on his chest. The crowd shouted their support.

The Red dragon, made up of youths of similar stature and skills, had now reached the site of the Dragon King temple. They were focussed on the prize packet at the rice shop. Neither team intended to give way to the other.

Both fiery dragons were shaped by candle-lit lanterns, hand-held, creating from the darkness the lines of the dragon's body. They wove their way among the crowds; tails swinging wildly and heads thrusting high, they pranced and danced. The leader of the Black dragon was somersaulting, bare-chested, on the cobbled ground, and the dragon became a fiery circle.

Red equalled Black's performance. Following the embroidered ball, lunging to and fro, it became a giant centipede attacking some living thing.

The rattling roar of the strings of firecrackers ended, and thunder bangs were thrown from the crowds. The performances also came to an end, the contestants panting and sweating like eels out of water. The Reds had planned their charge for the packet, and in one bound snatched it from the pole. The local Black team felt humiliated. They had lost face. Their anger boiled up, and loud swearing among the teams replaced the discharge of the firecrackers. It became obvious that the Dragon Dance had been an expression of more than competitive skills; the teams had a strong antipathy to each other.

In the intense atmosphere the crowds parted; fighting was about to break out. Women screamed for their children and rushed them indoors. Dragon team supporters in black T-shirts were moving to the front of the crowd. This small town was the power base for the Black Dragon team. Last year they had proudly proclaimed their superiority over the Reds by winning the contest. This year, they had bullied themselves into a position where another win was sure. The surprise move by the Reds had shaken their smugness and infuriated them. The Reds were not acting like a defeated side! – It was as if last year's humiliation had not happened.

The Black Dragon troupers were losing face. Rubber truncheons began to appear. Stools used for gaining height at the back of the crowd, left behind by the fleeing women, were passed forward as weapons, and the crowds stood in hushed shock at the sickening thuds and cries that followed.

Village feuds split open. Family and personal vendettas, both ancient and new, poured out. The black T-shirts were now in small gangs, moving among the crowds, bullying, threatening, demanding. Petty jealousies were exploited. The lust for power, advantage and revenge was fulfilled, both openly and secretly.

The storyteller says that the story could go on and on; for he is making it up.

So, this is only a story?

Yes, but it is true, for the storyteller tells people about themselves without betraying who they are. The ambition for power over another is always there. So are the bullying tactics that exploit this, from the politician to the bus driver.

This must cause deep resentments, and an endless search for approval and favour, ever upward, so that the balance of power can even out ... if it ever does.

As a boy, my father taught me not to acknowledge certain neighbours, and even relatives. I did not question why, but was simply led by my family's pride. I did not consider being true to myself, for I did not have a personal self, just a collective family self. We were just a poor steelworker's family, but family pride told me that others, who were also poor, were in some way inferior to us. I found that by simply refusing to acknowledge them, I had power over them. I was fighting my father's war, or my grandfather's war, or even my great-grandfather's war; I am not sure which. To win this war I had to become a victim of it.

I have also seen starving people refuse food and clothes, and make a joke of it against themselves among people who have plenty. They were fighting some hidden war, and in order to satisfy their pride they had to become victims and suffer impossible consequences.

It is like walking through a swollen river with tangled tree roots on the bottom. It's hard to tell where to put your foot without stepping into someone's hidden war.

When we step into another's wars and carry with us our own, confusion deepens further, especially when we meet on the pretence of helping them. I have, incredibly, seen some of my young Chinese friends bullied by a business hitman into paying a large sum of money for a product so poorly made as to be unsuitable for their use.

We are all affected by each other's disposition, anger and moods birthed in inner wars. Sometimes we don't know how or where to be who we are. When we fight on ground which belongs to people we are pretending to help, we bully them into accepting the conditions that exist in us.

It seems so destructive to let our emotions invade the inner landscape of an innocent person.

Yes, but it is always happening ... however, there is hope. From a single spark of realisation, light can thicken as it dawns upwards.

THE FAR CITY
- Reflection from a Boeing -

The hours pass. I am in the company of three hundred others, all strangers – a can full of aspiring adventurers, ten kilometres above the earth. Tour operators' placards held head-height wave for their attention, and in two weeks a 'Great Wall' T-shirt will announce to America and Europe that they have successfully survived the smog of China's show cities.

It is sad to be sitting in the belly of a Boeing and enjoying no more of the romance of flying than we would sitting in a railway station waiting room. Babies cry. Children run along the aisles. The queue at the toilet lengthens. Still, as we hurtle in an ark across the sky, I have good reason to be proud to be British. The tornadoes stirred by our wing tips make their statement in the sky. We banish kilometres at many hundreds every hour, for slung beneath our wings, thundering us through the solid air, are the bulwarks of British achievement ... the Rolls Royce aero engines.

I choose not to take this boastful thinking further, for I have been told that if I were in the position to look for the manufacturer's insignia authenticating many of the components, they would carry the three instantly recognisable words: *Made in China.* In fact, I believe that some European airlines have their aircraft serviced in the Philippines, while an American airline plans to open a service base in Beijing.

The biggest surprise of all, however, is the announcement in *China Daily* that Airbus, pride of Europe, will sell off some of its shares to China and move the design and production base for its A320 range to one of its main cities ... while Britain negotiates the sale of its remaining shares to Germany.

Over the tannoy, the muffled voice of the chief steward apologises for the breakdown of the video equipment and assures everyone that he will attempt to fix it. I play with the idea of something similar happening to the hydraulic system, spiralling the aircraft out of control, or the engine management system, or the navigation system.

I once heard of a passenger who suffered a panic attack when he saw a coffee stain on the side of the plastic cup served to him by the air hostess. He reasoned that if the cabin crew were that careless in sight of their passengers, what might be happening among the mechanics in the engine compartments? – I cheer myself with thought of the chief steward clinging to the cowling, pliers tucked into his belt, screwdriver gripped between his teeth, fixing the engine as we fly.

We wing our way ever eastward, across the Ural mountains and western Siberia. Russia's anonymous towns of featureless concrete and rusting municipal heating pipes give way to the Mongolian Steppes, the horse-whipped plains where wolves howl and the sounds of the great Khans may be heard on the wind.

My colleagues who await me south of China's Great Wall will have already lived much of the day which I have just begun. When I scramble for my rucksack at Beijing airport, it will be tomorrow, yet I will not have aged a day. When I return I will recover the missing day ... still packaged and unused.

I have a deep love for China and, with the passing hours, the sense of coming home grows stronger. As a young man I volunteered to join a war against Chinese communist insurgents. Time has reversed my role. I am no longer young, and the communists are now the government and may regard me as the insurgent. In fact, the reversal of roles is even more profound as the West's dependence on Russian energy sources deepens and our manufacturing base moves to China, which is also busily mopping up the world's gas and oil resources – especially in Russia and Africa – yet without an anti-pollution policy. Since March 2007, foreigners have had to rehearse to themselves the hundred and sixty-five new civil offences which have been introduced. Failing any one of these could lead to their deportation.

When my view is reduced to the back of the seat in front, and I have read the overhead locker number a hundred times, to rerun memory of a pleasant past is a great escape. Not only can time be rearranged, but distance also. By the brilliance of modern navigational systems, our precise moment of touchdown in the east of China has already been calculated while, at the same time, memory can set me down in an exact location outside a city in the west.

Here mountains rise directly from multiplied thousands of square miles of a sand-and-stone desert. These mountains have huge crocodile tails. Scale-covered, they weave across the desert floor. Jagged saw-edged teeth follow their spine upward and over their humped backs. If dinosaur bones had not been discovered, they could be imagined from the shape of these mountains. From a distance they look like gigantic prehistoric creatures attacking an even higher mountain range. Wind-blasted and ice-capped, their sky-piercing spires of rock stand out defiantly in the red, yellow and grey of naked barrenness.

With such a small percentage of China's land being arable, it is not difficult to discover those areas that are not. Yet weaving among these unforgiving pinnacles is one of the most ancient highways in history. It traverses mountains and deserts, and once bridged two great centres of civilisation: Chang-an, China's ancient capital in the east, and Rome, in the west. Thus the humble worm of the east supplied the Roman elite's insatiable appetite for silk which, during its months or years of journey along the Silk Road, appreciated in value more than gold.

Along this ancient trail Christian faith spread eastward, culminating with Alopen, the Nestorian monk, who presented himself to the Chinese emperor in 635. Islam later travelled the same route, as did the various forms of Buddhism. From the Mongol cauldron, Genghis Khan's horsemen followed this trail and poured their fury on Central Asia, and even threatened Europe.

I am picturing this city in the far west, one of the last outposts in China before this timeless highway rises among towering sentinels, nature's boundaries with Central Asia. It was to this point, some seventy years ago, that visionary Chinese walked almost the width of China before being halted by the Red Army. Some were imprisoned. None made it across the formidable mountain range. Their goal had been to carry their faith back to Jerusalem, from whence it had come. These were given the nickname of the 'Back to Jerusalem Band'.

The embers of the vision kept their heat through the years of the communist purge. When the wind blew freely through China again, and faith began to spread among the village farming communities, the embers began to glow.

The Silk Road is among China's historical treasures, and the movement towards Jerusalem a holy dream. A dream is essentially a personal experience; it happens within the darkness of our inner sanctuary, where there is no natural or artificial light. It is meant to remain in the darkness until it is properly interpreted and providence signals its hour. When dream is spoken before the time it is usually lost. I was to learn that this was the reason for my visit to the tea house in this far city.

We had responded to the invitation of Chinese friends to meet them in a quiet quarter of the town. An inconspicuous teashop was the setting.

The proprietor had awaited our arrival, and led us into the privacy of a back room. As we settled with our friends, two men pushed their way in and sat at a corner table. Inside the cloud of strong tobacco that smoked them, they swilled their tea and argued roundly. They could afford to, as their ears were tuned on us. My friends restrained what they were about to say, casually passed the time of day, and left. I left later.

Two days passed before we met with these friends once more.

"They were secret police," they whispered, then continued: "Please suggest to your Asian colleagues that they consider not coming here. They are causing us some difficulty."

Sadly the wish, expressed by these Chinese friends, went unheard. Their dream, commonly referred to as 'Back to Jerusalem', has created news in a sensation-hungry world where perhaps not many dream, and where the romance of another's dream can sound an attractive proposition, particularly when a seeming unlimited financial resource is available to follow it. If my reporting sources are correct, several hundred descended on this sensitive Islamic area during the summer period, all from the nation our friends had hoped to dissuade.

The same Asian colleague who reported the number of visitors also shared with me the following moving story:

In a yellow dress, on a raised drain cover in a market place near the mosque steps, stood a young girl from one of China's minority groups. She had been there for some hours, her small hands covering her face, sobbing deeply.

"She has lost her father," said my Asian colleague, "perhaps he is in the mosque."

"She has been abandoned," said a Westerner, who had experience of abandoned children.

Where they found a silent agreement was in that the pitiful figure, so alone, found no hope or consolation among the swell of people involved in the zeal of Friday worship.

I wonder if this incident, though emotionally disturbing in its own right, is a parable illustrating something far wider that my Chinese co-workers are hoping we will understand. Surrounding their hopes of journeying west towards Jerusalem, and in the cause of 'helping them do it', is a buzz of foreign excitement which has an inherent life of its own which, in the end, leaves the Chinese like the child on the drain cover wondering where they belong.

The outcome? When my Asian colleague finally left the square, the girl on the drain cover could still be seen, alone and frightened. At the same time, a new ruling was issued and enforced by the police. There could be no communications between local inhabitants and foreigners without written permission. What my Chinese friends had feared, had begun to happen.

Such are the brush strokes that paint the compromised religious life of China. Wild foreign triumphalism has intruded into stabilising silence. 'Bigger and better' has sacrificed the purity of honesty. Envy is a prolific plant that grows seeds of deceit. Religious conflicts are often fought on other nations' lands, usually at the expense of the local people. Celebrations can sound the advance of that which dream may not have inspired.

The artist's pain can be seen in the colours on the canvas.

Somewhere below my seat in the sinking Boeing the undercarriage smokes the runway of Beijing's Capital Airport. We have weaved our way through the sky, leaving only a fleeting shadow on earth, unaware of unseen obstacles in the jet stream that the aircraft's sensitive electronic systems, linked to sources outside itself, have recognised. Yet familiarity numbs my mind to this incredible achievement.

I brave the stone-faced immigration control – men and women who have been trained in a hundred different ways how not to smile – and the luggage reclaim scrum. I follow my name, held high above the taxi and hotel tout men. A plush car stutters me through Beijing's gridlocked intersections, to an equally plush guest house. Kindness showers me. My crumpled, unshaven, jet-lagged self scavenges for the tact to show proper appreciation.

My co-worker hosts are a different nationality. I am the lone foreigner, unable to speak their language. From around the world they have gathered in Beijing for consultation. I know that the sessions will be punctuated by lavish acts of hospitality and evening entertainment in prestigious restaurants so typical of the generosity of my friends. Yet they also happen to be the nationality from whom my Chinese colleagues in the far city have sought to escape.

I battle against tiredness and attempt to tap into that reserve of inner stillness which I so often fail to maintain. It's the stillness in which that unexpected voice can be heard. It is apart from the confused babble of sound that saturates the air. It is where spiritual sensitivities are heightened.

How can I – without language, without the intuitive under-standing inherent within a culture, and without giving offence – communicate heartfelt matters with a heart-controlled tongue? Usually, silence is more effective than ill-chosen words.

Once, a flustered colleague told me that he considered that I had about as much pastoral ability as an ant. I thanked him for his generosity, for that was far more than I had allowed myself. Today, however, I am hoping that he meant a really large ant.

I want to assure my dedicated co-workers that this may be opportunity's hour to lay aside the pride of national ambitions and the popular concepts of success, so often fuelled at a host nation's expense; to lay aside personal wars and bear the cost of forgoing that perceived success; to allow the Chinese, with their support, to fulfil their own dream.

The source of wisdom appropriate to China's future is unlikely to come from a far-off seat of power, but rather from the ordinary man who, without anyone's knowledge, submits himself to whatever discipline may bring.

I feel that my extended years can be validated only by standing tall for the young, black-haired bunch of Chinese smiles I have around me as I write. Their innocent freshness of hope and vitality, free from pride and politics of achievement, will naturally sow faith into the environments in which they live.

My personal desire for gain seems to have diminished in proportion to my age. If I could have envisaged the freedom this has brought me, I think that I would have chosen a deeper discipline in my younger years.

There is presence of eternity in the unchanging truth which simply says that ... we fulfil our personal dream only to the extent that we enable others to fulfil theirs.

VOICES ON THE BREEZE
- Xinjiang Province -

When my Chinese friend whispered to me, "Please ask them not to come," his eyes glanced across my shoulder and wrinkled into a smile: "all except those two. They have the same heart as us, tell them to come."

I half-turned and, standing talking to each other in unaffected innocence, quite oblivious to the value this prominent leader was placing on them, were two of my Asian colleagues whom I had grown to appreciate considerably. They were already progressing in the Mandarin language, but were also from the same nation that had been the source of the difficulty.

The route to the far city lies south-west of a large industrial metropolis. From the budget hotel, I can see across the city to the mountains that ring the horizon. Below the mountains, cooling-stacks fume. It is early morning, and the shamble of irregular buildings disappears into yesterday's pollution haze. Below, a bus station begins to breathe and the heavy diesel engines of a hundred parked buses cough into life. A tide of passengers is making its way through the entrances. In rivulets they approach the bus stands.

To one side of a square is a row of familiar shops, all reputedly hairdressers. They will not be open yet, as they specialise in late-night trade. My colleague says he needs a trim. I advise him to look for the shop with the oldest hairdresser, as they seem to be mainly young ladies. He is already in the chair before he realises that they can't cut hair. An hour passes before we rescue him, held to the chair by three bullying females demanding an exorbitant amount for his escape!

Each night our room telephone crackles into life, offering a massage. Doubtless it is from the young lady hairdressers again. It is the only time the phone has use.

Once, as a mixed team, we spent the night in a similar hotel. The receptionist confused the room numbers, and the females settled into the male room. We decided not to change back. Before turning in, I checked the balcony outer doors. I discovered clean cuts through the metal insect netting, just big enough to slide a small hand through.

That night I lay awake and, in the strong moonlight, watched a shadowy figure climb silently over the balcony rail. We were at least three floors up. I worked my way to the balcony door and waited for him to enter. He must have sensed my movement, for he vanished. I dived onto the balcony but he was nowhere to be seen, nor was there a visible escape route.

His intention had been to break into the female room, not knowing of the mix-up. I suspect he would have entered silently, then opened the main door from the inside for others who might have been waiting.

We start our journey south-west. In earlier years, this would have taken three months in set stages across desert and mountain, always by night in the hot weather.

Burning grey-stone desert runs to the horizon in all directions save one, where it stops abruptly at the foot of towering peaks. Jagged and sterile, they probe the sky. They are the bones of a dying landscape, torn and ravaged by the sand-laden wind, shattered by relentless sun and frozen winters. Their reach is never in sight, for they melt into shimmering haze. It is the haze that swallows every horizon, sometimes as close as you could throw a stone, or as distant as where the sky drops below the earth's curved surface. A lake appears, unaccounted for by the maps, its grey-blue water suspended above the desert. It disappears as instantly as it materialised.

Zephyrs play on the desert floor, as erratic as prancing foals. Sometimes there is no horizon, but a swirling, blinding terror to which all other movement submits. Stone dust is hurled into the air to stain red or yellow the glacial ice that forms around the highest peaks ... which guard the secrets of the far city.

A Son of the Yellow Earth

Uig is a man at home with the soil, and I often find myself wondering about the source of his likeable difference. Perhaps I am unconsciously letting him into the warm image I carry of Wil 'Lotment, but I rather think that Uig stands in his own right.

His hands can read the history of the earth: of the centuries of peasant labour; of the ravages of passing armies; of the subjection of his own people by advancing Islam. With sensitive understanding he can read its sorrows, and exchange them for promise. It is his nature to cultivate life.

Uig and his six companions are all people of the soil; university students studying agriculture and completing a period of field work on a small, local farm. Today, however, is a rest day in recognition of their extremely hard work. To celebrate their holiday the girls have dressed in colourful national costume. After joining together for a simple meal, oblivious to the fact that we do not understand each other's language, lost in each other's company, we wander around a local lake. The open entrance to the pagoda, its elegant pillars and arches outlined in blue, red and gold, invites us to sit amid the lush greens of the lakeside growth.

Softly, a colleague begins to sing. It is a Korean song of his own composition. Our new Uyghur friends begin to clap. A spontaneous appeal for another song, then an Uyghur song, a dance ... and a celebration of being alive has begun.

Amid clapping and laughter the dancers take to the stone slab floor, sometimes singly, sometimes in twos and threes. Black headscarves and red and multicoloured skirts swirl around the pirouetting figures. Framed in the crafted archways, the backdrop of sky, mountain, lake and desert come together. The skill and grace of the entwined raised arms and hands seem to be inviting nature's presence to dance with them. A love poem, delicately performed to the wild landscape that raised them to be who they are. A display of the pride and dignity of what it means to be Uyghur.

Uig is a head taller than his companions, his features clean and youthful. His strong arms and large hands clap with controlled explosions. His shoulders begin to move with the rhythm. His smile reflects his relaxed concentration, and leaves his sense of enjoyment in no doubt.

As the excitement mounts, his whole body resonates to the ancient music. It is a melody of romance, both to the surrounding mountains which, like warriors with no fear, spear the sky, and to the mysteries of the moving sands of the great Taklamakan, which reaches before us to an eastward infinity. It is music that has no sound. It is what the inner ear hears, its sounds hidden in the breath of the wind. It is what the composer hears before notes appear on his manuscript. It is what the roadside artisan feels in his tingling fingers as he delicately shapes the instrument and stretches the drum skin. It is how the feet of the sailor read the sea, and why wisdom literature states with uncluttered simplicity, 'Spirit to spirit, you speak.' Little wonder that the project-orientated Westerner can cause him unnecessary suffering.

He was born here, and his life expresses a love of belonging that makes me feel adrift and insignificant. His seat, on the low wall of the open pagoda which holds back the searing sun, can no longer restrain him. His arms outstretched, his hands gesticulating, his feet stomping, he joins in the dance which swirls in crescendo before me.

And why not? They are young Uyghurs, and the far city is not without reason called the City of Song and Dance.

In the rapture of these moments, in the free air and the sun, I think time stands still. The dancers are interpreting to me the landscape and the sky I have experienced on my days of journey here. With life sculptured by the creative hands behind nature's awesome fantasies, they wake, play and sleep to a thunder of the torrents that, with unbridled power, force deep, impenetrable gorges through the mountains, yet also to the silence of the delicate spray-drenched ferns that daily defy gravity as they cling to the crafted rock slabs in a never-ending quest to meet the sun on its short visits.

The dancers see deep beneath the wind-harried desert of rocks and bone, the fissures that for hundreds of miles have rushed the clear snow meltwater to where oases bloom crimson with grapes, yellow with melon, and green with rice. These jewels of the desert are where indigenous communities have been nourished for longer than history records, each one unique in its importance to the mosaic of life reflecting in infinite detail a master design.

And what of the sea of sand? – It is as far away from the sea of salt as it is possible to be. It is where the dunes, like migrating waves of an endless ocean, mount up and break at the boundaries of landfall. Cities of ancient civilisations, whose wealth and importance grew up with Silk Road trade, are buried forever by their mountainous crests.

'Buried forever?' I ask. Even though I already know the answer, I wait for the dancing figure to tell me again in a picture painted by artistic gesture.

By gentle breeze, by playful whirlwinds, by angry tornadoes, sometimes in secret, sometimes before a million eyes, a slow transfiguration takes place. Grain by grain the mountain of sand, like a wave, begins a long migration. Then, to the sky and the stars, there is restored a landscape familiar to those alive several millennia ago. Among them lie their tools, their pots, their sacred images, and their graves.

The dancers now move from person to person. Their eyes flash an invitation. Their bodies lean forward, arms and hands adding welcome to their call. I would love to join them in this song of the earth. They are offering me more than an interpretation of their culture. I am understanding the clay from which they are made – their hidden, but true, identity. I want so desperately to join their dance, but with limbs so stiff and clumsy, with eyes too misty – perhaps with age, certainly with emotion – I feel I would devalue the offering of those I mean to serve.

So I let my spirit soar with theirs, in the hope that when it returns, it will inwardly instruct me more clearly into what it means to be Uyghur. I am a stranger, but they have chosen to open their treasury to me.

The Long Valley

There was a moment when I fancied that my heart beat to the same rhythm, but it proved only a fancy. These Uyghur twenty-year olds had opened a door to a dark valley through which they had travelled.

Among China's millions they are tolerated as a minority group, and their land as an autonomous region. The centre of their far city has been cleared of traditional Uyghur buildings, and a Tienanmen-like square has been built in honour of Chairman Mao. High above the surrounding buildings, above the artificial lakes, the flowers and gigantic red lanterns, he stands. Gleaming white in the sun, his dead arm and hand extended, the dead smile of achievement on his dead face. Some historians claim it is an image of the most successful mass murderer of the past century, before which all must bow.

Before our day together closed, Uig had suggested he show me their main mosque. One of the girls wrinkled her nose. She stayed outside. I paid my ten yuan and, as an entry ticket, received a postcard of the mosque, already stamped for postage.

My trainers joined the blitz of sandals dropped at the mosque door, many wearing old car tyres as soles. I walked barefoot through the prayer rooms that surrounded the courtyard. At the exit I turned and looked back at the route I had taken.

It held a significance I had not dreamed of. Memories of Mao's regime are passing into history with the death of his generation, and a nation is recovering its poise. The dominance of Islam, however, represents a journey back along the Uyghur trail far longer than Mao's reign. Islam's expansion advanced rapidly eastwards through Central Asia, until in 751 the Islamic armies defeated the Chinese, and the Christianised Turkic-speaking Uyghur lands fell under their occupation.

I had travelled perhaps another stage in the journey back down the Uyghur valley ... but who knows what distance still remains to the quarry from which their clay has been dug?

Their song of the earth had preceded Islam. In the language of the heart, was there a cry to God who, in the wildness of his own dream, had made a wild world with untamed people who wanted no more than the affirmation of his love? I suspect that Uig wanted me to know for myself that the mosque stands as a visible symbol of what the centuries have tried to persuade them to accept as an integral part of their identity, culture and spiritual life – something it has only achieved superficially.

With wet eyes, we stood silently and watched the crowds in the mosque square absorb the colour of our young Uyghur friends. They too, lost in the mists of their thoughts, let their tears speak feelings no words could adequately frame.

I wrenched a hole in the silence; perhaps I was not meant to. I asked quietly to anyone who would hear, "Will you keep in touch with them?"

"How can we?" came back the answer I could expect but did not want to hear, "we cannot speak or write their language."

Without thinking I looked across at So-young and Son-mi, the two that had made the Chinese leader smile as he had glanced over my shoulder and whispered to me, "Those two have the same heart as us, let them come."

Both had their heads bowed and their silence carried the conviction of those for whom destiny's search is over.

Silently we made our way back to our lodgings. The street was beginning to fill with people emerging into the cool evening. Bakers had fixed up their open-air ovens; brick-built, inverted domes. Each baker took measured amounts of dough and flattened them against the inside of the dome. These loosened as they baked, and catching them was part of the skill. Cobblers treadled primitive stitching machines. Fruit and produce stalls jostled for pavement space, whilst skull-capped men with hessian shopping bags haggled over each item. Coffee shops spread their tables and chairs in the remaining space . Families of two, three or even four, on a single cycle, wobbled their way to their own 'somewhere'.

Tonight was a night for celebration, but not on the streets. Each one of us had already retired into our personal inner hiding places. Together with our new Uyghur friends, we had crossed an invisible line and had awakened to the fact that the future was already in us, inviting us to keep walking through our tomorrows and to let it unfold. From words of ancient wisdom, I overheard the promise: *You shall have an agreement with these stones of the field.*

The Two Stones

The next day I wandered alone some way into the desert, and from the floor of a great sand pan I picked up a million years of history. It was in the form of a common stone. Drenched in the sun's heat, it burned my fingers as I slipped it into my rucksack. It was a visible confirmation of my invisible secret. It was a stone from the field.

As the stone fell to the bottom of my rucksack, it found place alongside another I had already collected from an entirely different location. As I shouldered my bag and returned to the city, the 'chink' of the two stones gave me an inner chuckle of faith, and a smile I could not hide.

TWO SMOOTH STONES
- An Altar at the end of China -

Kallie ... our first stone

The massive diesel engine had hauled our quarter-kilometre-long line of carriages across the plain of sun-tortured barrenness, where dried stream beds, like gnarled fingers, reached out for our help. When our conversation, like the landscape, had dried through the heat, Kallie appeared.

It was as if she had been wandering through the carriages looking for someone. She carried herself with the air of a free spirit, confident to the point of being cheeky, yet in such an endearing way, no one could take offence.

"Hello, I'm an English student. May I sit down?"

We moved along our bunks to make room for her.

We quickly learned that the tall, slender visitor was indeed an Uyghur in her mid-twenties. Her open, honest expression made her most attractive. "My home is in the far city" she explained, "but I am a student in Beijing."

As Beijing is the whole width of China from the far city, and a horrendous train journey, I asked the obvious question: "Why Beijing?"

"The environment is good for learning English" she replied, "for there are many foreigners studying there."

As China was then in the grip of the SARS pandemic, with all students confined to campus and with travellers having temperature checks every few hours, I did not dare ask her how she could be returning home even before university summer recess.

Kallie was as delighted with my young colleagues as they were with her, and conversation took off in all directions at once. I turned my gaze to the carriage window.

Outside, the landscape appeared more friendly. We had left behind an undeniable hint of oil exploration and a forest of wind-generated turbines and, for an hour or more, had followed an incline along a valley floor. Sparsely spread tufts of green had encouraged sheep among the boulders, the shepherd, head scarfed, squatting low in the shade. Impossibly steep trails mounted the foothills, and puffs of orange dust, shimmering in the heat, signalled movement of vehicle or animals.

It was a startled pause in the conversation that snapped my attention back to Kallie.

"How long have you been learning English?" someone had asked.

"Just about three months," came the articulate, confident answer. "Yes, just about three months now," she affirmed.

The conversation was punctuated by an audible gasp from everyone. It was Kallie who again broke the silence that could be felt. "Have I said something wrong?" she asked.

Kallie, too, was part of earth's chorus, but with a difference. The wild storms that bore in from the desert were in the air about herself. No swirling skirt and black headdress, but jeans and a Western hairstyle.

"I will be your tour guide to the far city" she said. "I will show you how our traditional instruments are made."

Unwittingly, she had uncovered her own roots.

"Do you sing and dance?" I asked.

"Yes," said the musical laughter in her voice, "all Uyghur girls do. Sometimes celebrations are held high in the mountains with our traditional music, our folk-songs and our dances."

Kallie had trained for a banking career, like her father and sister, but had given it up and returned to university. She now studied economics, with English as part of this degree. "An Uyghur proverb says, *We live on a goldmine, but with only pennies in our pockets.* We may have more oil than Arab countries," she said, "but we do not know how to use this resource. This is why I study economics."

The straining locomotive had now wound its way up the head of a valley. I looked back on miles of spiralling track; we were in a mountain pass – another marvel of Chinese ingenuity and determination, though I could not help but wonder how many lives it had taken to give me this effortless ride. I dwelled on the image of Chairman Mao's fabled Long March. Carried on a litter across high mountains, the peasant soldiers – with the front shafts on their shoulders, cut, bloodied and exhausted – had climbed the rocks on their knees to keep his litter level!

The soil here unrolled its sweet green towards its surrounding guardians, their fierce snow peaks hidden in the streaming dark clouds that preserved their mystery. Nomadic yurts dotted the landscape with animal herds and flying horsemen. A river played over boulders. A large bird of prey hung in the air, and the breeze carried voices. Before beginning its onward and downward plunge to the desert basin, the train halted and large flakes of snow began to fall. Yet this was June!

Lunch, on the day of the guided tour, was sumptuous traditional Uyghur fare with Kallie's family in a modern apartment near the much smaller Tiananmen Square lookalike. Kallie's mother, a medical doctor, had with Uyghur generosity laid out rugs and mats for us to sleep on after the meal.

On the streets, in open-fronted workshops nearby, families of craftsmen – apprenticed sons and grandsons – using eye, hand and ear, built with precision the most delicate musical instruments. Heat from a wood-fired stove on the pavement edge bent wood strips of various sizes into intricate shapes that captured the voice of the wind, shrill among the peaks, mournful among the rocks, frightening as vicious storms. Of torrents that with the sound of giants' laughter gouge the mountain slopes. Of galloping horses. Of clapping hands. Of dancing girls. Of a clear sky, ablaze with a million stars for every grain of sand. Of the song of the earth. Oh, that the advance of electronic gadgetry should never denude man of his spirituality and inherent creativity!

Kallie spoke of the inevitability of marriage among Uyghur women, often at sixteen, sometimes at twelve. Many are illiterate and expect nothing else. Then, with an indignant toss of her head and a fire in her eyes, she spoke to all who wanted to hear:

"Everyone thinks that I should be married now, for I am becoming old, but – waaaaa! – I am not ready yet, and besides, I must choose my husband carefully ."

We made our way to the bazaar. "Over there" she pointed, "are where poor people live. The mud and wood houses are two hundred years old. We have many beggars. I avoid them, as I do not know what to do."

I wanted to tell her: *Follow your heart, Kallie, just follow your heart.*

"Buy a knife," she commanded me; "they are crafted here. Look, I carry two!"

It startled me to suddenly see them appear in her hand.

"We all carry them" she assured me.

I bought a few folding knives with red stones embedded into their brass handles. I would give them away to each one who would promise to pray for my two colleagues, for whom Kallie was unknowingly affirming a destiny in this far city.

Kallie held the stall holders in an incessant chatter which kept me interestingly informed, until her mobile interrupted. "I must go now," she said, with a finality that did not allow for objection.

We exchanged email addresses. She gave me three, and suddenly we became aware of the wide space she had occupied among us in just a few tantalisingly short days. I wondered if she had engineered her own mobile call, which had neatly brought the interlude of our togetherness to a convenient end, for fear we might intrude on her fierce independence. With equal deliberation I searched for a suitable stone from this city where Kallie had been reared, and for the moment my rucksack would be its home.

I cannot claim my thoughts on the two stones to be original. About three thousand years before, a Syrian general travelled to the Jordan river. There he discovered a profoundly elemental spirituality which completely altered his personal thinking. Before returning, he asked if he could take with him as a gift two mule-loads of earth. Wisdom's literature had allowed an altar to be built out of earth or uncut stones. I chose the uncut stones.

You shall have an agreement with the stones of the field, said my inner voice once again.

Two seasons of snowmelt from the frozen peaks of the Tienshan have flooded the gorges, and the desert oases have bloomed. My two stones, symbols of hope, await the fulfilment of promise for desert and city. Meanwhile my two young colleagues, in a city some distance away, have continued the study of Mandarin and begun a small recruiting and training base. One has wisely decided to remain, to expand the base and supervise future training. The other, with a companion, as the mountain snows begin their new season's thaw, will leave for life in the far city with the desert ... and their story awaits its time to be told.

RED CRINKLED PAPER
- Shaanxi Province -

The city is not my chosen habitat. It seems so unnatural that the horizon should be the view of the other side of the street, except in some cites where that might not always be possible until a fresh wind clears the traffic haze. Where people always seem to be on their way to somewhere there is not enough time to reach. Where the best places to shop and eat are always on the other side of the city from whatever side you happen to live. Where the span of the sky is tailored to narrow strips by houses that follow roads. Where we live in tightly-packed rows of rooms stacked on top of each other, like over-planted seedlings that reach ever higher in pursuit of the sun. Yet these are the places to which all of us at some time gravitate.

Where Wisdom Hides
Someone waits at a busy street corner. If I do not appear soon, he will leave. I alight from a city bus. Without raising my head, I follow his heels past a uniformed guard, an iron gate, and through a narrow passage that leads downwards into a bare room ... the home of an underground family church.

Unorchestrated, subdued singing begins, punctuated by spontaneous weeping and prayer, smoothing away apprehension caused by a foreigner among them. The presence of faith fills the room. I have been invited to teach, but since entering this hidden closet I have not ceased to be taught. I am emotionally overcome.

They understand that tears have their place and, like something holy, they make room for them. They are not a sign of weakness but so often an honourable badge of suffering. Mine are from powerful emotion. I lose track of time.

Eventually the people begin to leave as they had arrived: inconspicuously in ones and twos, filing into the busy lane. A presence smiling directly at me draws my gaze. Lined skin under grey hair and wrinkled eyes, offering me more than her outstretched hand. I take the crinkled red paper, but my gaze remains on her, an elderly lady – doubtless a daughter of communist ideology. Perhaps with high expectation she had faithfully worn the communist hope all its grim years, but the Chairman became the new emperor, and her hope died.

Inwardly, however, I know that this is unimportant to her and is not what she wants me to know. She watches me open the red, crinkled paper. She has cut out a Chinese character that spells ... *happiness.* Her eyes search mine for that gleam of understanding. I think it is there, though defined by more tears. She is no-one's slave, yet everyone's, for she has chosen to be among faith's family. Divinity within her responds to divinity without, and I suspect this time it is eternal dream she has begun to dream. Happiness now characterizes her days. She has found an inexhaustible source from which she can draw for others ... including me.

This gentle introduction to a personality who, through suffering, has been refined to a rare purity and hidden by Wisdom's genius, has kindled in my dull orthodoxy a little of its own flame. Natural life seems like living a simple parable, when sudden insight reveals the deeper reality which the parable is meant to convey.

I realise that my understanding of spiritual life has been gleaned mainly by viewing the wrong side of a tapestry. All that can be seen are the knots in a confusion of coloured thread. The intrinsic value of the poor, the ordinary and the unimportant, is only understood when the tapestry is viewed from the finished side.

I feel that I have been in the presence of such a work of art.

I take time to filter into the passing throng and to recover my anonymity. I pass the guard, the iron gate, turn a corner and inwardly begin to unwind.

Meanwhile on the Pavement
Along the pavement a small boy lies face down. His legs, knotted

like gnarled tree roots, lie in a tangle behind him. His chest and tummy rest on a small oblong of wood with wheels attached. He cannot raise his head, but can move his eyes, which look up at me. At the end of a crippled arm a hand is cupped. With the other he pulls himself along, keeping pace with my unhurried steps.

I notice this boy because he moves, but there is another who has no piece of wood and wheels. Someone shouts to the boy at my feet. His eyes turn again to the pavement which is just three inches from his face. I am not sure of how I should feel, for I am told that the boys are owned and put out to work begging for their employer. This does not stop a wave of guilt passing through me.

I have seen similar sights elsewhere. From a pavement in Manila to the hard-pressed cities in Africa, I was told that children have been maimed and certainly drugged and used for begging. I met a young African who kept an ulcerated leg wound open, selling the antibiotics that charity had bought him, for by his wound he kept his family alive.

I wonder if the boys who hover above the pavement have had their legs bent, scream by scream.

There are many poor who survive by living on the pavement. I know of one father who packs his family into a cardboard box each night. By day he sells cigarettes from a makeshift table ... one at a time. I learned his story when three of us shared a room in a hotel on the opposite side of the road, for a total of three pounds a night – which included breakfast.

Then something I have not seen before. A mother with a young baby strapped to her back is kneeling before a low wooden footrest. By her colouring and features she may not be Chinese, but from one of the many minority groups. Her faded clothing and flat green cap probably confirm this. From a distance I watch her at work. She is tying the shoelaces of better-off children. A parent looks on, radiant at this act of subservience to her son. Perhaps the kneeling mother also sleeps on the pavement, and the footrest will be her pillow. Then what of her own child ... ?

An older woman kneels in front of me. She is holding out her hand, pleading ... for the equivalent of one penny.

There is space for a bus pull-in alongside a small concrete

building. Against the wall and close to the bus someone has made a low lean-to of rags and plastic bags wired together. Underneath sits a sad, elderly lady; her feet and legs are swollen, and there is no room for her to lie. Someone pulls aside the plastic sack she uses for a door and pushes a small round bread into her grimy hands. She makes appreciative noises. Passengers also use the space between the bus and the lean-to as a toilet.

I step into a small, open-fronted teashop and pull a metal-framed chair to a formica-topped table. At the corners, the formica has begun to curl back. An aluminium kettle bearing the coal-black scale and dents of years pours hot green tea into a plastic glass.

A broad set of teeth grins a welcome over a greasy apron. Her husband stands before an oil drum that looks to have grown out of the ash-littered floor, at the entrance to the one small room. Against a wall of black grease, his hand reaches for an equally black switch. A supply of air drives flames upward through the coal briquettes.

His wok is already warm. Soy bean curd, water, oil and vegetables fly. Five or six pinches of different spices follow. They are shaken together while cooking, and in moments empty onto a plastic bag-covered plate, which lands on the table. More tea follows. It is delicious, but far more than I am able to eat. The cost of everything ... about twenty-five pence or less, and the hot green tea keeps coming.

There is an open honesty about such small places that I like. It is Mum and Dad who serve you. Mum will sit at the table and talk with you if business is slow. She may tell you that the little shop keeps her daughter attending school. They also grew up in Mao's China. They have both been reborn in their daughter. They gladly work twelve hours a day for seven days each week. They find their hope in their daughter's future. Sometimes in the evenings the daughter will help serve, and be introduced with much pride, but usually she will study. What about the apparent lack of cleanliness? – I have never been affected badly by such meals. Mum and Dad's honour would be at stake should I be ill.

I am in no hurry to leave, so the green tea keeps flowing. I watch the people who pass, and soak up the homely ambience. I cannot keep the kneeling mother and child out of my mind. Perhaps I should pay for a meal for her here, or a week's meals, or a month's, or a year's? Then what about the crippled children, or the elderly beggar-lady?

In a village, I once watched an ancient hand loom at its slow work. It took so many different strands of thread to make a metre of cloth. Infinitely more complex is the diversity of strands that make up life in China.

Where Underground isn't where it Seems

From my table I look up at the top floors of a small number of apartment blocks. In the gloomy grey skies of China's autumn and in the dust-laden air they look frigid and uninteresting ... but looks can be deceptive. Simmering in one is a cauldron of pent-up energy.

Springs of irrepressible faith quickly become streams, then rivers. Sometimes the waters are temporarily diverted into hidden reservoirs, small but deep and still. These are the training locations for China's underground mission movements. At the approach of danger, the little reservoirs empty ... only to be reformed quickly elsewhere. I know of few training locations that compare with China.

I slip past the guards, into a small estate of mid-sized tower blocks. With some difficulty I select what I believe to be the right one. It is beginning to get dark. A grey cement staircase offers the only route to the top floor. As I begin the ascent with as little noise as my laboured breathing will allow, an uneasiness begins to settle on me. *This could be anywhere in the world*, I ponder, as I look at the footprints etched in the dust-powdered corridors. A black door looms through the failing light. I am about to graze my knuckles on its sound-absorbing iron when my unease grows too strong.

My knuckles are saved, and my cover is not blown. I descend the flight of stairs quickly; the entrance gate is still open. On the approach road I look about and realise that I have entered the wrong block. I choose the right one; finally, a heavy door opens a little and I slip inside.

From around the room, many pairs of eyes search for mine. I take the stool offered me. It is just nine inches off the floor. The small room is crowded, and smiles beam a welcome from every angle. A few wear the excited response of recognition.

As last light fades from the windows, we settle to some hours of study. They are visibly tired, so I choose a suitable teaching mode. In response to my request for shared dreams, Caleb – the tallest of the young men – says that he wants to 'sound the horn of the dawn over China'. Something in me understands, without knowing what he means. At the close of a long day, after a small team has taught in turn morning, afternoon and evening, Caleb's statement has in it the force of China's future.

For three months the little group had hardly left their top floor hideout. Then suddenly police activity tightened, and all changed. The rooms of this little reservoir emptied of smiling faces and hushed laughter ... only miraculously to form elsewhere, in a location secret to all but the trainees and the thin stream of those who share their lives with them.

My focus is almost entirely on the development and growth of Chinese teams. This future force, though underground, is potentially one of the world's largest. Through hundreds of small centres there is more training taking place in the provinces of China than ever before. A Chinese colleague has more than twenty centres under his supervision. Some move frequently between tower blocks. Others operate under the guise of other interests. Yet more, hidden far into the country, are deprived of heat and most things considered as basic necessities.

Faith will continue to point the way, and allow China to fulfil a divine destiny on our world's frontiers.

Where Leaders Serve

It was in the back of a primitive agricultural vehicle that I first met Joe, and so gained my introduction to the leadership of one of China's main House Church streams. The sky broke, and rain flowed in torrents. Our journey was across country, and mud threatened to swallow our vehicle. Joe laughed as he leaped from under cover and his strength eased the wheels out of the mire. He need not have done that. In fact, he needn't have been in the vehicle at all. It was a dangerous mission. Any hint of his involvement would have added more years to his prison record, which already stood at six years' hard labour.

Joe is casual, relaxed and friendly; his mellowness belies his rank. He wears his authority not as a uniform, but as a comfortable old coat. Because he is secure in his position, his humility reverses the power pyramid structure. His satisfaction comes from enabling others to get ahead of himself. People feel safe in his decisions and, without thinking, model themselves on his strengths ... which is the most potent form of discipleship. Similarly Joe, without realising, has developed the code that 'showing is better than teaching'.

Joe introduced such a warm image of leadership into my mind that, ever since, I have been eager to learn from others ... and I have not been disappointed.

Some years ago, in an intensely poor rural village setting, I was an unseen witness to a generous act of leadership. It was at a secret training camp when the cold air, dampened by incessant rain, clung to people and buildings alike. The unsurfaced roads and fields, awash with mud, had not deterred the numbers of people who had made their way under cover of dark.

On the final morning, while the absent sun was still warming countries to our east, faint sounds had drawn me outside the barn in which I slept. Two figures, black shadows in the darkness, were busy clearing the earth-surfaced yard, and in particular the open primitive toilets. Few words passed between them. Finally they returned their tools and washed in the cold well water.

I recognised them; they were both rural farmers. The lady was also an underground pastor with wide responsibility in her area. The police were aware that she was active but so far she had escaped arrest. The previous day I had learned that she was quite ill. Now she had to leave; she had a ten-hour journey across country astride an open and unprotected iron-framed three-wheeled vehicle, steered by both hands on a heavy iron bar, and powered by a large, single-cylinder diesel engine which must have been the world's most primitve agricultural vehicle.

But not before I had watched her become the servant of all at the camp.

I love her world, and wish to earn the right to a place in it. My insight into her hidden actions trains me how to serve. She is a unique person, and that moment my unique opportunity to be taught by her. Outside the farm compound, the close darkness her only witness, wrapped against the rain and cold, she cranked the ancient engine by hand, mounted the iron frame, and the dull thud of the single cylinder grew fainter in the mist thick air.

Perhaps she is giving you permission to serve also, you say. *Our value is determined by our hidden decisions. Sometimes we gain by losing, and lose by gaining.*

Yes, but my service may be unreal. It may be patronising, or boosting some kind of perverted pride in me which will pollute the spiritual environment in which they have chosen to live. It may not be permission to serve that I take, but permission to be arrogant.

I returned to my place in the barn, warmed by the thought that, to follow her dream, she had chosen to serve. She had allowed herself to be different, so could give others permission to be different too. She understood that no one dreams the entire picture. Her dreams were the crumbs, for the whole loaf is shared between many.

I love the earthy humility that accompanies her faith. It is where I belong and feel secure ... and I would judge that the hundred or so she holds in her care feel the same way also. The faith that gripped the steering bar of the tractor, and the eyes that in the darkness focussed on the trail, were like those of the one who steered a donkey towards Jerusalem – untroubled by doubt.

THE BLUE DOG
- China's Old Streets -

This Central China city has no sky to roll out today. Instead it is in the hug of a deathly grey mist – a toxic mixture of brick dust, vehicle fumes and factory emissions. Lustreless acid droplets form rivulets on rusting metal and insidiously sap a building's strength. Smoke stacks, designed to disperse their pollutants over the countryside, are now dwarfed by higher buildings. With ghostly surrealism they rise from the ground into nothing.

What will happen, I wonder, *when tower blocks, like old men, grow tired together?*

I feel the fangs of the freezing mist. Occasional snowflakes drift in the wind. At midday the sun, eaten by the acid air, drips tears of weak light which may penetrate here and there, creating short-lived islands of warmth. I succumb to the temptation to stand in one of them.

Within my stark block of flats the temperature seems lower than it is outside. I live wrapped in my heavy outdoor clothes, and shiver. We have not yet reached the official start of winter, so the external heating controls await their hour to be opened. Still, cities are generally better provided for than the smaller towns and villages, where eighty percent of the population live. They have no heating of any form.

China's old streets welcome me from the night chaos of neon, and I have a deep contentment walking through their scarcely-lit maze. Blind corners offer the imagination journeys that could lead anywhere. The scent of the day still hangs heavily in the cold air, and my breathing resonates against the thick slurry of the mist.

By day, the street is filled with the din of bicycle bells. Cyclists here seem to have been born with skills unknown elsewhere. Slung with heavy sacks, they weave among handcarts and the bag-carrying throng, to the shouts of the hawkers under the awnings. The sounds are loud and colourful, and mingle with the traders' bargaining, joking and laughing.

I breathe in the smell of country vegetables, chickens, boiled pork and soy sauce. Narrow shop fronts line the street: pineapple shops, oil shops, egg shops, rice shops, vegetable shops. Shops scrunched up one against the other, selling Chinese medicine, meat, silk and cotton, clothes – tailored on a treadle machine while you watch – tea, rope, pottery, incense candles and shoes, rusty iron tools, hair-dryers and soapy liquid of some kind in gaudy, plastic bottles. A flying wok supplies instant noodle meals in a plastic bag, and the inevitable circle of squatting card players shout as they throw their cards to the floor. Children with bare feet, indistinguishable from the black stone cobbled street, stand and stare. In a vacant space, rice noodles dry as they hang from wires.

It is when the harsh glare of light has retired that the soul is released from the day's stress, both in me and in these lanes. This is a fruitful time, when healing and bonding occur. I find a kinship between darkness and light. They are entwined strands of the essential thread called life. Both nature and spiritual life have common laws, with one giving great depth of insight into the other. From the dark soil of the womb we have emerged, but not entirely. Friendly darkness shields my inner life, for it lives in continuous night. All my thoughts are born there. From the womb of the night the day's creativity emerges.

A handcart leaning against a wall, its worn shafts dully reflecting the ambient light, tells its own story. From the shadow, soft grey hair and a wrinkled face emerge for a moment, caressed by a wisp of light, just long enough to leave an image fixed in time. Then, smooth-skinned innocence and feet that refuse to keep still – a child, barely visible. Hands glow from the light of a struck match. In the darkness, a voice, invisible. It evokes an image only inner eyes can see. Each its own brush stroke without the confusion of detail.

I turn into an unusual lane: long and straight. I judge by the diffused glow of moving lights that there is an arch at one end which meets a busy road. The low buildings lining either side of the lane, long and straight, are one-room shops that open onto tiny pavements. It is very late, and the shops have dropped their shutters against the night – save for one, whose light still warms the pavement and infuses the mist with luminous glow. It has caught my eye, and I am tempted to follow.

Behind a plate glass door, with an air of indifference that can be felt, a small dog with long white silken hair sits and patiently watches for passing feet. During my early years in China, almost the only dogs I can recall were for sale in the live meat market, where they would be displayed along with frogs, snakes, cats, rabbits, chickens and trapped wild animals I could not recognise. To choose a puppy meant that it would likely come despatched, skinned and wrapped.

This one, however, has so far escaped the wok. Its head of hair is dyed blue and brushed over its eyes. Its ears and feet are purple. I allow the shadows to enclose me while I stand and watch. From its space on the floor, its responsibility is to look for feet. Veiled by the hair, and having no neck, it can look no higher. When a pair of feet turn into the shop, it is the signal to stand and to wag a pink tail. When two pairs of feet walk in, its pitch of excitement rises. Its tail becomes a blur and, leaving its place, it greets the new shoelaces.

The shop is modern, though quite small. Light explodes from mirrors and stainless fittings. Swivel chairs line the walls, filled by young men and women – probably students from the two universities along the main road. They are having their hair cut and dyed, perhaps blue, and their nails painted, perhaps purple.

I step from the shadow and the young proprietor acknowledges me with a nod. He is smartly casual, with white shirt, dark trousers and permed hair. He follows my gaze to the dog and smiles, not apologetically, but as someone who knows he has succeeded. He does not need to give account for what he does, for around him his personal dream is being fulfilled. He offers freedom to express an image which his followers queue to buy, even into the night. He is selling them difference, which may be their key to a locked door behind which their own dreams are imprisoned. He has a paying membership of those who are proud to wear the badge of blue hair and purple nails. With his influence, both young men and women are changing the status quo, a wildness that pushes back frontiers – at least in the local universities. He is demonstrating a principle that may possibly be unlocking the idealogical stalemate that is China's normality.

Though I shall keep my silver crown for as long as it chooses my company, as strange as it sounds, I cannot deny a feeling of affinity with the young man and the blue dog.

THE SMART, THE FOOL
AND THE SLAVE
- A Philosopher's China -

In the molten swim of my thinking are the conclusions of the Chinese author, Lu Xun, which I am using as a broad framework for a foundational understanding of life in China. In an article published in 1926 entitled *The Smart, the Fool and the Slave,* he defines three categories of person with three distinct attitudes.

The Smart Person, like ambitious politicians, may sacrifice responsibility for personal gain. They know how to present themselves in a pleasing manner and how to say exactly the right things, but only for their own advancement. They smile over the Slaves because they need them, but do nothing to ease their circumstances.

The Slaves complain bitterly about their position, but generally are powerless to do anything about it. And the Fools have no place in either society. They are the activists, the true revolutionaries, who accept the dangers and are prepared to run with what they believe.

China, writes Lu Xun, by tradition has just two groups – the Smart and the Slave. What China needs is more Fools.

"We are among the Fools," says my colleague, looking over the mound of fifteen heavy quilts she has just bought for the poor to wrap around themselves.

In his own way, so is the young man with the permed hair and the blue dog, if only for the students around his street. Perhaps those who follow their dreams will need to accept that, by Lu Xun's definition, they are Fools who fit nowhere, but inspire change.

Inwardly I have a nagging question, for I wonder whether, from among the genuine seed of the Fool, a weed can appear. The roots of some forms of organism refuse to die. From a single cell they can begin to grow again, the difference only becoming obvious as they mature.

I am thinking of a particular peasant boy who, through great hardship, became a student and who, for a short while, looked as if he were fulfilling the role of a Fool. At the age of twenty-four, however, he began to explore the inner structures of his dream. He believed himself to be responsible only for the reality he enjoyed, to have a duty to himself alone, and absolutely no responsibility for others. The voracious hunger of a new Smart Person had begun to appear.

People are here for my benefit. My desires are there to act upon without consideration for anyone.

He began to show a sadistic appetite for brutalising the Slave, which gave him the adrenalin rush he craved. Before he had reached thirty, his rallying call to the villagers was to *kill! kill! burn! burn!* – and the first of his many purges had begun.

Looking for the favour of Moscow, he followed Stalin's directives and incited the classes to kill each other. Change, he taught, would only come about through the destruction of people, towns, countries and the world. As the years brought their changes, his lust for power developed. At the close of his reign of genocide, torture and totalitarianism, seventy million had died.

His legacy lingers in the bullying bureaucracy of China's government. As one journalist wrote, 'It is impossible to be unafraid of the future while the face of Mao Tse-Tung still appears on Chinese currency.'

The Fool became the Smart Person; the new emperor appeared in different clothes. The hopeful Slave simply changed his master. The structure of China reverted to what it had been, though infinitely more brutal, and scarce freedom was found only behind bars or in hiding. Those who professed faith of any kind were numbered as the new Fools, a threat that had to be eliminated.

Not all of the older men of faith that I have known, who have subscribed to the Fool's way, have been fortunate enough to receive just three years' imprisonment with hard labour. Once, I attempted to console one who had spent twenty years in prison, but I quickly became unglued.

"It was my freedom," he said. "Mao's Red Guards did not put to death those already in prison."

I dither under a street light that tonight refuses to be friendly. Behind me, a fountain does not celebrate. Both have stopped working. Around my feet a halo of frost grows on the grass. Polished ice covers the road, and my breath smokes in the frozen air. My reluctant feet must turn in the direction of my welcoming doormat. My mind still feels threatened by the suffocation of sleep, but common sense argues that my questions need the light and experience of a new day.

My future is not a challenge to engage with all I see, but to refine my focus to the one thing that holds meaning and purpose. For the remainder of that night, sleep becomes a restless wait until morning. It is half past seven before the weak light of dawn has penetrated the smog.

Some hours earlier, neighbours in the flat above me stirred into their daily routine. Clog-like shoes journeyed back and forth across a cement-tiled floor. The echoes rang and jarred in a way that made me feel like a fly trapped between the skins of a drum. There followed what I imagined to be a hard onion being finely chopped on a cutting board. I gritted my teeth, thought unkind thoughts and pulled my sleeping bag around my ears. It is not that I object to waking early, as the time was already long past my normal routine. Rather, it is that I have reconciled myself to being a coward when it comes to my feet touching the cold tile floor.

I reach for my outdoor jacket, drape it over my shoulders, and decide to concentrate on the space within me that a breakfast of warm soy bean drink will not fill; the space reserved for the silence out of which my focus for the day will emerge.

I reach for my notebook on the bedside table, and the book I would never want to be without. This is not the hour for study, but for quiet contemplation. Scriptural meditation offers knowledge and assurance through inspirational insight, rather than academic pursuit. It allows light to fall on the reasons why, which usually is the purpose for which events with all their details have their being;

for He, himself, is the Why.

As I expected, my Bible is already open and I read the words: *In the beginning* ... As far as I know, it is the only text which can make that statement with authority.

I find a home, in that uncluttered beginning, which leads me to myself. In the darkness of interior, light shines, and multi-layered reality comes into view. A network of stars appears within the universe of a single truth, but every attempted explanation distorts that truth. Here the whole world of discovery is but a minute eclipse of the moon, and the value of any conclusion is about as complete as knowledge gleaned about all the deserts of earth from a few grains of sand.

Nature is itself a book, a fathomless expression of eternal thought and the source of all scientific discovery. Yet there is another book written by the same creative author. It is the book of origins, commonly called the Bible. Incarnated into the story of our physical universe, it is the source of truth and reveals the invisible spiritual reality which gives time a framework, and nature its meaning.

Mingled among the words I read that do not appear on the page flows my personal story of China, eased into my experience in measures I have been able to accept, though not always understand. Unknowingly, my life has become a product of this union.

As I luxuriate in the delight of truth and experience, unknown to me, it is also a fortification against the disturbing thoughts that providence has allowed into my day.

THE RESTLESS MAN
- Which Way New China? -

I gasp at the sight of my watch dial. My moments of quiet meditation and reflection have swallowed hours. I find courage to face the cement-tiled floor, the cold water in the tap; the icy temperature inside the flat. There is an urgency in me I cannot understand. I do not realise that I have an appointment to keep that I have not made. An event is to become part of my experience which will forever blow away some of my naive assumptions.

It is afternoon. Three men in dark clothes walk stiffly towards us. My colleagues, who have been expecting their visit, welcome them to a table. After a round of introductions and informal conversation, they invite me to join them – a meeting that will lead me to consider many possibilities which I have lacked the courage to face.

I take a seat across the table from a short, middle-aged, restless man. His expression, mannerisms, and the uncertainty of his nervous eyes speak a language I can understand. He does not easily smile, and seems relieved that the table preserves distance between us. My confidence wilts, as though I am either about to be judged in court, or to hear a serious lecture.

He is accompanied by two younger men who seem unsure of their relevance, or even whether they have any. They balance on the edge of their seats like pieces of fragile pottery.

In an attempt to wave a flag of truce, I join their conversation. Or at least I think I do, before it becomes obvious that I have struck hidden rocks. I feel like a hard-of-hearing elderly uncle who is noted for saying the wrong things at the wrong time. I wonder if I am increasing their bad experience of foreigners. Making the restless man more restless seems to be my only achievement.

Thoughts of what he is about to say stiffen his posture. He tightens his hands and lays out his arms, edge-on across the table.

"We come from a province in the east."

Such a statement can carry with it an authority. It is in this area of China that the so-called Jerusalem of the East exists, regarded – especially by distant non-Chinese nations – as the heartlands where the growth of underground church communities has been felt the strongest.

The men have arrived in Central China to help village people who migrate to the cities in search of employment. They also intend to begin an underground family church here which will express their parent group's distinctives.

A mobile phone invades our privacy and irritates for attention. It seems to please the restless man, who heads for the corner of the room. I use the unexpected freedom to restore my confidence by asking the nearer young man about his employment before he joined the team. He misunderstands, and lists the cities he has visited. I try again, giving him my age and a little of my experience in China and elsewhere.

He relaxes, slides back in his seat, and with a smile says, "I am just twenty-six," then confides with a whisper: "I also dream of becoming a missionary."

Silence in the corner announces the imminent return of the restless man. The younger man's conversation stops, but his smile continues.

Without looking in my direction, the restless man slides into his place behind the table. I find myself testing the air. I have the growing feeling that I may already have bungled this meeting, for my conversation with the young man may have trespassed his reserve. With tightly drawn lips, he begins to denounce the practices of another non-Chinese group, his arms thrashing about with a force that could have put daylight between himself and the seat. His eyes, wide, look unseeing at the table.

Why is he so critical of others, and especially to a person he does not know? Perhaps his telephone conversation holds the answer, I muse – but I know that this is not the case.

A table meant to be every man's altar of friendship through sharing a simple meal is becoming increasingly uncomfortable. I am hoping it may be no more than a cultural misunderstanding. I may have not properly understood his expectations of me, and my interpreter may have misjudged the position he assumes.

When the fresh innocence of imagination is wounded, the wholesomeness of balance between head and heart is disturbed and old clichés of religious legalism become law. I had hoped that we could meet together as human beings who could appreciate each other's unfinished condition, which is continually unfolding. Then our experience together could be mutually enriching.

I wish that it were possible to photograph dream, then I could visibly show the restless man what his younger companion has seemed so relieved to deposit into the soul of a stranger. But it is imagination that captures the possibilities of inner hopes, and for the moment the restless man may not want the presence of my words on his canvas.

I think that my feelings have moved through disappointment to where confusion swarms, and fears have begun to glue themselves to my spirit. Then I recall the words of a young Korean writer friend, words that have been hovering near, waiting for space to enter my experience. "*I have learned to love what I write,*" she had said in answer to a difficult question I had asked her, "*then I leave my writing on trust to the God whose purpose I pursue.*"

My lack of experience looks like an untrodden field; a blank piece of paper that I can fill with what I love, not criticism of what I do not understand. In the still darkness beyond my clean sheet, I see a graffiti of stars in wild random thrown against the sky, each one a promise brilliant in the night.

From the folklore of the Kalahari, I once read a story which serves as a parable that does not judge, but offers a humbling insight from the rich wisdom of the bushman. It captures the essence of what disturbs me.

A bushman farmer had several black and white cows of which he was very fond. The colours and markings of the animals were important, and his black and white cows held a strong spiritual significance. Each day he led them to graze; at night they were enclosed in a thornbush corral.

One morning, he came to milk the cows and found they were dry. He changed his grazing ground, but the following morning they were again dry. On the third night, he hid himself near the corral and watched.

A silver thread dropped from the sky, and down it climbed several beautiful young women. Chatting happily, they began to milk his cows. He ran to the corral to stop them, but all except one escaped up into the sky. The last one, who was carrying a basket, he caught and eventually married.

His new wife proved a great help to him, and they were happy. While he grazed the cattle she tilled the land, and each night brought home fresh vegetables. She had married him on condition that he would never look into her basket – until she felt it was the right time. He had promised never to do so. However, the temptation overcame him and one evening, before she returned, he lifted the basket's lid – and burst out laughing.

When his wife came home with the vegetables, she sensed that he had broken his promise.

Weeping, she asked him: "What did you see in my basket?"

He burst out laughing and said, "You foolish woman, there is nothing in it!"

With much sorrow she picked up her basket and walked slowly away into the distance. Heartbroken, the bushman did not see her again.

"You see," said the storyteller with great heaviness, "in the basket was her dream, which she had intended to share with him when the time was right. But the bushman could not see the things of spiritual value. He saw only his cattle."

Some historians believe that, at the end of the Warring States and the unification of China under one emperor, free-thinking scholars became a threat to the emperor's security. As a result they were buried alive, and most of their books burned. Criticism of the government was severely punished. The 'Hundred Schools of Thought' and the study of philosophy were banned in favour of the development of Confucian philosophy into an autocratic ideology. This conditioned the individual into subservience to a clearly defined hierarchy.

During the early twentieth century, the few precarious routes into self-expression were further eroded as the sacrifice of self was promoted in the form of patriotism. This was followed by the Communist Revolution. Under the carefully engineered strategies of the Cultural Revolution the surrender of the self to the collective mentality became the entrenched habit, and the annihilation of personal expression was the new norm.

Somewhere in all of this, the restless man has found a home which he instinctively defends.

Possibilities of power are not always balanced with responsibility, except to eliminate threat to that power. China's history is ablaze with examples of the oppression and murder of those whose commitment to meaningless obedience has been lacking. At each level of authority the competition to gain favour is unrelenting. Promotion is rarely for the benefit of the people, but to satisfy the conditions of favour.

Again I borrow the thoughts of a Chinese storyteller, for it is not hard to envisage China's Fools of vision manning a small boat with practically no freeboard. It is on a river that flows deeply and powerfully through an endless gorge. The rowers put all of their strength into the oars, but the boat makes slow headway against the current. There is nothing about the river that favours the upstream journey; yet this is where destiny waits, and it is the Fools' faith in their own dream of reaching their destiny which will change thinking about what is possible, and so model an alternative freedom. I must take seriously the temptation that faces Fools of vision, for the human spirit works against its own river of human frailty.

As the river bends there is a sandbar and, beyond, a beach where slack water plays gently against the shore. There are a few houses in a tree-filled valley. Smoke is rising, and there is a smell of cooking. A stream of clear water flows into the river. Several figures on the beach beckon them ashore. Tired from pulling their oars, they make for the quiet water beyond the sandbar.

"Where are you heading?" they are asked.

"For the source of the river," they reply.

"It's the same here as it is there," say the villagers.

They rest, eat and drink and prepare to launch into the fast current again. Two decide to stay, so the others work harder to make way against the current.

Unwilling to be beaten by the Fools of faith, a communist Ministry for Religious Affairs exists which has authority to recognise communities who will register with them and submit to atheistic controls. Through platitudes of caring concern, they appeal to the tired rowers. When the boat changes course by just a degree, the distance between it and its original course grows with every sweep of the oars, and it eventually arrives at a different destination. Those who respond to a promise of freedom are imperceptibly drawn into a newly-named old Slave habit.

I claim to be no more than an observer, and not a Chinese scholar, but even from my dismally poor understanding the prospect fills me with despair ... I do not know what to do, but equally I cannot watch and do nothing.

I once stood inside the entrance hall of a large old building somewhere in China, where someone had written a notice on a wall which read: *To remove this wall could greatly endanger your health.* I looked up at the high ornate ceilings and thought that the warning was probably right, though I could not work out who would be likely to want to remove a wall!

A journey into the last hundred years of Chinese history is a story of invisible walls being built by favour-seeking communist officials, each with a share of the Chairman's omnipotence; walls built overnight; torture and death facing millions who attempted to remove them.

Fresh in my mind are the writings of Dietrich Bonhoeffer, a German theologian, who became one of the last martyrs of the Nazi regime. Before capture, he had helped keep faith alive among young German men through underground training camps. He wrote of two forms of godlessness – 'hopeful' and 'hopeless'. He described 'hopeless' godlessness as 'pious' godlessness, where religious trappings replace faith. 'Hopeful' or 'promising' godlessness persecutes the 'religious' godlessness and in a sense, if only negatively, defends the heritage of genuine faith.

You come to my aid. You ask me if am convinced of what I am saying. I have to answer. I am ashamed at my thinking. Opinions are unsafe. I am drawing conclusions that my inexperience does not allow me to make. I take the coward's way out and wish that the meeting had not taken place. I hate being in a position where the easiest route is to make judgement of another's belief and intentions. If I am wrong then I trust that I do no harm, but at least I can say that my naivety is in shreds and can admit that, even in the close persecuted world of underground faith, two possibilities still exist and, through one – the old order of the Fool becoming the new Smart Man – may even now be rising. I want to shout, 'China, why aren't you angry?'

Three men walk past my window, the restless man in the lead. As the two younger men follow, they turn to me and raise their hands. I read it as a gesture of bonding. The seamless honesty of at least one, or perhaps both, has woven in a thread of hope with that of disappointment. For us, at least, the table has brought us together.

Around me are a number of young Chinese, some from a rural background, others from the city. Guilelessness glows through their laughter and easy relationship with each other.

"These are the new Fools," says my colleague, who has introduced me to the philosopher's writing, "and we find our place among them."

A protective emotion has surged within me which has overflowed into a resistance against the men in dark clothes. *But I am a foreigner protecting them from their own kind, and that's crazy ...* explodes my mind against my feelings.

No, answers reasoned thought, *I love their innocence and am protecting them against shipwreck on the rocks of the old order which may rise again, over which the spectre of Mao stands smiling ... in respectable pious dress.*

'China needs more Fools,' spelt out the words of the writer ... perhaps with prophetic insight. Could he have worked out what the nation's strategists have planned for China which will, within two decades, hold the position of ultimate power in a resource-stripped, energy-hungry world being eaten slowly by pollution's worm? Alternatively, did he see what the steady march of faith might achieve in peaceful integration, just government, and shared prosperity?

In the broadest sense, these realities swim together into the day that follows our evening. When this happens, will we continue to walk in the sky as well as the water? Then these two alternatives have always existed. The most ancient Wisdom available to us suggests that what has been done before will be done again. To the place from where streams come, they will return.

The man with the key guards it jealously. He will not open the door, for the key means power; so many millions of Chinese have fallen outside the category of success.

Even so, China moves ahead rapidly. The majority have little opportunity to calculate where their journey may take them, or where meaning lies. Siblings separated by just five years belong to different generations. Pushed on by the momentum of the crowd, any escalator that offers upward and onward movement will do.

At Beijing main railway station, shunted by the crowd, I was edged onto a wrong escalator. It had no onward transport connection except for a man with a delivery van, who was waiting in the hope of someone like myself arriving on his pitch. I had no choice but to accept his deal. After much distress, I arrived at my destination with just ten minutes to spare ... after two and a half hours of assisting his deliveries from the back of his van.

My story of the restless man has arisen from a genuine incident which has served to help me realign my perspective on future work in China. However, for the moment, it is just a stray draft of his presence that blows cold, more noticeable in the warmth and hospitality of China's normal environment.

A few weeks later, there was a strong note of sadness in my

colleague's voice when she told me of the deaths of three men. Two had lived, and ended their days, on the streets; one from a cancer within in his skull which had grossly disfigured his face, another from an undiagnosed illness which had weakened his resistance to the chilling cold. The third was the young man who had secretly shared with me his missionary dream. Perhaps his sense of urgency had arisen from an inner knowing. A heart attack had called him away from his wife and child; a tender sapling cut down before it could give its shade to many. I continue to measure the responsibility I have for enabling his dream to be transfigured from imagination into possibility, to be lived out by many others.

When the opportunity arose, I shared my heart-searching with an older Chinese man, who had survived the Red Guard death squads and beyond. I asked him at what point foreign overlay would begin to suffocate the spontaneous spirituality of the Chinese, and unwittingly introduce its own forms of hierarchical control.

I told him that in the east of China I had once visited a new church building that looked like a hand-crafted Welsh Protestant chapel, embellished with the peripherals of a Korean Presbyterian church. Knowing a little of the strong hierarchical systems of pastoral power in Asian churches, I felt inwardly dismayed by this. Later I heard that the church building had been demolished. I wondered if this might have been an expression of the German theologian's 'hopeful godliness'? Anyhow, the rebel in me was pleased.

Then what of the possibility that a new generation of self-important Chinese leaders may gravitate to the old order, and dominate the freedom of spiritual life, living in hierarchical isolation, to whom faith would be a stranger, altogether unrelated to the common man?

He suffered my outburst graciously and, like all wise men, listened for longer than he spoke. Eventually he broke the silence between us.

"Do you know what VIP stands for?"

Knowing that he was about to answer his own question I did not interrupt. After some time, not lifting his gaze but with mirth in his eyes, he said, "Velly important potatoes! Yes, *velly important potatoes!*"

DARK IS NEUTRAL
- Shades of Night -

I have a good friend. Based on an intuitive sense of purpose which, as far as I can remember, we have not even discussed, we have worked together for almost ten years. Both he and I have driving passions – and this is where our similarity ends.

He is a medium-built Filipino and an American citizen, whereas I am a tall, stringy Welshman. When we have a group photograph, which always happens when we work together, he will be smiling from the front row in a smart dark suit and tie. With careful searching, you may also find me looking bewildered between the row of heads at the back, my Oxfam shirt unbuttoned at the neck. He loves the light, I shy away from its gaze. We work well together because, in silent agreement, we respect each other's desire to fit where we feel most comfortable.

On closer scrutiny, not even the direction of our personal passion gives us common ground. I listen with amazement to the reports of his familiarity with the national figureheads of just about every country he visits, while I report on the number of unwashed, unshaven men in crumpled clothes that I think could be the president of the United States had they been raised in different circumstances.

Some time ago there was an incident that had about it a touch of humour that so clearly illustrated how we direct our energies towards the opposite edges of life. We were both heading for China on roughly the same dates, he from America and I from Wales, each of us on separate programmes. He headed for the Ministry of Religious Affairs, and enjoyed the company of its vice-president on his travels. I became the last passenger to crush into a dangerous-looking bus, and headed for the streets to satisfy my hunger for the friendship of the homeless people. His keen eyes were roving over the banqueting halls where he might entertain party officials as his guests, while my eyes roved the pavements as I wondered where I could sleep and gain acceptance among the poor without arousing police suspicions. We both feel comfortable in the environment of our passions that are at either end of the spectrum through which we interpret life.

Passion is the key to wild inventiveness in whatever area of life it exists, and I continue to learn how to trust its gravitational pull. To serve the disadvantaged has been my consistent driving force. Through my mission-building years, my passion has been to help the less privileged young person find the front-line of success within their calling. Later, I was bold (or foolish) enough to devote myself to help non-Western nations arrive at something similar.

It is sad that the usual drift of our Western church life is to some middle ground, where passion exists for itself and our prayer is conditioned by a 'please give me' mentality. In the narrow culture this produces, religious language becomes restricted and clichés fall easily into areas where such language has least developed. Words form a pathway of the spirit, so language which is recycled back into itself does not explore truth, and the music of truth is seldom heard. Thus, offers of prayer 'for the present, and heaven when you die' cost nothing, and can take the place of a warm coat or a meal for a cold and hungry cast-off human being.

When we are blind to the presence of the poor, we do not realise how lost we truly are. So too the poor are blinded to the image of the Creator that defines the uniqueness of the human being. To explore their world does not need a heroic up-river expedition, or a dangerous mountain trail. Their borders may fall just a metre from your door, where your Lazarus waits, with a dog's lick the only healing for his wounds.

So, allow me to introduce you to the characters on my street.

Yin has a village background. He is of average height and quite lean, with a generous nature and a worn face that smiles easily. Life has not been kind to Yin. His right arm and leg have withered and he walks by swinging his damaged leg in a shallow arc, then standing on the ball of his foot. While still a boy he fell from a tree. His family did not have the money to pay for medical attention.

Yin has no home. He is among the many thousands of men, women and children who live on China's streets. He wears whatever he finds: a blue cotton Mao suit, usually. He sleeps wherever he can find some shelter from the rain, the glacial winter winds, and summer's dehydration. Daily survival is by collecting waste paper, cardboard, plastic bottles and, best of all, coke cans. His disability does not allow him to move easily, yet he walks many miles each day to find the seventy or more empty plastic bottles which he can sell for a total of fifty pence. Competition at the most productive rubbish bins is fierce.

Yin once owned a village business selling small amounts of petrol. Through the economic upheavals of change he lost his business, which left him with unbearable debt. He made his way to the city in the hope of finding a job that would release himself and his family. Years have passed, and he has not found an employer who will tolerate his disability.

One of the essential features of being human is that the signature of eternity lies within us, and this has a bearing on every other aspect of life. We pray because we *can* pray, and this gives that eternity a voice. We seem to be an inseparable mix of spiritual and natural. I used to think that the physical gave the spiritual a home. Now I am not sure. I am a swimmer out of my depth and distance. When I meet another person I meet a face and an outstretched hand. However, there are times when I am aware of meeting a presence which seems to extend beyond the physical and which, for need of a more suitable word, I call 'soul'.

When we meet soul we become immediately aware of many points of contact, which I would find hard to put into language better suited to the material world. Sometimes I think that it may be more realistic to say we *see* physical appearance but *meet* soul. In modern Western thought, the soul resides in some confined space within us. More ancient thought suggests the opposite – that the soul extends beyond the body. There are times when this seems to be true. These things are elemental aspects of life, each contributing their richness to our humanity. The invisible is a pure form of the unknown which often we learn to cope with ... by ignoring.

Yin has undoubtedly begun to respond to the pull of the eternity within him. It is as if he has discovered the core of himself that gives everything else its place and meaning. He is finding that the Bible is a book about life, written from eternity's perspective. He carries it with him in a discarded make-up bag he found while searching for coke cans, and sometimes he can be found reading it in the street.

Yin has also begun to pray. This is deepening his contact with himself and is awakening in him a wider sense of responsibility. He has begun praying for his street-sleeping friends, and some have been restored to health. Most are infused with his life and encouragement. Faith grows imperceptibly, and Yin is slowly realising that he has begun to live in a dimension that brings its own form of completeness and meaning to himself and others.

At my first meeting with Yin, he put his good arm around my waist as if to help me cross some mental threshold into his street world. Since that time he has become a comfortable friend. As winter's unforgiving grip grows stronger, his Mao suit looks so pitiful ... I think of giving him my warm jacket, but then its Western cut gives me some doubts. I have no wish to make him look like an outsider in his own world.

I have a small amount of money set aside to buy mementos for my colleagues in Wales. I then think that it may be a better idea to invest this money on their behalf in a warm jacket for Yin. A visit to the old streets soon gives me a choice of warm coats that main street shopping may place beyond my reach. A passing student of English, eager to practise his skill, gives me the bargaining ability while his girlfriend listens. Both the shop assistant and I are happy to agree on half the asking price, and the student receives a small gift that shows the proprietor's appreciation. The difference between the student and myself is that I have some money, which, as a wealthy man expressed, is power folded in a convenient form.

Some metres away from the shop, the student and his girlfriend call to me. They want to thank me for giving him the opportunity to speak English.

"This is the first time that I have spoken with a native English speaker. So ... the shop owner gave me this small gift. I would like to present it to you," he says, pressing a silk tie into my hand.

A plastic smile covers my disorientation at his thoughtful act. Knowing roughly where I might find Yin on the streets, I make my way to him and help him on with the coat. His face beams gratitude.

The cold is now penetrating. I have no desire to leave the streets yet, but it is quite late, I am tired, and I know there is a room and a bed with clean sheets, pillow and blankets awaiting me.

Huddled under an arch I see a solitary figure. He is sitting, his knees drawn under his chin, his back against the cold stone wall. He has no thick coat, no hat, no blanket, not even newspapers spread on the stone slabs; no food, and no water. I wonder if he knows it is dark, for he has no sight either. He holds a makeshift cane, but has no gloves, so is a likely candidate for frostbite.

The dark is friendly to me. I can take just a few steps and the dark will dissolve him from my sight, and the thick mist absorb the sound of his shivering.

I guess he is about late thirties. Later I learn that he was an unwanted child, beaten from birth, kicked in the face while defending himself and losing his sight as a result. He has learned to repeat the Lord's Prayer ... who knows how or where?

The temptation is strong. Darkness will take him away. I turn up the collar of my coat, thrust my hands deeply into my pockets and step out towards my flat. As he fuses with the darkness and the arch ... I try to forget.

My door slams shut and a hot cup of soup seems like a good idea. Not being a natural chef, I have bought a large plastic bag of soup sachets that looked promising, from a market stall. I read the ambitious description of the contents and this settles my choice, though its main ingredient described as 'fried flour' does raise a question. I read on:

> This product is this kind of best one
> The taste is pure and delicious
> And nutrition is rich

116

Put bag into 300 ml of boiling water ...

I discard the bag, as it is plastic, and empty the contents, but when the mixture immediately thickens so that the spoon stands upright I begin to wonder if the instructions about the bag may well have been right. Determinedly I squash the lumps against the side of the cup until it has the consistency of brown cement ... and a taste to match!

Serve to friends as a present, continue the instructions. I am beginning to feel that this may be a good idea, but I have no friend I dislike that much!

Then, with bold pride: *This recipe has been handed down for four generations,* and a voice inside me adds: *Being able to keep a product running this long without improving its taste must be something of a record.* An open drain smiles welcome to the fried flour soup, and both the cup and I enjoy green tea.

It is only a few minutes before I remember the blind man, and I wonder how much more of China and its culture I am willing to see by looking at the back of a tapestry. Perhaps I am frightened to disturb the comfort my ignorance offers me. I pour what I do not understand, or what offends my Western sensibilities, into the nearest drain.

Darkness returns quickly during Central China's winter months, and daylight has already weakened by the time I venture back onto the streets. Through the night and most of the day I wrestle with the issues that my contact with the blind man have raised within me. It takes all the courage I can muster to plunge into this abyss of self-examination, but if my final years are to find meaning in this context, then my spirit has to be able to rise to meet the challenge. I need to feel comfortable with both the ownership of myself, and what I do. I need to know that I am apprenticed to faith. It would help if I could find an example of faith at work, free from the overlay of the power struggle of envy, or of foreign opportunism.

I am looking forward to seeing Yin again, and the thought of this makes me hurry out of my flat and down the darkened road. The temperature feels near freezing and the mist has not lifted. At the main road, heavy diesel engines breathe in the remaining oxygen and pump a monoxide cocktail around my feet. The air tastes acrid and my eyes water.

Cars that make statements about their owner's or company's search for identity fill many empty spaces in the traffic stream. They are long black vehicles with dark tinted windows that shout out, *Why occupy one traffic space when you can have two?* and: *Why run on ten miles per gallon when you can run on five?*

The chauffeured men wear immaculate black suits, black polished shoes, black ties, and starched white shirts, cuff-linked two inches below jacket sleeves. They walk slowly and bend stiffly to slide into the back seat. They speak coldly and deliberately. They do not laugh, but have perfected the chilling smile that can make their clients freeze on the spot. Filtered of emotion, they are able to zero in on their instructions, whatever the circumstances at whatever distance. Through night or day they are transported around the city to any point where they may be needed.

Am I looking into a frightening future, when China may boast more vehicles than the rest of the world put together? – *China ... when will you recognise the ambitions of your new Smart Men?* They have little interest in anything else when their priority is the domination of world markets.

I am making my way to a location known only to my colleagues, myself and a number of street people. At least that is what we think, as we filter carefully so as not to arouse attention. Some street children see us, and decide to tag along. They are not so security conscious. We divide up, but not before I spot a figure in normal dress with a small case on wheels, making use of the street lights to video us on a mobile phone. I look straight at him before I realise what is happening. I attempt to hold his attention in the hope my colleagues will turn away. Years of experience mean they instinctively do. Before he moves on, he reruns the video clip. The dark is neutral, and as he steps into oblivion, so do we.

We have received a friendly word of caution from an underground leader. "The PSB know what you are doing," he reported.

The video incident strengthens this opinion. Perhaps for the moment they may have wider interests, and are not yet ready to reel us in.

The Bent Tin Badge

A Chinese colleague and I take a detour to pass by two families whom I know. One is an elderly couple who seem devoted to each other. The wife, clad in tattered blue Mao dress, is active and busily tends her husband. He is on a makeshift trolley. It is waist high and has a chair-like back against which he leans. It is not entirely a chair, as his legs lie out flat before him. It has four small wheels. He is dressed in heavy clothes. Ragged blankets cover his legs. He has a long beard, and his face carries lines of suffering. They have no home, no money, no food.

I usually find them under the same railway arch, except when there may be an important visitor due, or officials from the tourist department − or an influx of tourists. Then they are moved away. They have no value as people, except perhaps to each other, each one feeling valued because the other needs them. In the headlong rush for prosperity, they are an embarrassment. But who knows their history?

Their age makes them survivors of the Mao regime, of the years of the Red Guards, of Mao's purge and torture of his opponents. Perhaps the lined face and useless legs are a badge of honour, worn proudly but with no acclaim. Perhaps in a reality that few, if any, may recognise, the disabling scars, rags and homelessness are an effective disguise.

Mother Theresa taught her disciples to see divinity behind the mask of the suffering poor. My colleague offers them some soup, bread and fruit. In their presence I feel unworthy. I stand as near as I dare. They return my smile and I think they understand that I am the one who will walk away, dirty and without honour. My badge tells it as it is ... it's made from bent tin.

This elderly couple, whose lives seem to be suspended by a fine thread and who may not survive the winter, have neighbours − another family. In terms of distance they are very close; possibly less than a metre separates them as they share the limited shelter the arch can provide. In terms of neighbourly appreciation, maybe they have something like my memories of wartime bomb shelter camaraderie that softened the threat of death from the sky.

Or perhaps not. A family may come from the country, or even from different parts of the same city, and speak a different dialect. In their two-family world there may be a story of a history and a present that will die with them.

The second family are parents, with a boy of about eight years old. They have already spread a blanket on the concrete-slab pavement, and a stitched-up quilt covers them. They are fully dressed, with the boy between them. I make a move to approach them, unsure if I have permission to enter their private world. The little boy sits up, fear flickering in his empty eyes. He quietens as my Chinese colleague rescues the situation by handing them soft rounds of steam-baked bread. Eager hands receive these and hide them under the quilt.

In one hand I carry a plastic carrier bag filled with empty coke cans. My colleague counts out five. Their contents already having met another's thirst, the cans can be resold for about one penny each, an income of five pence between both families.

I recall a time when, in a north-east African country, I had trained myself to live on one penny per day for food and a further three and a half pence for drinkable water. But I did have a place to stay, and I did have clothes – and what is more, I had hope.

So my badge is still one of bent tin. It seems a contradiction to say that I need these who have been shaken to the bottom of Chinese society more than they need me. I need them more than my finest teachers. By serving them, I have reason to exist. Beyond knowledge, they give me meaning.

Perhaps I should continue to wear my tin badge, for more than anything else it identifies my misplaced pride. The elderly couple and the unwanted family are as fragile and vulnerable as a young child, and this child becomes father to me.

I find my way through narrow lanes of tired, damp buildings to our solitary hired room. I am surprised to see that inside it has been redecorated by some of my very close Korean colleagues, during part of the time they should have spent on honeymoon! Save for two wooden-boarded, springless beds, the room is without furniture or heating. It is already two-thirds full of both younger and older men, who choose to sit on the floor rather than the beds. Like their clothing, they are China's cast-offs. For a short time they have escaped their world for ours, but can only bring with them the characters their hurt minds and emotions have created.

There is a disturbance at the door. A disabled shoe cleaner, who sits each day on the pavement at a city intersection, has piloted his wheelchair through the maze of blackened streets, and found us. He needs help to wrestle himself from his wheelchair to the floor of the room. He has found faith and hope, and has asked if he can speak to others in the room about what this means for him.

The room continues to fill as men trickle in. Eventually the coat I look for makes its entry, with a profusely smiling Yin looking over the collar. His eyes thank me, but the creases in his forehead and the gestures of his hands are telling me something I am unable to interpret.

Then I notice that he is helping someone else into the room. It is the blind man I walked away from yesterday evening, but whom I have not been able to forget. They sit opposite me on the boarded bed. I am both elated and ashamed, but tempted to be grateful that neither of them know that last night's footfalls, which hesitated by him and then passed on, were my own.

The room fills, until the door cannot be closed. As most cannot read, we read to them from Yin's Bible. I teach them a simple prayer they can use to start each day. They repeat each sentence until they can do so from memory.

I feel that if they can experience the beginnings of prayer, they might allow their own dreams to continue to guide their prayer. We finish with each man placing his hand on the next man's shoulder and praying for him. To this degree, each stands on the threshold of unlimited possibility. The blind man, whose eyes are always closed, has perhaps learned to depend more on the sight of his inner eyes, as he prays distinctly and with confidence.

As the room empties I find in a nearby lane a grease-blackened oil drum, still burning with coal briquettes. In moments, a wok has produced noodle and vegetable meals. From plastic bags, Yin and his blind friend celebrate. There will also be two empty spaces on the wind-strafed pavement tonight and, for once, it is not because of winter claiming two more victims. The men have exchanged the pavement for a hard, boarded bed, but without mattress or bedclothes. When another street sleeper asks Yin about the room, he says, "Father has given it to me."

For myself, I have waited for a miracle of assurance which is now taking place. It is as if that miracle has placed its first footprint into the void within me. In this wilderness of wasting people, where outsiders' footfalls scarcely enter, I find blooming an exquisite example of faith. As always, contrary to human expectation, divine intention unravels its perfection. One of the stars I had snatched from the water has contained for me the seed of promised incarnation. There, hidden among the pain-torn millions within this great nation – which with reckless abandon races for wealth and future – go I, an aged adventurer desperately in need of new inner maturity that matches my years.

On the way home tonight I turn over in my mind the illusion that communist propaganda has deceived the world into believing: *Under communism, every poor person has their bowl of rice.*

Some movement in a foul-smelling rubbish skip catches my attention. An elderly lady is turning over the contents, looking for something to eat. She is hungry; her hollow eyes and shrunken skin match her ragged thin clothes. My Chinese colleague invites her to come with us. We will buy her something at the bus station. She follows, but at the sight of the food we intend to purchase, disappointment lines her face. She shakes her head and raises her hands. Her remaining teeth have rotted away to the gums; she cannot even bite soft bread. We buy her some soup, which will at least see her through the night.

In an attempt to gain centre stage in the leadership of world communism, Mao engineered his 'Great Leap Forward' when, to gain favour with countries that would support his political ambitions, he gave away millions of tons of Chinese food, to the applause of Western political celebrities. As a result China's death toll through starvation was counted in tens of millions, and much of the rural population survived by stripping trees bare of leaves and digging up grass roots.

Could there be a hint of history repeating itself, you ask, *though not on the same scale?*

I am saved from having to admit that I do not know the answer, as two boys, each about twelve, edge their way into range of the street lighting. They are looking around nervously. My stilted vocabulary will not honour their survival spirit if I attempt to describe their condition; they have taken on the colour of their normal surroundings, and it is too painful to think of what those might be. The brittle thickness of the grime on their hands has cracked and there is Chinese skin beneath. Chinese hair is discernible in the matted locks. They are looking hopefully at the skip. One of them is climbing in ... perhaps they will find their bowl of rice.

I see myself walking away from myself. I know that my feet are going to follow, shock and the frustrated anger of helplessness ruling my emotions.

I hope the boys help you find an answer to your question, I reply, and walk away, leaving them to the democracy of hunger.

Whilst relating Yin's story to a group of Korean trainees at our centre in Wales, I had to answer an expected question.

"How do we pray for Yin?" someone asked.

My answer, like no answer I had ever given before, had to be: "Pray that he might find enough empty coke cans, plastic bottles, cardboard and old newspaper to stay alive each day."

PORTRAIT OF A CHINESE SERVANT
- Sichuan Province -

Many who have growing interests in China are surprised to learn of the hundred million or so minority people who are not of Chinese descent. In fact, until 1500 BC there was no Chinese race, just many tribes of people who were spread throughout the land. Over centuries of integration the Chinese nation grew, as new people, for a variety of reasons, moved into the land – from Jews in the ninth century who braved the rigours of the Silk Road through Central Asia before crossing the width of China to the east coast, to the Mongolian descendants of a detachment of Genghis Khan's army who still live in the mountain pass they defended centuries ago. Today, half of China's land is occupied by almost five hundred distinct minority groups, although the Chinese government, for administrative simplicity, calculate just fifty-five. Some provinces have larger ethnic concentrations, such as the Tibetan Buddhists and the blue-eyed Muslims of Xinjiang, while the greater numbers live in remote mountainous regions.

Driving on the wrong side of a road is not one of my normal inclinations, yet an Egyptian friend, frustrated by Cairo's traffic soup, launched his car into a street where every cyclist, scooter, car, truck and bus were hurtling towards us with apparent intent. When two cars abreast were about to ram us and the only option I could see was to choose which bonnet to go through, he mounted the pavement. No one seemed perturbed – not the pedestrians, nor the police. This explains why most Egyptian cars are built in the shape of a brick. This one, however, had not escaped so lightly, as it looked like a brick with rounded corners.

Still, that was Egypt, where morning begins at about noon and attitudes are generally laid-back. Now I am in China, where city life does not stop and claims more than a hundred thousand road deaths each year. As someone pointed out, very few wars have a death-toll that size.

Some years ago, when Tibetan borders were unfriendly to foreigners, some colleagues were attempting an overland entry in two Beijing Jeeps which they had hired with drivers. These were the days when out-of-town traffic mainly drove with lights off; perhaps the logic was that if you were going to drive around bends on the wrong side of the road at night, you at least would not know what hit you. My colleagues had the horror of rounding a bend to find that the lead Jeep was nowhere to be seen. It was only by peering over a cliff that they saw the survivors squeezing through the windows of the rolled vehicle.

More recently, I had been unnerved by a similar incident. With the best of intentions I had gone to the help of a stranded driver. His truck was facing the right way amid a traffic flow on a fairly busy country road. The odd thing was that the truck had stopped near the centre of the road, on an approach to a bend. The howling tyres and the brakes and horns of traffic speeding by seemed to do little to alarm its driver.

Dodging the traffic, I made my way to the front of the truck. Behind the wheel the driver, a neatly-dressed young man in a blue shirt, seemed to be following my progress. It was only when I was near enough to notice that his eyes did not blink, that I became suspicious ... I was right, he was dead. The front of his truck bore the scar of an impact, probably from a vehicle rounding the bend – on the wrong side!

The oncoming vehicle had evidently reversed and driven away. It was difficult to tell how long the body of the young man had been there, or how long it would remain. At a casual glance he was sitting upright, looking forward, eyes open, with his hands gripping the steering wheel and no visible wounds. To all passing traffic he would have appeared to be alive. Death had shown no respect for the man's few years. It had kept its appointment, suddenly and with finality.

It was late afternoon and, at the driver's home, no doubt a meal had been prepared ...

Today I am among a small team hurtling north-east in an oversized delivery van. The landscape is hilly, green and flowing. It reminds me of Wales. Towering behind are mountain summits, bare, grey and angular. The weather is pleasantly warm, but dabs of dark cloud set the mood of the peaks.

The road reaching ahead, friendly in the sun, ribbons along a valley. There are many bends. Deliberately, we steer into them on the wrong side of the road. I am not sure how many we negotiate like this, but when I judge my face has become as white as my knuckles, I politely ask Meng, our driver and friend, if he thinks we will lose much time by driving on the right side of the road. Meng says nothing but looks hurt and I feel bad. I have expressed mistrust.

I am continually surprised by Meng who has a placid laid-back nature. When behind a wheel, however, the vehicle becomes a projectile designed to carry him between two points in the shortest possible time. Brakes, he seems to believe, are for parking only.

Eventually the countryside stops rolling and swaying in the vehicle windows, and abruptly starts a chopping motion. We have left the dubious security of the tarmac for a track worn into the hillside.

"Don't worry," calls out Meng encouragingly, "I have fitted special shock absorbers."

I wonder what kind of shock absorbers will bring us safely around corners on the wrong side and will make a difference to the width of the track that, by a hair's breadth, allows the outside wheels to stay in contact with the ground.

The track now becomes end-to-end bends. Without changing expression or speed, Meng slithers through mud and rocks in his unbothered way. He spins the most unlikely vehicle ever to leave the tarmac across ruts and gullies, while the vertical drop to the valley increases in depth with each metre we travel.

Around the hundredth blind bend, the trail climbs up a rock outcrop. A threatening wall of wet slabs angle down to the cliff edge and the valley below. My mind says, *This is where we park the vehicle,* but no such thought has occurred to Meng. Driving straight at the rock slabs, our momentum carries us part-way up. The back wheels, searching for grip which is not there, begin to slither towards the drop. The engine stalls and the vehicle comes to a halt, angled across the slabs. The side door opens directly above the valley floor below.

Meng's eyes occasionally smile, but usually look sad. I think they reflect his experience of life. Whatever his mood, they give those who do not know him the idea that they have a permanent tired droop. Now they are no different, or perhaps it is the way he holds his body that adds to that impression. Tall for a Chinese, though slightly stooped, his arms hang loosely and his torso bends over a little to one side.

In the bright sun and clear air, his slender frame spikes a hard shadow across me as I lie on the wet slabs to assess our position. Stones I dislodge take an age to crash into the valley below. I feel sick. One rear wheel has come to rest a fraction from the drop; the other, daylight bright between it and the ground, spins uselessly.

I make a guess: the way forward is to use up the precious inches between the back wheel and the drop, by rolling it onto a carefully placed stone. If this works, it might force the opposite wheel back into contact with the ground. If Meng could then inch forward and everyone push, we might yet have a vehicle to drive home.

Wrestling gravity, we make the top. Meng seems unmoved; in his experience, life that consists continuously of disaster and near-disaster is normal – a million miles away from the expectations of a Western lifestyle.

By the time I gather myself, Meng has turned the vehicle around and it stands, poised, ready to slither down the wet rock on our return. He has already announced, "We must walk from here. One hour to the village."

We set out. An hour passes, and we seem to have climbed very little.

"About an hour to the village," he announces again.

This happens at least twice more before the sight of a cow herder and villagers, with colossal baskets on their shoulders, indicates that we are reasonably close. These are not Han Chinese but one of the minority groups, this one no more than a blip in the Chinese population census.

The minority tribes, though fiercely independent, had united in their opposition to the advance of communist troops and hotly defended their highland stockades. Their buildings, now daubed with the sayings of Chairman Mao, are ever-present reminders of their defeat and humiliation.

Meng has mentioned his work among another minority group. I ask him where their village lies. "Two days in that direction," he says, pointing to a pass high in the hills. Given his calculation of time to this village, I wonder how many days would make two!

During the final hour, the track descends below the skyline to where trees and bushes proliferate. It flattens out onto a ridge overlooking another open valley. Usually the rocks and soil are yellow, but here they are mainly red. Homes are sprinkled wherever there is sufficiently flat rock to hold them. Most are built of stone and plastered with clay. Some seem to be built of baked clay blocks. Almost all are roofed with crude, curved tiles. Some are two-storied, with room for animals on the ground floor.

Between the homes, pathways rise steeply. Polished broad-leafed plants with tall orchid-like red flowers add a three-dimensional effect of colour and life. An older lady, her long clothes decorated with faded flowers and noticeably worn, walks slowly along a path with two heavy buckets of water suspended from a carrying pole across her shoulders. Here is a beautiful, primitive loneliness, empty of all imposed meaning.

Far down in the valley, vegetation has been cleared, making way for what looks like handkerchief-sized fields. Reds, browns and greens patchwork the valley floor, climbing the far slopes over the opposite ridge and disappearing towards the blue haze of high mountain slopes. Distant black specks move slowly. This is where most of the village men and younger women spend their days. When the mountains cast their shadow into the deep valley the upward trek to the village begins, each with an enormous cone-shaped basket fastened to their shoulders.

As the lofty figure of Meng, with his unusual gait, nears the houses, the village comes alive. Ladies with wrinkled brown faces and missing teeth, their bunches of black hair coiled above their foreheads, stand in doorways and wave a greeting. Children run past them, hugging his long, trousered legs, skipping and calling in seamless chatter.

The track continues to plunge downward, past homes and animal sheds, to an unusually level piece of rock with a semi-completed building at the far end.

"My school!" announces Meng, and we enter the building.

It is two-storey, compact but adequate. We look around the sparse classrooms, where he is the only teacher. He opens the door to a small ground-floor room. A bare bed lines one wall; a chair and table complete the furniture.

"My home!" announces Meng, as he welcomes us inside.

Across the open ground comes a fair-skinned little girl, dressed in white and pink and embroidered with beads. Two bunches of black hair swing as she runs. She is not among the first children to meet us; obviously her mother has dressed her for the occasion. She greets Meng, and us all. Then, encouraged by Meng, and with all the confidence of an impresario and the eloquence of her rich culture, she begins to sing and recite: a timeless poem in praise of the history and hopes of her nation, trilled by innocence's sweet young voice ... in a language that, in my poverty, I do not understand: a thorn that digs where it hurts most.

Two large brown eyes receive our applause. A rare orchid, blooming on the slope of a valley among deserted mountains. Unaware of such presence, our world rushes on, our pride a loud statement of our ignorance.

This is where Meng spends most of his months. The tribe is poor beyond belief, but open-hearted and welcoming. They have no mail service, no telephone, and virtually no access in and out of the village. These are Meng's family. He speaks about his school, his feeding, clothing, water and Bible translation projects, all paid for by himself. The village expresses their love to him in any way they can, and he responds as he can. He seldom negotiates the trail to a town without buying winter shoes or clothing for all the children. Meng is truly a remarkable man.

During the eventful following weeks, besides beginning to gain experience of the diversity of China's non-Han Chinese peoples, I also begin to understand Meng, and my appreciation of him grows daily.

Meng's ancestry had filled high positions in China, entwined with at least one of the emperors. His father was involved in government and so a ready target for Mao's Red Guard purge of educated, thinking people. As a nine-year-old he watched helplessly as his mother and father were led away and slaughtered by boys not much older than himself. His home and belongings were confiscated. Fear ruled his community, so friendship was scarce.

Faith lay deeply hidden in the Korean Chinese man from Manchuria who befriended him. He was a skilled tinker, who made small amounts of money by walking between villages repairing pots, pans, buckets and farm machinery. In this way Meng learned his simple trade and, more significantly, slowly embraced his faith.

Later, for three years Meng lived alone in a cave dug into the soft rock of a hillside. Each morning he would leave for local villages where he could employ himself. Sometimes he waited at the foot of a hill, where he could help push a heavy cart to the top for a little money or food.

A kindly elderly lady, expelled from her village, had made her home in the next cave. Noticing that Meng had not left for the village for a few days, she visited him and found him ill and near to death. Her care and cooking of what food she could scavenge and herbs she could gather saved his life.

A coal mine offered him more permanent employment. Like mining in Wales some two centuries ago, it was primitive, dangerous, and demanded his whole life. It was excruciating hard work and had impossibly long hours. There was the constant threat of roof fall, gas and flood, as well as ingrained grime and the killer coal dust.

Once, someone allowed him a sight of a Bible, carefully wrapped, disguised and hidden in a drawer. He asked if he could read it but the owner refused. It was illegal to own a Bible, and to be caught reading it would mean prison, or worse. However, he asked again and the owner relented, and allowed him to have it overnight. He read it all night before handing it back.

On one occasion Meng was imprisoned for his faith. He was abused by staff and, as with most new inmates, he was beaten up by the prisoners' regime. While he was being punched, they asked him what offence he had committed.

"It's because I have faith," he gasped.

The gang leader, who had been listening, called his men off.

"If he's a Christian, he's a good man. He can sleep on the floor next to me."

Meng did not realise at first what that meant. There were more than fifty men in the cell, with space for just two to lie down. The gang leader, and himself! Stripped of all belongings, most of their clothes, and starved of food, fifty men – unwashed and sweating – waited month by month in an airless, confined space. Lice powder and soap were among the most coveted gifts.

He did not speak of how, eventually, he escaped China to become a refugee in America. Perhaps there were others involved who are best left nameless. He attended school, learned good English, found skilled employment, and bought a home. Then he let his heart rule his head, and returned to China.

And so, for some time, it is my privilege to walk through China's towns and villages with one of the most extraordinary men I have ever known. He is extraordinary because his suffering developed in him the charm of unpretentious ordinariness, a rare quality.

His loneliness brings an ache to my heart, yet he is not a team person. When pressed in this way he appears awkward and ungainly. His knowledge of China, even to the detail of cities and streets, seems inexhaustible, but is a poor second to his knowledge of China's religious history and its missionaries – even to their uncles, aunts, their graves and surviving relatives.

He owns little. His rucksack holds few clothes, yet his generosity I find painful, as it unmasks my deep roots of inherent selfishness. He carries an air of childlike innocence, but I know that it is reflected light from the surface of a deep well which I have not fathomed.

He seems always to be inwardly alive to something. Guessing what that might be is fruitless. When I think that his conversation offers a clue, the event has already become history. Starting a conversation with him is not easy. I feel I lack his permission to follow a route into his depths – which probably marks a level of his confidence I have not entered. My words sound cheap, and often foolish. They are like vessels without a cargo. They come from thoughts which tumble around my head like empty cardboard boxes. He has found humility, not before the great but before the small things in life. By knowing him, I have begun to appreciate eternity in a different way.

Meng knows the temperament of these mountains, and I can see by his frequent glances at the sky that he suspects rain.

"If the rain comes," he says, "we may have to stay here."

He does not add that he has already planned to visit government officials who have jurisdiction over another village where he is building a water reservoir.

Some of the men have begun to return from the fields, their huge baskets containing produce and their working tools. Several are leading slender horses that seem at home on the narrow paths and steep slopes. Most villagers wear thread-bare clothes, the women often in green Mao caps, the men in a mixture of odd clothes and blue cotton Mao suits.

Three children are in extremely ragged traditional dress, their bright colours stained to a dull grey. Dirt ingrains their hands, arms, legs and faces. Their feet ooze with mud. They cling closely together at the track side, their expressions distant, vague and fearful. The eldest fumbles a small piece of cardboard tube between her fingers while the younger two look on longingly. It is their only toy.

They look as though they lack a mother's attention, perhaps a father's also. Here are three more rare and beautiful orchids, growing uncultivated and wild, seen only by the stars and the birds and a sprinkling of stone houses on a mountain ridge somewhere in vast China; faraway in distance, and perhaps time, from the raucous crowds and neon-washed city streets.

Does the village know their secret? When the sprawling mists that inhabit the mountains hang like a curtain of smoke, where are they then? Or when the terrifying dense darkness of night encloses a totally primitive chaos, where there is no sky or earth, trees or rocks, no top or bottom, no right and left, for all are wholly caught in this void – where are they then? I wonder what demons torment them? If they had someone who listened to a child's fears, what stories would they tell them?

Three ladies, in thick long skirts, have boiled water for tea. By gesticulating hands and the occasional push, which we cannot fail to understand, we are guided to a waiting table. A man, proud of a large plastic washing bowl full of honey and broken combs, invites us to dip our fingers in and try. That day Meng has introduced me to two minority tribes, an experience from which I have never since wanted to retreat.

We are about to leave the village when a three-wheeled agricultural truck appears. Its owner wants to take us back to our van. I stand in the rear box; it is like being in a small boat in a heavy sea. It climbs unbelievable gradients and leans at impossible angles, its single cylinder not missing a beat. We are in sight of our vehicle when he decides he does not dare go further. Meng climbs aboard our own and, with uncertain steps, I follow as we slither crab-wise down the steep, wet slabs.

We journey north by train. The six-berth rough sleeper has its normal assortment of hard-smoking, loud-talking travellers. Four men and a young lady student are unusually courteous towards me. I suspect my silver hair has something to do with this. When two men and the student leave the compartment to walk the corridors, the remaining older man, looking at me intently, crosses himself, puts his hands together and bows his head. Without altering his gaze he does it again. He smiles, points to himself then to his son. His son smiles. They want me to know that they have both found faith.

The train enters the province that is home to many races of minority peoples. It is also recognised to be one of Tibet's important gateways. Here our small team divides, and we arrange to meet again in a northern city.

It is not straightforward. My close Korean colleague becomes trapped by horrendous landslides on an overland journey from Lhasa, and suffers much through sickness and cold. Others are raided by police at night, and later stumble onto a mountain region reserved for sky burial, where a corpse is dismembered and spread on rocks or grassland and vultures summoned – unless the vicious Tibetan dogs arrive first.

Meng, who in his usual style says that he needs to travel by rail to Beijing, still manages to meet up with us on time. He had gone to the aid of a small boy travelling alone, who had pulled the railway carriage urn of boiling water over himself. He could do nothing to help himself, and no one had offered to take responsibility for him. Meng advised him to leave the train at a stop where there is a hospital in the town. I don't know if he did.

For myself, somewhere down in the hush of my being, an unmistakable urge sends me in search of every spare moment from each day's activities so that I can be alone and listening with an inner ear. This retreat behind the doors of my inner room helps me to explore areas of myself which I have seldom visited, there to raise questions about these forgotten peoples which can dramatically affect my borrowed tomorrows.

Sometime later, by prearrangement, we all meet up again in a small Chinese pavement restaurant. We celebrate with one very large bowl of soup between us. We aim our chopsticks below the oily tide mark, then surface, some clutching a chicken's scaly, clawed foot and I, a whole chicken's head still wearing its pre-execution look of horror.

Meng continues to be one of the most unusual Chinese men it is my privilege to know.

WHERE BELIEF DIVIDES
- The Secret Mountain -

The Community that Loved Me
Where are you going?

I am leaving the bare room I have hired. It has a bed, a table and chair, but it is soulless. It has been put together for foreign visitors in order to earn rent from a night's sleep. It is an invasion into the privacy of this community. It feels cold, and has no trace of the intimate touch of care. Even so, I have paid a heavy deposit against anything I might break or steal.

You mean the bed, table or chair?

I walk out into the narrow lane. It feels much warmer, its atmosphere more inviting. Being awash with neon would not help this street. It would lose the intimacy of its dark corners, from which a sense of belonging can grow. This is not a glass-eyed shopping wonderland of polystyrene mannequins wearing city suits, of mock-designer leather handbags, and of glossy evening dresses. It looks more lived-in than shopped-in. It invites the older man to sit, drink green tea, and become absorbed into the presence of real-life characters working and playing on the road and pavement, bringing the street alive. I have to force myself to believe that this life, like the tide on a million shores, will continue, as it has for hundreds of years; even when I am not here observing it!

The thoroughfare is narrow, and its side streets even more so, designed for cycles and trishaws rather than mechanised traffic. A variety of 'live-behind' shops, adequate for the community, front both sides of the street. Some have eaten away at living accommodation to provide a fair-sized trading room, whilst others have open-fronted trading areas a couple of metres deep, making me wonder whether the shopkeeper clears his shelves every night, or sleeps in the same space.

Many contain permanent tanks of live fish. Air plays in through plastic pipes, yet the scarce water remains cloudy and it is the glazed-eyed, belly-up fish amid the lively specimens that draw the gaze. There is nothing to stop fish jumping between tanks, or landing on the silver-scaled, stone slab floors, only to be re-captured by a long handled net and dropped back into water; but at least here it is not the practice to display split-open, heart-pumping, lung-working fish.

Uneven pavements supporting another tier of traders, tumble outward to meet the repair-scarred road. Motorised trishaws, with drivers who know their population, wait at the kerbs.

A bicycle repairman kneels beside an upturned cycle. Searching for bubbles he grasps an inner tube still attached to the rim, and holds it like a black eel in a bowl of black water. Cobblers, three or four of them, sit behind ancient hand-operated stitching machines on tiny stools no more than a few centimetres above the ground, with hammer, paring knife, tacks, glue, and rubber heels littered around them. Key-cutters, four or five of them bunched together, chatter and laugh. Each has a cutting machine, self-owned or hired, and a long necklace of blank keys, tarnished with age. Customers are few, but there is no harsh competition.

Though the sun is diffused, an elderly lady sits on a small square of cloth on the pavement under a faded parasol. Her head and shoulders cannot be seen. Perhaps she does not want to be known. She shares her cloth with a few well-spaced trinkets. She may need money, and these are some of her prized possessions. They have value to her, but perhaps to few others. No passing feet slow down for her.

Then there are the eating stalls. Many sell fruit. Pineapples are peeled, dissected, displayed submerged in water, and are eaten off sticks. Apples, oranges, tangerines and bananas abound. Though we are in the cold north-west, south China is tropical.

There are noodles boiling. They are served in a thick brown sauce. At a low table and chairs four schoolgirls busily wind their noodles onto chopsticks. Several stalls sell long red sausage. Some have cuts angled along their length, others are cooked whole. They too are eaten on a stick, but have tough skins. Others sell potato crisps, cooked and spiced by Muslim men. Less than ten pence buys enough for a family treat.

In the shadow of a handcart, tethered to a leg, a little dog complains in its sleep. Its long hair would be white if it stood in the rain. Tied to a lamppost is a cat of a similar shade of white, sharing its space with a man shouting into his mobile phone. The cat stretches full height, both paws tapping the water bottle he carries in his other hand. The shouting man, engrossed in his personal battle, leaves the cat disappointed.

A rusting, channel-iron, charcoal-fired kebab grill stands on an ash-blackened pavement, its heavy metal frame making it a permanent feature. Beneath it is a mound of fresh charcoal pieces. The kerbside chef juggles kebab skewers on the grill. He holds six in each hand. The small pieces of animal innards sizzle to a pleasing sound. He splits open a roundel of bread, paints the halves with molten animal fat and toasts them in the heat. The charred-black meat pieces slide off the wires into the bread.

At yet another stall, some young people are eating Chinese-style pizzas out of paper bags. One man rolls out dough in a clear space on a dusty table. He passes it to another, who bakes it on a hotplate. As he turns it, he dips a paintbrush into a tin of brownish-orange liquid topping, splashing it onto the cooked side.

For the equivalent of fifteen pence, I get more than a meal. The sheer pleasure of eating it as I walk? Priceless!

There is a thunderous whining roar above me. The road, the pavements, the shops, the houses, the whole street are acting as a sound box. The fish, the birds, the dogs and the people are unperturbed, but the daylight is fading. I alone stand looking up at the sky, as the nose, belly and wings of an airliner begin to creep over the houses, the black-tyred wheels almost leaving tread marks on the roofs; a tall tail fin with rivets that can be counted, and white-knuckled passengers, all silently praying. For ten minutes at least, there are few atheists aboard flight CK 147 as it lines up with a runway. Perhaps, literally, this is the most prayed-over street in the province.

As I leave, I step out of a community that has preserved its identity ... a rare sight and feel of Old China. The villagers who live with a focus on the street are unable to control what happens in the sky, which will eventually dramatically affect their private space.

Tomorrow, an Asian colleague will guide me into a mountain community. I sense that there may be something significantly different about this.

The People on the Hill

It is another morning, and the world swings into view again. The sun lacks determination, for the day has set in an overcast sky. Or is it in fear of the pollution? – At least a diffused sun will make the mountain journey easier.

I am heedless of yesterday because of my elation over today's possibilities. We board a town bus – or rather, are pushed through the doors by the conductor, who gathers up everyone on the pavement. There is no room for him inside, so he clings to the outside bars. With only one entry and exit point, he will collect the fares as passengers leave. Pressed chest-to-back in the crush, we become easy offerings to pick-pockets.

Near the town centre it is as if the buses change *us*, as we are bundled from one onto another. There is more room on this one, but for standing passengers only. We follow the Yellow River. The mountains are never far from this town; sometimes they feel only inches beyond the tip of an outstretched arm. In the river valley, they rise steeply on either side.

The bus halts, and we start on foot up the hill. To enter a distinct community is like being born. At the moment of entry we begin using up the only time we are going to have. We need to mature quickly, and learn to relate. We consciously cross a threshold, and become sensitive to the mood of the community.

There is a tension in the air which is reflected in the faces of the men on the street. I do not immediately see any women. The men wear dark, baggy work-clothes and white skullcaps. They are not Han Chinese, but part of a large minority group. The figures, disturbed by our intrusion, wear a scowl. Walls are unpainted and accumulated dirt seems to be reaching out from every corner, and from behind every stone. The pungent smell of stale animal blood hangs in the air. Ah! . . . a return to yesterday is already beginning to feel a better choice. I don't think I am meeting the people, but rather the brooding suspicions raised by a foreigner.

The uneven hillside road is bordered by broken pavements, neglected houses, and an occasional shop. Tied to the walls are numbers of sheep. These are kept without food and water prior to their slaughter. The stench is quite strong; they are terrified, and nudge each other in an attempt to be inside the safety of the herd. To one side of them a wet-blooded mound of sheepskins rises higher, one by one. Another sheep is taken, a knife slices its throat, and within moments its blood is running. They are slaughtered, gutted and skinned near the pavement.

Passing a double gateway, we instinctively look into the yard beyond it. Rows of small, two-storey buildings stand on two sides. The top floor looks like accommodation, the lower dissolving into the chaos of the yard. Amid the gut and slime, cauldrons boiling on wood-fired oil drums steam a sickly scent. A woman works among heaps of animal intestines that cover the floor. She lifts armfuls into the cauldron.

A group of men beaver away at something I cannot see. More sheepskins grow into mounds where they have been stacked. Another tends an open fire on the yard floor, out of which he hooks blackened sheep skulls. He growls unwelcomingly, with gestures to match. I am not sorry to round a corner as we continue to climb the hillside. I look back, and where the modern roof line of the town sharply ends, this crumbling community begins.

I am beginning to feel an old insecurity rising, which I know could develop into a disturbing, irrational fear. I wonder if my colleagues feel the same way. Then I reason that they are Asian, and can pass for Chinese, while a lanky, grey-haired Westerner may not mean good news to this community.

When my personal focus has been with the Islamic races of the Middle East, Africa and Asia, I have built many strong friendships, and within them seldom felt insecure. Cultural difference apart, we stem from a pool of common humanity and are able to reflect on the brutal realities that seem evenly spread among the adherents of all religious and non-religious philosophies. Humanity streams and mingles together in this sea of universal sadness into which Europe's two world wars have contributed liberally.

You confide in me: *I feel that I am trying to walk through a mangrove swamp with a tangle of tree roots beneath the surface of the water. I am suddenly unsure of myself. I am confused over what may be acceptable or not, or why there should be a sense of antagonism in the air.*

I know the feeling, *I reply,* and to arrive at the end of such a time as this just deepens the confusion, and still there is no clearer understanding of what it has been about!

Some years ago, in the sticky thick heat of a late afternoon in a Middle Eastern refugee resettlement, I stepped out onto the narrow roadway, among low houses. Their stones were returning the sun's energy to the cooling air. My head and emotions had also reached boiling point, and were in need of cooling.

It was some years before, when we had begun to explore ways to serve refugees, that a warm glow of friendship began in a small town in the south of Israel. We had been greatly impressed by the love of life and optimism we had found in a number of young Palestinians. This eventually led to an arranged visit to a family home within the refugee settlement.

Although a perimeter fence defined the camp, there was no evidence of the heavy tangle of razor wire we associate with the West Bank. It was more a tangle of legal status that had denied these people access to the villages of their birth.

Inside, small stone or cement block and wood houses jumbled around a vague roadway. Achmed, our local Palestinian translator and chaperone, pointed to a neat, freshly painted house, its open door reaching out a welcome.

"Salaam Alaikum" greeted our footsteps and a lady in a knotted kerchief ushered us in. She smiled warmly through a tired, lined face as she introduced herself as Maria, then her extended family and their children. Among the crush of people in the room, a small table appeared with home baked snacks and coffee.

We exchanged pleasantries, asked and answered questions, and all seemed eager to join in. But their hurt was not far below a lightly dusted exterior. Conversation soon moved around the familiar story of oppression, dispossession and loss. As others came and went, they added more texture and colour to their heart-wrenching tales.

"Are you employed?" I asked the young man leaning in the doorway.

"Yes, I build homes for settlers on the hill. It is the site of the village we came from. My grandfather owned and farmed the land."

We thanked our hosts and, silenced by all we had heard, stepped back into the road and made our way to the town. On the hillside, it looked as if a designer's dream of Milton Keynes had materialised. Achmed caught up with me.

"What do you think?" he asked, "how will you help them?"

My mind and emotions had melted together into streams that ran in all directions simultaneously. I was familiar with Israel and held the nation in highest regard, but had often questioned their collective opinion of their neighbours, which sounded rehearsed, and amplified by extreme fringe supporters. Yet the same is true of the Palestinian opinion, given over again to willing listeners with well-rehearsed timing.

The boundary lines between both are razor sharp and anything but regular. Fuelled by pain that succeeding generations have not been able to heal, and fanned into flame by a hundred external opinions, it is difficult to make judgements on either position. But it is not difficult to attempt to walk the narrow paths between them and to end up feeling like an insignificant figure entangled with a team of high-powered time-share salesmen.

I wanted to be alone, so I left the little town and the hillside, immortalised by ancient literature, and found streets that had not digested the day's heat. They lay deep among tall houses. My concentration was focussed on slowing down my racing thoughts, so I did not at first notice a young man step out before me, nor the heavy chain wrapped around his knuckles, nor the loose end scything the air, nor the wild look in his eyes. We weighed each other up. I stepped forward; so did he. We passed each other by, and both saved face.

141

This incident deeply disturbed me. He was a young man; I was not his enemy. I had come as a friend, genuinely wanting to understand and help!

When I returned to where our two small rental cars were parked, it was in time to see two more similar-aged, fresh-looking young men being hustled into the back of a patrol vehicle. I rushed across the road, part in protest, part in enquiry. A soldier signalled to the underside of the cars. I lay on the pavement. There were thick, sticky brush marks from the door sill to the petrol tank. From a tin of baby food, the soldier poured some thick fluid that looked like contact adhesive. At the touch of a lighter flame, it immediately flared. The two innocent-looking young guys, with a carrier bag, a paintbrush and a harmless-looking tin of baby food, were waiting for us to drive off. I would probably have joked with them both before doing so. Why not? – It was out of an act of genuine friendship we were there.

Yes, the undergrowth is very tangled, I agree. I can only believe that the source of this confusion does not lie within people, but in the fears bred by their cultural beliefs.

Higher into the hill, along the winding track, elements of historic China survive the communist devastation – yet, by remaining, they add to it. I stand outside the chained gates of what looks like an old mission compound, a monument to the courageous faith of a past age. At the time of the revolution it was confiscated and brought under government control.

The low church buildings and their accommodation are now an island of nominal Christianity encircled within an Islamic community. The caretaker unlocks the heavy gates long enough to allow us to slip through, but our presence is quickly absorbed into the advanced decay, and we feel impotent before the triumph of Mao's regime. It is as if these imprisoned buildings are kept alive to commemorate the death of faith. They are allowed to host one short course each year, with permission granted by the Ministry of Religious Affairs. It makes me wonder if an honourable burial for the bones of one of history's heroic missionary achievements would be more appropriate.

To one side, below the walls of the compound, are the sights and smells of the slaughter yard. On the uphill side, pressed against the boundary wall, stands a mosque, the shadow of its onion-shaped minaret adding to the gloom of this tottering symbol of hope. The caretaker accompanies us back to the chain, the padlock and the high gate.

There is nothing to steal here, save perhaps a lingering memory of what has been, more than a lifetime ago.

Perhaps discouragement has stolen a question which, when answered, could explain a profound reality that underwrites the working of genuine faith.

What is the question?

Can the gains of faith be lost, even if they suffer a lapse of time's decay and may be overtaken by an unsympathetic generation? It is difficult to make judgements of right and wrong, or gain and loss, outside eternity's frame. Genuine Dream or Vision is based on Promise that will be honoured. Faith is our signature to an agreement with divinity. Genuine missionary advance is rooted in this principle. Our conclusions, based on the short-term views, are sometimes inaccurate. We live in a time trench. It is necessary occasionally to take an unhurried gaze over the trench walls and into the distance, or else the trench will become imagination's grave. Communist ideology places man at the centre of everything, its leaders worshipped in place of divinity.

This piece of imprisoned land reminds me of Israel, which is also surrounded by religious ideology which in its fundamentalist extreme belief is working towards Israel's extinction.

Yes, perhaps Israel illustrates the point ... it is a land inherited by Hebrew people, yet through its history it has often been ruled by other nations and their descendants. The present population has had to undergo the painful process of recovery, but has never been lost. If their belief in *El Shaddai* has proved unreliable, then hope is groundless and we are reduced to no more than being reasonably well-evolved life forms, clinging to the paper-thin crust of earth's surface, whirling in open space at about seventeen hundred kilometres an hour.

The caretaker stands with the chain over his arm, the padlock in his hand, the gate slightly ajar. For a rare moment I am glad that I cannot speak Mandarin, for it will be a distraction. The farewell I want to convey to him has nothing to do with the hijacking of the compound by the secular state, nor of political aims. I want to convey the hope of the positive outcome of divine purpose. It is to the touch of my hand in his that I commit this responsibility as I step back into the Hui community, and the trail that winds upwards.

We reach the point where the path levels out into the first plateau, which sweeps to our right. Ahead of me, my colleague is pointing to an obelisk. Tall and needle-thin, it reaches into the sky and pierces a red star.

"We make for this," he says, and I follow.

Domestic and commercial waste litters the open plateau, but I am growing accustomed to the heavy scent of decay. At least there has been no rain, and underfoot the wind has dried the mud.

The needle stands on a platform at the head of a flight of steps that rises against a background of the steep slopes of the higher mountains. It is surrounded by enclosed parkland. It stands as a monument to the Red Army and its horrendously costly victories in the north-west. This region, once the terminal for massive supplies of Soviet arms, is today a memorial to the expendable peasant population, lost in a revolution they did not want but from which they could not escape.

We follow the hard-packed mud and stone track that runs along the foot of the steep slopes. Below us is a valley which could not be seen when we first reached the plateau, into which the town's refuse is carried. Just over the valley rim, there is a small village of houses built from discarded materials. As the valley fills, the tide of rubbish advances to engulf the villagers.

Dark-clothed, white skull-capped villagers scrabble among the refuse. Plastic materials are salvaged and put into sacks. The wind seems to do little to dissipate the stale air. Rodents swarm over the land. Scavenging birds circle overhead, hunting them. Higher still, bald-headed eagles hunt the scavenging birds. A row of toilet cubicles discharges waste through holes at the back. It is collected into heaps alongside the track.

The desolation of the landscape and life is profound. It evokes my bad memories of Manila's notorious Smokey Mountain, and of the dependent population it sustained.

After walking along the hard-baked mud of a saddle, the trail rises again to meet a rocky outcrop. This is a vantage point overlooking the town. From it, the energy of mountain rain flowing on its way to the Yellow river has deeply carved its signature in the soft, yellow soil. Many tombs have been dug into the ravine's steep banks; I think that many more will come.

TEMPLE IN THE SKY
- Secret Mountain -

At the presence of the mountain the landscape shrinks, and we are like grains of dust blown by the wind. The rock outcrop looks forbidding, as if it possesses the soul of the sky's dark mood. Then, from the thick haze of this wasteland's rubbish fires that swirl and eddy as if from the pages of the chronicles of another time, materialising, illusion-like: the mirage of a castle, a temple, or ... what? An arresting chord, frozen in time, seizing our senses and stripping our liberty: a surreal world within our world.

Two octagonal towers, several storeys high, reach skyward. The floors are separated by jutting eaves, the lower supported by bronze pillars. Below them, at varying heights, lie heavy concave roofs of buildings and archways, each having wide eaves with dramatic upswept corners. Symbolic creatures line the ridge tiles of each corner. Even at a distance, the presence of the buildings seems to capture both the past and the future, while defining the present as a gateway through which time dare not enter.

We continue to move towards them, amazed by what we are seeing. Behind an outer wall a huddle of temple buildings grows taller. In an attempt to display more courage than we feel, we enter their courtyard and are overcome by their scale. Flowing roofs, heavily timbered and delicately carved, overhang the courtyard. The wall and door arches are heavy with intricate symbolism. Slabs of light-blue stone with detailed carvings are fitted together to make up a single gigantic picture. Dragons, deer and mythical animals in different poses abound.

The courtyard floor is similarly decorated, and interspersed with trees and shrubs, balustrades and railings. Large, naturally-formed stones define the heads of snake-scaled bodies which rise from the floor, the heaviest in the shape of a turtle which weighs many tons. I remember that in the Orthodox cave churches in Cairo a naturally-formed stone bearing a resemblance to a mother and child is equally regarded as a divine omen.

Two elegant stone stairways with banisters curve upward through three richly-coloured archways, to buildings on a higher level. A large cauldron of sand stands at the entrance to an inner courtyard. From it, blue smoke spirals upward and perfumes the air with incense. A chequered, tiled floor with two raised gardens in decorated surrounds leads to three further cauldrons of sand. The central one is circular, with three legs; the other two, oblong and altar-shaped, stand either side. More incense smoke curls into the air. They stand before a low flight of steps which rises to a third building. Bronze pillars frame highly-decorated red doors, overhung with curtains.

There is movement at the far end of the courtyard. Two men in black, with white skullcaps, are standing in the archways. They light incense sticks, then kneel. Rising again, they slowly walk the length of the courtyard, audibly reciting prayers. They add more incense sticks to the central cauldrons, then climb the low steps and kneel before the curtains and the red doors. Then, their act of worship over, they retrace their steps.

The layout of the buildings has a familiar feel. They could be modelled on the Hebrew temple. If this is so, then the small building behind the curtains and doors may represent the Holy of Holies. It has no Ark of the Covenant inside; it is the mausoleum of its founder, before whom the rituals of worship are performed.

I look up at the concave roof, the elaborate carvings, the flying gables, the curious creatures on the corniced eaves. Into view comes the pagoda-like tower that rises above the carved roofs. It has a dome like an upturned flower, each petal tip forming its own eave, beautifully inlaid with gold, the stem as straight as an arrow, piercing not just the sky, but the moon in its early crescent. Over this strange hint of Hebrew temple, into which has been woven Buddhist and Taoist themes, a spire stridently reaches upwards, supporting the Islamic symbol of the crescent moon.

With my feelings and understanding in confusion, I look for a way of escape. Without thinking, I train my camera lens on something that pleases my eye. It is a brick-built circular archway, beautifully crafted, surrounded by a wide border: the Chinese symbol of completion.

I am about to take the picture when five men walk into the viewfinder, all dressed in black. Four have the tight white skullcaps, the fifth a black one. The man in total black I judge to be an imam of some rank. Two men make up his entourage, and two stand either side of the arched doorway.

The imam, catching sight of my camera, gestures to his attendants to stand back, and poses for his picture beneath the arch. I take the picture, and through the long focus lens take a closer look at the pattern of the surrounding border.

What I see releases in me the horror of a seven-year-old's memories of a wailing siren and the roar of German war planes as they swept out of the sky, low over our hilltop on their mission to bomb the town below.

It is the swastika, with left hand crampons joined in an endless formation. To the Buddhist, it symbolises the toe print of Buddha.

Outside the perimeter walls, the rubbish-fed desolation begins almost immediately – except in one area. Here work the craftsmen, the stonemasons, and the carpenters. I read somewhere that they have been building this temple for fifty years.

Ancient Taoist and Buddhist texts, powerful Chinese symbolism, along with Arabic tributes in praise of Islam, are still being carved to adorn newly-built walls. Tree trunks, numbered, dated and laid out to season, await their optimum year before being formed into roof beams, lintels and doorposts. This is a building crafted to last a thousand years.

Which way does the wind blow?

I am unsure. It can come from every direction. It blows steadily, then it doesn't. Each mountain has its own sound, and on this rocky promontory, where the wind blows from all points, it carries the sound of a lament.

We seem to be at a summit of confusion. Here on this rock,

where the four winds circle and eddy with nowhere to go, we are in a temple in the sky where four major world faiths combine ... with nowhere to go. For above these rises the obelisk, a monument to atheism and to the capitulation of a nation; to a government which has suppressed hope and replaced it with an ideology empty of faith.

The minority people of this small plateau have new Smart Men, but remain Slaves. They live on the refuse of others.

The Dance in the Shadows
What is the wind doing?

I seem to think I can see it blowing a tide of cloud that is hugging the mountain. It is a thick cloud, rolling down the mountain side at the speed of a galloping horse. Soon this temple of shadows will be as if it were not here. I have an uneasy sense that I am crossing an invisible threshold ... beyond it waits something to be understood.

What can you see now?

I see eyes in the cloud blown by the wind. I cannot look at the eyes. They are bright, but not beautiful. They are calling me, and I feel drawn to them, but to what? I think that they are the eyes of a dancer I first sensed at the time of the the New Year celebration. She can be any nationality she wants to be. She is dressed in silver and is heavy and muscular but, in a strange way, appealing. It is as if the grotesque movements are coordinated by an outside source.

Like a shadow puppet?

Perhaps she is a shadow puppet, and if I follow her I will become shadow too. No! She is silver, and not reflected onto the back of a screen. Perhaps the dancer is in my mind, for I feel as if I am in a cloud of confused consciousness. The outline of my own body, the familiarity I have with myself, the identity I have not doubted, is rapidly diminishing into the dance. The hideous prancing back and forth is like a giant mantis teasing its prey, devouring my mind, until I am swallowed, until I do not exist outside the dancing figure.

Where is she dancing?

It is hard to tell, for the light is behind her and her darkness shadows the stage, but I think she dances on a bed of flowers. Their beauty is gone, for they are broken. Their value is in the eyes of the gardener who planted them with purpose. Each broken flower a book full of story. A lily damaged, a beauty abused. A tulip with hanging head. A blackened moss. A heather trampled. A rose unpruned. A shrub cut down. A tender plant bitten by frost. An unwanted root drying in the wind. Each with potential of becoming whole.

As the wind blows from one direction then another, so the dancer's mood changes. I don't think that everyone can see her, but she is there. It is the same ugly dance, uglier than anything I have seen. There are no graceful, whirling pirouettes, a blur of colour spiralling upwards. No defining the essence of all that it is to be human by the turn of the hand or the sparkle of the eye. No beckoning eternity to fill a moment of time. I am aware only that it is the power of pride that controls this dance.

There is anger in the dancer now. The shoulders are hunched, the face reddens, the gaze looks down, the body stiffens, the actions are mechanical, the feet are stomping the earth; the flowers suffer. The anger seems to bring its own source of energy. The figure is like a toy re-wound. The ungainly leaping and bounding continues. She is drowning in perspiration. She is destroying the dance, destroying herself; destroying the invisible only she can see. Her arms lash this way and that; a hundred grotesque idols look through her face. They fight for a place in her eyes. The broken flowers tremble, the stage trembles, the temple trembles, the mountain trembles at the energy of her fury. There is a sound of weeping in the wind. Everyone touched by her anger is hurting, hurting, hurting.

The wind has changed direction, and the mood of the dancer follows. She draws energy from the wind, from her surroundings, and from us. Her movement is slow and deliberate. It is the accuser who is now on the stage. Her eyes are roving all around. She is not staring, but searching with an intensity. Like a hunter, she is stalking. She looks for fear in any gaze she meets. Fear becomes her door to the soul through which she will enter, violate and accuse. There is the energy of jealousy about her demeanour, and resentment is the fire in her eyes.

With subtle movement, her actions follow her gaze. She selects the broken flowers, one here, another there. Her heels grind them into the earth. One by one she selects people ... The dance has a compelling rhythm and no one knows what to do.

While I watch, the figure of the dancer begins to dissolve, and in her place I see an old man my colleagues have saved from a lonely death on the street. The outline of his body replaces the dancer, and it is his arm that is outstretched. He has a finger extended. It points straight at Yin. He is in a jealous rage and falsely accusing, accusing, accusing Yin of selling street children. Yin stands silently under the weight of his condemnation. He offers no defence. Yin is a damaged flower, but is determined not to die!

Seduced by her smile, subdued by her authority, terrified of becoming her victim, we sing in a chorus: "We do not want to know what to do, for the dance is pleasing us."

The wind is blowing cold now ... the mood of the mountain is changing. A mountain can be both beautiful and treacherous.

Now she smiles at me, eyes brimming with hypnotic brilliance. Arms and hands beckon me to join her in the dance. Her step is lighter. With subtle elegance, she is careful not to step on the flowers. Her appeal is growing stronger. Alluring looks flash in one direction, then another. She is calling to people whom I cannot see. Soon they begin mounting the stage, one by one. She leads them in a simple step. They are dancing behind her. Bells tinkle at her wrists as her arms wave gracefully in the air. She has an engaging, endearing smile. She makes me feel as if I am the only one who counts. I am beginning to trust her intrinsic honesty.

She wears the smile of cunning. She has light in her eyes, but it is the light of deceit.

Now they flash a dark panic into me. She exudes the grace of an angel and the ethereal light of a promised dawn. She turns in a wide circle and the dancers keep following. They are young and they are old, from different nationalities. Some have much, others little. A few have only themselves, but they all want to give to her. Around she glides, her slippers scarcely touching the floor, but with each movement the circle tightens.

Still they follow ...

The knot of dancers is at the centre of the stage. Her dance reaches a triumphant finale. She is poised with both hands extended into the air. Her look is that of one who has achieved. She is both the soul and personification of pride. Her aura encapsulates the innocent and sensitive. She holds her poise as she lets the moment of her triumph settle over her, and over her audience. They applaud her performance and bow in respect. They are her willing prisoners.

"We will follow our shepherd," say these lambs, not realising that the shepherd is in disguise, and is the most ferocious wolf of all.

Angrily I respond to the deception, though I know it is pointless. "Go away," I shout, "you do not belong here. Let the prisoners go!"

My voice is weak, it lacks authority. No one turns a head.

If you do not have the authority, you are helpless.

The mist has begun to dissolve the stage and to entwine the dancer and her prisoners. Only the light in her eyes remains. Her gaze is fixed, but her eyes are moving, as though she is inwardly seeing a future which attracts her, yet she is intensely aware of the present. There is deep deception at work, unfathomable, impenetrable. She is more than two people in one. She is a hidden self, with a purpose from which only she can benefit. She will meet others on whatever level they approach her. She sees only lambs to be sacrificed to her purpose.

I see fresh fire beginning to burn in her eyes. She has already sensed the warm trail of unsuspecting innocence. She turns in their direction and stealthily begins her approach. She is predictably true to her cunning nature. For a moment she looks back at me. She says nothing, but there is a hideous smile playing around her mouth and eyes. She is giving me the impression that she is leaving, but there is frightening energy in that sly glance that is telling me something I don't understand.

There is a sound I have not heard before, the deep rumble of a drum, deeper than anything I have known. It is reverberating from the earth. The earth trembles. Above my head booms a heavy bronze gong, struck by a wooden pole suspended by ropes; a call from the snows of some high peak. The dancer has the power to call the sky and earth together, and there is no escape. It is also the sound of the tempest that is raging in my own surging blood.

The uncleanliness of her presence lingers in the air. It is the uncleanness of deception. It is in my clothes; it is in me. I feel ill. My head is in my hands. I have pain over my heart. My capacity for hurt is already full. I want to cry for the broken flowers, but I have no tears.

Why are you are angry? – for the dancer has only portrayed human nature. It is the mind of humanity that has decided the culture of the valley, the poverty on the plateau, the death of religions in the temple of the sky, the domination of the ideology which has captured the nation. She has demonstrated the power of the human being to deceive and to destroy. She has exposed you and me, for we also have descended from the same clay and have both trekked down history's common trail. Perhaps there are no depths to missionary life where the dancer cannot be found, for there are no elements of human nature that she has not touched.

"I want to get away from her, and from you too!" I shout, while in my mind I see a door of escape opening.

From the heavy unnatural blackness that has been slowly feeding itself on who I am, from the horror-inhabited void within me, from the stage where I have become another broken flower, I see my Chinese friends, the long black-haired bunch of smiles. I want to take them away from the vile intentions of the dancer. They must never become broken flowers under her feet.

Away, away, away! my inner being cries.

I see myself in Wales, on a hill under the shadow of a castle. Below me there is a transparent gold crescent of sand, lapped by the sky-rich sea of Carmarthen bay. The warm invitation of the soft music of the curling waves is calling us.

"We would like to swim," they say.

"Please do," I answer, "for without you this replayed pageant of Eden could not fulfil the purpose for which it was created, for it has a need to be enjoyed, enjoyed, enjoyed!"

Down the hill they run. I follow them, my blackness lifting,

lifting, lifting. I am beginning to feel alive again. Then suddenly ...

Rowland, do you realise who is following you?

"Is it the dancer?" I ask. "Is it my bunch of smiles that she has fixed in her gaze?"

Yes, it is.

"Does she also dance in Wales?"

Yes, she fights her personal wars on everyone's ground.

"Where is she hiding? I cannot see her, though I feel her shadow and it makes me shiver."

She is playing her master card of deceit, for she is hiding in you. Remember, we are made from common clay.

"O God! Can I continue with this life?" I cry ...

Only you know, 'machgen i, says a voice from the dark. You have climbed to your Disgwylfan. *You are standing on the summit.*

I have remembered the dream that has troubled me, I answer. I dreamed that all things were as they appeared to be.

That illusion has dissolved and you are pained by the ugly realities of now. You must decide if shalom still holds, for this is the route to you wide sea.

This is not what I want to grow in my soil ... but the voice that calls to me from his dark, the voice I hear in my head, is the trusted voice of Dan.

I have climbed my *Disgwylfan*, without realising it; but I have no feelings of achievement, only a heightened sense of my inner struggles and the ragged road of my history that sweeps into the dust of distance. My way upward to *Disgwylfan* has been a plunge downward into the darker reaches of myself.

I know, says Dan, but you are in clear air now, no longer where spirituality is reduced to what can be seen, and goodness a mere description of behaviour where words like 'nice' and 'sweet' are acceptable. For the divine can seem awkward and contrary, most active in individuals who rouse our feelings of disappointment and of judgement of ourselves.

My personal sense of being owned by my ugly life is too strong, I argue. It resists Wisdom's way of dying. Yet that is how it will be transfigured into another reality that will have meaning for my young Chinese friends.

Only you know this, bach. Find your holy place, for the prayer you need for this time was born with you, and has been waiting for this hour to be prayed.

Dan's advice supports my inward desire to escape to the solitude of my prayer mountain, away from the mocking empty echo of pious words I have grown to distrust, from the sequence of religious clichés meant to be a stairway to hope. They will rob me of the oxygen my soul needs to breathe.

Warm in my mind is a memory waiting to be relived. I climb to the brow of a hill, and to a familiar place in the shelter of a large mound of rocks. The wide sea, white, blue and green under a dappled sky, spreads to the horizon. My Celtic ancestors prayed here, many carrying stones to leave at the mound. They symbolised concerns shared in prayer, then left behind. It has the aura of timelessness. The white and green lichen give the limestone rocks a soft appearance. I feel their welcome. I have not carried a stone to add to the mound except, perhaps, the ice-cold stone I feel in my heart.

Though the hilltop is exposed, it is a private place. I have not seen another person during my climb. Solitude's fingers are already reaching me. They have a settling effect. I feel the primal chaos within me, like music, beginning to take its own form, and my thoughts become a foothold on the path that faith and time would have me tread.

Prayer is never arrogant, for it arises from the longings of our common clay, and our humanity recognises the poverty of our language as we attempt to give it expression. A person kneeling in prayer is a picture of total vulnerability. The essence of prayer lies beyond the requests generated by need. It grows from the desire to put words to the longings of eternal love. Silence is important, for in it we overhear the voice of divinity. Words are the signposts that lead to where we may find that silence.

I am not sure how much time has passed when, like a soft wisp of curling mist, a delicate female voice drifts into my consciousness. Surprisingly, I am not startled, although I am sure that there has not been another person on the hill. It is a soft voice, but firm with latent energy. It is fluid in the wind. Though I cannot distinctly hear her words, they have the tone of someone at home in her surroundings, questioning and imploring. I do not want to move and become a clumsy intrusion into her holy moments. She too is in prayer. She is filling the silence with a sound that brings a harmonious support. It is as if she is providing another vessel that will help carry the cargo of my longings.

Prayer's invisible incense mingles like smoke from wood fires that drift upwards. Dan's words again visit my thoughts.

Your prayer for this time was born with you. It has been waiting its appointed hour.

I sense that the hour may have come, and I am not alone. A new dimension of prayer filters into my understanding. At my crucial hour, just twenty metres from me, someone I do not know nor have expected has flowed into the life of my prayer. Twenty metres, twenty miles or twenty thousand miles – it does not matter. Coincidence? No! The miracle would be the same, as distance does not invalidate prayer. Then how many people are sharing in my prayer and, just as easily, I in theirs?

Perhaps an hour passes, and the prayer from the other side of the rocky mound thins into silence, but I am reluctant to leave the sense of presence which has accompanied it.

Eventually I make my way to the hard-packed, stony lane that follows the ridge past the mound. There is no-one in sight save a young mother, making her way slowly down the hill. She carries a baby on one arm while another small child walks alongside, holding onto her skirt.

I watch her go, but do not dare call after her. Home for me lies in the opposite direction ... without my ice-cold heavy stone!

I am walking again through one of China's subterranean passageways. Yin, the lame man, holds my arm. He is accompanying me to the vehicle that will return me to my flat before he returns to his place on the pavement.

"Can I sing you a song?" he asks.

From a piece of folded paper, in a rusty voice, amid the sounds of vehicles and people who scurry from the night, he sings a prayer of gratitude and hope to the love that has not failed him. Further along the pavement a dumb, homeless man, a friend of Yin's, runs and hugs me.

"I can speak, I can speak," he says in Mandarin.

He means that he can speak more clearly than he has spoken before. Yin has prayed for him, and perhaps for me too, for I am back among my loving friends.

SONG OF EARTH AND SKY
- A Village Wedding -

It was the day when Ya Juan, one of the bunch of smiles, was to be married. "We will call for you at six in the morning," said one of her friends.

The dawn had not begun to silver the sky, nor had the cold begun to lose its penetrating grip as I made my way past the security guardroom of the block of flats where I was staying. The spy cameras silently flickered their captured images on the security monitor, which also reflected the guard stretched out in a chair before it, arms folded, head back, eyes closed and mouth open. The picture of myself walking through unchecked also flashed across the screen.

The attitude of the security guards can be unpredictable: sometimes extremely mean, at other times quite indifferent. Once, I approached a railway station with arm-wrenching books in boxes that advertised washing powder. My fully extended rucksack was also square with books, so heavy that I had balanced it on a wall to place the straps on my shoulders. That day all passengers were required to have their luggage examined by x-ray. I felt trepidation rising as I took my place in the line. The books had been printed in China, by an underground press. I had collected them from their hidden warehouse to deliver them to the villages where they were needed. Both press and warehouse were under police surveillance.

The biggest difficulty was that several in the line of people at the x-ray machine were doing exactly the same thing! I took advantage of my foreignness and began to walk past. A guard turned me around and pointed me back into the queue. I heaved my boxes onto the belt and my rucksack crashed after them. I passed to the offloading end, having resigned myself to being escorted to a waiting police vehicle. My horror deepened when I found that my colleagues, who had passed through ahead of me, were having difficulty removing the heavy boxes off the belt and luggage had begun to pile up and to spill over the floor.

Eventually the conveyor belt shut down through overload, leaving my rucksack filling the monitor screen, with the enormous number of identical study books that they could easily have counted. At this point, fresh guards moved in, cleared the conveyor belt and, complaining at the weight of the boxes, stacked them either side. I followed the example of the others, picked them up quickly and hobbled my way to the train; an unpredictable outcome that worked in my favour.

Later I learned of the seriousness of the situation. The press and the warehouse were closed down, and I believe that a Chinese colleague who for some of the journey had travelled with us, was imprisoned.

This morning I have no such difficulty, and right on time the lights of a miniature people-carrier appear. My Chinese friends are crushed into the back. I jam into the cab alongside the driver. The incessant chatter from the rear seats keeps him amused. We make a right turn from the local road network, onto a ring road. It is deserted except for a motorised trishaw, which has no lights and the distance between us is rapidly shrinking, but our driver's uncanny sixth (or seventh) sense works, and the trishaw continues to the market with its cargo of vegetables intact. I hope that its daily game of roulette with every oncoming car, truck and bus continues to pay off.

Some road stalls are already in place, especially poultry and pigs. Chickens in bunches, their claws tied together, are suspended upside down from a carrying pole. Their wings hang open and are entangled with each other. Their open beaks continually drip moisture. A small knife penetrates the throat of one, its wings flap, its blood speckles the floor. If fortune smiles for the vendor, in a few hours not one will be left alive. On another roadside table someone is selling a pig, already chopped into manageable pieces.

Then there is a live pig, the size of a small horse, trotting before its owner, who is steering it by means of a thin rope tied to the ring in its snout – another table awaits it. Someone else sells cooking oil from the carrier on his bicycle; every few steps he makes the same cry. The rat catcher is also out early. How do I know? He has a carrying pole over his shoulder; rats dangle from it, tied by the tails, interspersed with small packets of rat poison. This is the identifying insignia that hangs over his mobile business. Yet another has a cycle with a few very weathered tools attached; a piece of cardboard advertises his skills as an odd-job man ... Just a few moments' view of this tremendous diversity of life is enough to inspire a lifetime's contemplative thought.

We roll into a small town and bump to a halt. I feel like a screwed-up ball of paper; six more screwed-up balls tumble from the back. The air is crisp and cold. Snow, which has been shovelled into heaps, has now turned into ice. I wear a thick jumper under a leather coat covered by a fleecy-lined storm coat, a model for the original Michelin man, yet I am still cold.

The town is made up of several village communities, each preserving a distinct environment. This street carries the signature of communist influence, rather than of the old China.

The bride's father has built their house, but soon afterwards his own wife died. In keeping with village style the living area opens front and rear, with small bedrooms curtained off. It has no heating and very little furnishing. The bride's day has started at four in the morning. By five, she was made up and dressed. By seven, she is sitting in her thin wedding clothes at near-freezing temperature, receiving family and villagers. She looks stunningly beautiful. Her mind is in a complex ferment of emotions, but she shows none of this. Neither does she show the effects of the cold. Her eyes are alight with excitement.

To present her with memories of her special day, I have brought my camera. Her relatives and friends recover quickly from the uncertainty that a foreign presence may have caused them, but at the sight of my camera, immediately freeze and with expressions set in marble, line up and look at the lens. I think that this is the least inspired form of photography, but to please them I fire away. At the same time I look for those unguarded moments when the bride's expression really defines who she is.

Outside, a black limousine draws up. Its driver spreads himself across the front seats and falls asleep. He leaves the engine running, which smokes the frosty air. It looks altogether out of place amid the hanging columns of corn cobs and mounds of corn stalks that dry in the sun and wind, and overflow the space outside most houses. Inwardly grumbling about the black car, I almost miss the progression of the marriage.

The groom has arrived to collect his bride. He wears a suit and a tall-crowned trilby-style black hat. The bride and groom together bow to the seated father and the mother's empty chair, their acknowledgement of those who have brought her life and beauty. The groom then carries her to the car, so that her feet may not get soiled. They will not touch the ground again until she arrives at the groom's home. She will not return to her father's house for some days.

So full of potent symbolism, you murmur. *The wedding tells a beautiful story, its own and another.*

The black limousine slides out of the street. We re-pack ourselves into the complaining people-carrier and, with some effort, slide the door shut.

At the groom's house, the black car halts under a plastic gazebo. It is immediately sprayed with some kind of incense.

The past is over; she is crossing the threshold of her new beginning.

The bride now wears a red veil that completely hides her face. The groom leads her out of the car. They enter the living area and bow to the groom's mother, who sits on a bed in a curtained-off area. There is no one beside her, for her husband has died, and she has raised the family alone.

They then pass into another curtained-off sleeping room, where the bride sits on the brick and hardboard bed and is joined by her new family for a simple, cold rice meal. A neighbour hands me chopsticks to share the rice on the the bride's plate, watches for a moment, then changes them for a spoon.

In the rear yard, at the open end of the living area, large tubs are steaming over wood fires. On benches and tables, vegetables, meat and fish are being prepared by neighbourly hands.

By mid-afternoon another long metal-framed plastic tent fills the roadway, and plastic tables and chairs are set out. The guests fill the tent and overflow into what space they can find, and the wedding feast begins. Ten courses of country-style cooking swirls onto the tables from a team of willing helpers. The bride and groom make their appearance and slowly walk to the large table, where both their families are seated together. They bow to them three times while the master of ceremonies reads the official script. They also turn and bow to each other; it seems that the official ceremony is over, so they are free to mingle with the guests. The meal's end and the tent's instant dismantling seem to be the signal for the remainder of the village to pour into the space, and the meal starts all over again.

I leave the celebrations to look for the old part of town where there are low houses with wide curling eaves and broken overlapping fish-scale tiles that almost meet each other across the narrow lanes. There are shops that sell incense sticks, hell money, and paper houses for the deceased; toilet paper, cigarettes, rice wine and cheap watches. Ladies clad in padded Mao suits stand or sit outside on walls or favourite stones, with chopsticks and bowls of noodles – where chickens roam and peck, where pigs grunt, where cows in twos or threes are tethered and where the bicycle is king.

On an ancient fallen tree outside a row of concave-roofed cottages sit two old ladies. They have shrivelled parchment skin, shrunken eyes, and hollow cheeks. One is smoking a thin, long-stemmed clay pipe with a small smoking bowl. Between missing teeth, with lips hardly moving, they whisper to each other. Through age-misted eyes they watch a third younger woman clean a few vegetables in a little water.

They may be neighbours.

Their worn doorsteps are near, but I am not sure that they have always been neighbours, for a generation of fear and animosity may have kept them apart. During the dark days of the revolution, the strategists tapped into the emotions that underlie the surface of village life. They encouraged villagers – no, forced them – to make accusations against a neighbour, who could then be labelled antirevolutionary and cajoled to make public confession, be imprisoned, or worse. There was nowhere to hide in a commune, and some regions had quotas of villagers, who would be branded anti-communist rightists, to imprison or kill. Village cadres would themselves suffer if the targets were not reached.

But what does it matter now? Their field has already been harvested; these are just a few dried rice stalks left standing. They were once among the village princesses; they could tease the boys, for each one was a prize the boys longed to win. Now, life has run its course; nothing matters any more. Their space is needed. In the minds of the next generation, they are already ploughed into the ground.

The river bed below the bridge has only shallow pools of thick, grey, stagnant water. Plastic waste lies where it has caught among the stones. When the flood waters rush down from the up-stream villages, it will be replaced by yet more waste.

These old ladies know little outside of their own small world. They are aware that their visit here is about to end. Each day they sit and wait for the bleak, irreversible embrace that will lead them away. Like the waste among the stones, there will be nothing to hold them when the water rises. Others will take their place on the fallen tree. It will be as if they had never existed.

The hours have passed quickly and the bride, her wedding dress hung ready to be returned to the hire shop, stands at the door of our vehicle while we scrunch inside. I, a lone foreigner, have enjoyed being accepted into the life of the community. My clumsy mistakes have caused them laughter rather than offence.

Our vehicle begins to roll and pitch along the broken surface. We turn a corner where normally there is a deep mud hole the width of the road. In preparation for the wedding, the neighbours have filled it with building rubble. We pick our way across it, and pass a stall selling plastic shoes. I release the little shops, the incense sticks, the hell money and the two fragile ladies on the fallen tree to the droning engine, the melodious chatter of Mandarin, and the grunting agreement of the driver. I am thinking of the wedding, and of the deep symbolism which reflects the meaning behind the joining of two people.

It was the beautiful simplicity of the wedding that I found so inspiring.

Yes, the freedom from the forms to which we are accustomed gives room to think and to explore its elemental purity. There were no church buildings, no organ music, no marriage lines that we would recognise. Uncomplicated by pride and show, this bonding of two people felt as if it had transcended time.

Perhaps beyond that, it had an ethereal quality, as if it were happening in two worlds at the same time ... If I dare say it, as if two people were giving an earthly dimension to an eternal thought.

True, marriage bridges the beginning and ending of the poem in which we live. It mirrors the private celebration of one man and one woman at the beginning of time while, from somewhere in its depths, it also reflects the awesome celebration of God eternally united to his people at the end of time. Both ends of the thread of divine purpose pass through Ya Juan's village wedding. Its stark simplicity gives it a brilliant clarity. Suddenly, less became more. Yet to describe the future it projected into the present, and left me wondering if I was attempting to understand the sun, having only lived in the light of the moon.

How does the poem continue?

Despite our protests, the driver has decided to take us no further than a bus stop on the edge of the town. There is no concept of queuing. Everyone within a hundred metres runs and pushes for the bus. We stand in the bus, fifty or more deep. The conductress, imprisoned behind a cage, calls loudly in an attempt to collect fares twenty people away. I admire her tenacity, working over shoulders and under chins. I am beginning to thaw, and the sense of *aelwyd*, hidden in the meaning of the marriage, pleasantly warms my thoughts.

It is in the stone grey silence of the following morning, when sleep has begun to thin, that you remind me that I needed to finish our conversation.

I will tell you how I think the story unfolds. It is an allegory, for as I knock on the door of mystery I wear my bent tin badge as a sign of my ignorance, so I will only be able to show you the horizon beyond which your search may find truth. As I hear the poem within myself, I will speak it out and, if you don't mind, in the natural poetic rhythm of my Welsh emotion.

You nod in agreement, and say that is all that you could ask.

VEILED BEAUTY
- The Great Romance -

Ya Juan, the Village Bride

The houses had been raised from the earth as if sprinkled like seed, or blown by the wind. They were earth's colour and texture, each with its own mound of thick corn stalks waiting to be used as cooking fuel, and cobs that hung from the eaves, drying in the wind. In every direction the sky met the fields, trees and irrigation channels, except where a pall of smoke marked the nearest town.

The rich sound of children's voices lifted the cool mist of loneliness that hung in the air, for Yu Juan was preparing for her marriage, and the little ones were uninhibited in their excitement. The older ones were more restrained and whispered in huddles of twos and threes. Ya Juan, who carried the fresh innocence of a warm spring day, had captured the imagination of the villagers, both young and old.

A spontaneous breath of approval arose from the crowd that gathered around her father's house where she stood, framed in the threshold of the doorway. It was a subdued sound, for they were in awe not only of her unpretentious loveliness, but something more. It was as if an untarnished mirror beautifully reflected an image greater than her own, that had answered a question which had not even been asked. In the uncomplicated spirituality of Chinese country people it seemed as if, for a moment, immeasurable in length and depth, some pristine instinct began to interpret the mystery of marriage.

The Bride on the Threshold of Time

In the purity of earth's first dawn, when light swept a path through the dark and the sun eased away the mists of the primal day, the red clay yielded the first Adam. In awe his eyes drank in the sight of nature's welcome, and his spirit warmed to the presence that assured him that this was his to enjoy.

His awareness grew, and he searched for another like himself to share his home. In the mystery of providence, an answer awaited its time. It was not just space in the garden that Eve would need, but room in Adam's heart.

The Poet knew that the world would become unstable, and the powerless would serve the powerful, under whatever ideology or flag they would fly.

So he laid the foundations of love and said, "Let Adam share his body with Eve. Let him discover the sacred meaning of being, and find sweetness in the pain of giving himself so that another can gain her life."

So from his bloodied side she came, and he found sweetness in the pain, for he understood why the Poet had set her value so high ... she was never to be his slave.

When Eve awoke, a free and independent spirit with a garden and a world to explore, she thought little of the man who had given her life until, within Adam, there began to grow the wonder and the mystery of love. With the value of its currency, he bought Eve's affection. So a pattern appeared.

> *First there was one*
> *who became two*
> *who through love*
> *became one*
> *but as two separate beings*
> *and the divided flame did not grow less.*

What the Poet had called good he now called very good, and in the ambience of Ya Juan's presence was the silent echo of his pleasure.

The Bride on the Threshold of Eternity
When the ages, like rolled-out carpet, near their end and billions of

feet walk in its remaining, unsoiled time; when the carpenter's hammer blows and the computer keyboard's click join the growl of the dustman's truck and the throbbing bass from the radio of an open car; when frustration's pointless scream joins the sob of grief and the whisper of love, they all contribute to the cacophony of sound that besieges the mind until, unthinking, it believes that an endless source of tomorrows will continue ... and we rush on.

Yet around us hover sounds that are not confused with the roar of hectic pace. It is what our inner ears hear when we retreat into the silence within ourselves. It is the voice of another bridegroom. Where does it come from? I am not sure. What I do know is that it is heard on the wind that sweeps every sea and fills every valley, even amidst the roaring traffic that endlessly streams our sleepless city nights. It is the voice of the last Adam calling to his bride.

Come my darling, my beautiful one, come with me.

As silence welcomes the last bride, she stirs at the sound that wakens her fragile dream. It is as if she lives in an embroidery of dappled light, and the bridegroom's voice causes her pain she cannot understand. She is uncertain and awkward in her preparation, unsure that she wants the day to come, feeling undeserving of his language of love.

She wonders, if she were to be brushed again with the bloom of youth, would her confidence rise? But in depression's lightless moments, she knows she mirrors time's decay in the dying flame of her useful day. Her walk to the sunset has not slowed down. Eternity might just be footsteps away. She wonders and wonders if she can really be ... that chosen final bride.

The last Adam stands at the gate. Eternity beckons him through. He is a visitor to time, who wears the clay of common man. All creation waits in expectation of his bride, for in this final marriage lies the ultimate destiny of mankind, as purpose and meaning entwine.

Like the fragile moon behind a curtain of cloud, he feels the hesitation of his bride. Though she is his chosen one he does not roughly take her hand, but waits for her desire to arise, and with the currency of his love begins to pay her price. For every thought of her brings sweetness to his pain.

He finds comfort in the wood into which the nails bite deeply. It too has given its life to be cut and shaped to meet his final hour. The spear that tears his side has also been given up by earth to be formed by heat and anvil. Though those who watch are unaware, his tortured frame has nothing more to give except that to his bride he hands his flickering flame, and his last breath becomes her first.

The bride feels no pain as she is born again and finds herself breathing eternity's air. She arises with no thought for the man they carried away, but dances and dances away the days.

The Poet has been severe in the price he has asked for the bride. Her cost is greater than that of clay ... it is more, far more, than the man is able to pay. But the Poet is just and understands as no others can, when the scales balance against the man. Then, beyond the value of a heart of clay ... love begins to flow in the currency of pure gold. The last Adam, this visitor to earth, has held a secret which only he and the Poet share. As love flows and flows and flows, slowly the scales balance, and tip in favour of the man.

The restless swords are silent as the tomb guards sleep. When the night softens before the third dawn's glow, no one sees the last Adam arise and stand ... his hope transfixed into faith's longing gaze. Then, from every horizon across every hill, along every path, the final bride is making her way. By ones and twos, by tens and hundreds, by thousands from every tribe and nation, still she comes.

The Poet smiles. His decision has been honoured and the impossible price for the first Adam's race has, to the last penny, been fully paid. The accounting done, he closes the ledger and, with the air of confident finality, says, "It is finished."

It was when he reached across to clear his desk that his sleeve uncovered his hand and I saw an angry wound where a nail had pierced his palm. I suddenly felt alone, in shock, frozen by the sight. Embarrassed, I looked away but I could not resist his gaze, and as our eyes met, mine asked the question ... why? He looked down and his silence spoke with words that language has not been able to frame. The Poet, who had written into motion all the feet which had trodden earth and had also set their value beyond worth, had then stepped down into time ... and paid the cost himself!

That day I stood in the presence of a mystery whose threshold I have not crossed. It fills earth and sky and, since I saw the wound, it has consumed my every year. It is a mystery that has not yielded to intellectual argument, nor to the search of the ordinary man. Rather, in defiance of cynicism's objections, it has just grown and grown and grown. Beyond human consciousness, from eternal thought, the calculation had already been made. The bride price, the last Adam would pay, would be the full value of every human soul.

Through a silent look the Poet spoke once more.

This is a mystery that can be received, for I gave the human heart the capacity to believe.

In the Shadow of Divinity

In hushed tones you ask, *Can we see the final bride?*

As Eden was home to the first Adam's bride, so eternity will be home for the last Adam's bride. Only then will her identity be fully known, and her mystery fully realised. For the present, perhaps, her secrets live in her smile, and many more live in the symbolism that surrounds her. Symbolic language is extremely precise. It allows natural and spiritual imagery to weave together into multi-dimensional reality. The poem, of which we are a part, describes the final bride as both a woman and a city that descends out of heaven; a new Jerusalem, its gold refined to transparent glass, its walls of crystal, gates of pearl, foundations of precious stones, its tree of life, its river and streets and, most of all, its royal throne.

In awe you stare as if the city can already be seen. Then, with inspiration's insight yet with incredulous air, you say: *But on the city's throne I see the last Adam!*

Yes, that's exactly right, for the city is also the bride for whom the last Adam paid the ultimate price.

Among the powerful images in my mind I think I see Ya Juan, the village bride. Music plays in her eyes, a melody I have not heard before. She calls our attention with great emphasis and says, *There is at least one obvious reason why the last Adam is on the throne. Transformed by his love, it is the bride's decision to give the last Adam the throne of her heart. Remember, the bride and the city are one.*

As I turn to leave I catch sight of what I had not realised before.

The city, who is the bride, has no need of the sun or moon, for from the throne of her heart, through the transparent crystal and gold, light shines out and out ... In the shadow of the divinity lies our world, and the mystery of eternity. The Poet, *El Shaddai*, Almighty God ... and the last Adam, are one. God has made himself known to us ... as a man.

To take our place within the bride is the intended destiny of man. It mirrors eternal union between the Poet and his characters in the secure environment where his total love for them – his shalom – has been proved. So we return to that ancient equation on which life in time has been founded.

> *First there was one*
> *who gave himself to become two*
> *who through love*
> *became one*
> *but as two separate beings*
> *and the divided flame does not grow less.*

If it were possible to view eternity from some high tower in time perhaps we would see just two people: the bride and groom, walking into the distance hand in hand ... So, in the wild remoteness of Central China, we grasp the hands held out to us from the past and future, so immaculately reflected in a moment of present ... by Ya Juan, our village bride.

The bride holds many secrets which she does not give away all at once, and perhaps never to the casual glance. What I can confidently say is that, as the inner qualities of Eve may be understood by a beautiful but temporal Eden, so the inner qualities of the Bride are displayed by the new creation of an eternal city. Beyond this I cannot go for I still wear my bent tin badge.

Is this just a poem?

Yes, it is a poem in which we all have a part. It is wide with ragged fringes, which means that anyone can enter it at any point and somewhere within its romance they will find their home. No, more than a home, the *aelwyd*, the welcoming hearth of the home.

171

Sadly, it is often pain that leads us into the story.

In North Africa's High Atlas mountains, where only mule or donkey trails lead into the Berber villages, a few animal owners open a wound in the base of the neck. They press a sharpened stick into the wound. The animal responds to the severity of the pain, and will move faster or slower, right or left, accordingly. There are times when we, also, only make decisions by the pain we feel. Yet, lying bright among the unclaimed privileges of time, *shalom*, the unearned good will of our God, can easily be found.

What of the two old ladies on the fallen tree?

It is Dan's melodious Welsh voice I hear, answering in his usual style. *The Poet knows, 'machgen i, he knows.*

I cross a river by a narrow humpback bridge. Greasy with wet mud, it is not an easy crossing. Tottering before me is a frail, elderly lady, her gaze fixed on the far bank. As a child, her tiny clubbed feet were crushed and bound by Chinese custom. She fights onwards. I want to offer her my arm, but as this may frighten her I walk behind at her pace. She has seen the possibility, and I am watching it become a reality.

We make progress by leaving the known for the unknown. It is impossible to gain different results by forever covering the same ground.

How can there be so many levels of reality at work at the same time?

I happen to be standing near a slender eucalyptus tree. Its love of light has sent its branches foraging the sky. The bark-scented air is calm around me, yet its upper leaves change colour as they twist and turn in a steady breeze. Just ten metres above is an energy I cannot see or hear. Higher are cumulus clouds, white islands adrift in a westerly current in a sea of sky. Higher still are travelling clouds, feathered like wings of some Jurassic bird, splayed in opposite directions by the speeding Jet Stream; all energised by what cannot be seen.

It is a mysterious path that leads to the ultimate, and it is faith in the Poet's words that guides us to it. Only as the unknown becomes known, however imperfectly, can we begin to understand who and where we are.

Could this be the greatest love poem ever written?

PRIDE AND PRAYER WHEELS
- Tibet -

When People-shaped Smudges Shimmer in the Air
This north-west frontier town of China's ancient empire used to be a hazardous posting for the military, the strategic crossing on the Yellow River which in autumn still drapes the valley in a thick mixture of mist and smoke from the many surrounding brick kilns. Under its cover, invading horsemen could be at the walls or even the gates before the defenders were aware. Some weeks from now the frozen fingers of a north wind will tear through the streets and lanes shredding this eerie veil, like prayer flags in the mountain passes.

I feel like a minute, floating island, adrift somewhere in a sea of mist. One of the remarkable things about mist is the way it gives each one their private world. Mine happens to be on the broken pavement along which I walk slowly in an attempt to quieten my mind into the leisurely rhythm of my body. My comfortable private space travels with me. It gets no bigger, nor smaller.

I can hear the movement of traffic, which may be three metres from me, or thirty. It does not invade my space, so it doesn't matter. My mind, free to roam, imagines what might be there. People, like dark smudges, shimmer through the folds of this misty veil and share with me fractured moments of their lives. If I remember them, they will always be as I see them in these instants, ghostly figures, each within its own pose. Some are unaware of me; they have personal vendettas with mobile phones.

A handcart of apples that drip tears of moisture edges into my space. I hear the traders' cry and the scuffle of cold feet, but I see no-one. This is where I turn into the narrow brick lane, single rooms with tiny windows along one side, and the stale smell of neglected toilets on the other.

I trip over a box. A chicken is attached to either side by a cord to its foot. They peck the bare brick surface and lay eggs in the box. Despair looks up at me. Their world has never been wider than the narrow lane, their freedom just a few inches of cord. Their only value is in the eggs they produce. When they finish laying, that will be their end. Their heroic struggle to survive the wet feathers and the biting frost will have meant nothing. Perhaps they are the representation of life in this lane.

There is a commotion ahead. A small, round man drifts piece by piece into my space. He is also shouting into a mobile phone, more loudly than the others, like a preacher uncertain if he is being understood. One hand is curled up to his left ear while his free hand feeds strips of bread from a flat, round loaf into the corner of his mouth. His lips stretch as they attempt to shape words in a dialect of Mandarin. Time and distance are being compressed, and the round man has escaped from the lane to where there is warmth, friendliness and personal value. Perhaps this is why he can stand in a thin tee-shirt and braces, while condensation drips from his hair. He does not feel the cold for, as long as his subscription lasts, he can be somewhere else.

The lane ends in a tide of mud where the next street should be. I test its depth – it is above my trainers. A frail, elderly lady also looks at the mud. No, her attitude is different, she is not looking at the mud, she is searching for a way through it. She moves away; I follow her, and my space comes with me. She steps into a fresh tyre impression. It is leading to somewhere beyond. There is a way out of the lane. I am moved by her courage, so I also take the track and the mud slowly closes over my footprints. I leave the chickens and the man in a wet tee-shirt who, for the moment we shared the same space, believed himself to be somewhere else.

The fragments of silence within me, like small ships, each with a cargo of my disjointed thoughts, have come together into the same harbour and I think that I am ready to recount the story of my previous weeks; just one story, from a land awash with stories waiting to be heard. This one is personal, and I know that I will struggle as I tell it. Yet I need to tell someone, as it will help affirm me in the distance I want to place between my cultural pride and the freedom for which I search. Like the tyre track in the mud, my way disappears into the future and, like my space in the mist, the present will travel with me.

Morning is a dull glow in the east when I hail a roaming taxi. Speeding through the outskirts of the town, we crash into a barrier and limp to the bus station. The bus driver makes his way to the bus, following the glow of his cigarette stub; it dies under a twist of his foot as he coughs himself awake. He is a swarthy man, used to hauling heavy vehicles along trails their designer had not imagined. The diesel engine also shakes off its sleep, and coughs its way into the journey beyond the mountains that flank the valley, towards the lands of the warring horsemen.

The road snakes upward and the town sinks below the surface of the restless lake of mist. Minarets force their presence on the skyline as we enter the region of an Islamic clan. Some say that their tribal name contains the hint of hope that one day they may return to their own land. They are holding a morning market where skull-capped, bearded men argue in small groups. Others are killing and skinning sheep.

I have been here once before. It was summer then, and I wore a loose shirt. Some of the older men stretched out my arms and loudly discussed my faded army tattoos. Eventually, one ran to the mosque and brought a cleric to give his judgement. He inspected, then shook his head and frowned at me darkly. I had no way of telling him that I would probably agree with his opinion. Today it is the growl of our low-geared bus that disturbs them, and the passenger alongside me is sick.

A distinctly Tibetan presence evolves into the scenery. In a saddle between the hills, huddles of small communities are exposed to the raw winds. Their outside walls are daubed with yak dung drying for winter heating and cooking. In warm contrast colourful figures follow the rocky paths between the communities: men at one with their horses; women with thick black hair strain under impossible-sized sacks while leading goats or yak; a mother with a coloured headscarf has children playing prettily around her flowing skirt.

Tibet is not a new experience. It is where my focus has concentrated since childhood. Perhaps it is not unusual at that time for a young mind to travel imagination's pathways to unchallenged summits, to hear the grasslands sing when, in reality, my sky disappeared behind an industrial slag tip which fell away to a railway line and a stagnant canal. Here green did not exist, except in the weeds that survived the contaminated soil.

Untamed Tapestry

At the head of a pass, between two gigantic slabs of mountain that have heaved themselves upright, I stagger from the bus, drunk from the effects of altitude and hairpin bends. Ahead of me is the entrance to an ancient monastery compound, where the Mahayana form of Tibetan Buddhism is taught and practised. A hint of reflected sunlight flashes from the silver and gold adornment of a temple roof. Around the entrance untidy market stalls sell yak meat, yoghurt, apples, plums, pears, grapes and root vegetables, as well as bread in a variety of coils and twists. Second-hand clothes, shoes, boots, various sizes of rope, and rusting tools are spread out on plastic sheets. A row of small houses have shops squeezed into their living space. They all seem to sell the same things.

Vermilion-robed monks move around in twos and threes. Their toilets appear to be anywhere they choose to squat down under the cover of their long robes, regardless of the stalls or people. Long plaits grow from under floppy, cowboy-style hats, robes and scarves, as Tibetan men and women browse and bargain. A tall man in a traditional long-sleeved coat, and with red threads woven into his long, butter-greased hair, stoops to talk to his small son who is staring, wide-eyed, at the foreigner.

Then, standing out in her loneliness, I see a little girl of about seven years old – a nomad, by her features and dress. Dirty, with matted hair, she holds out her empty sack to each stallholder in turn. Dazed, her red eyes a history of tragedy, she does not know how to communicate. Bewildered, she is unsure of who or where she is. Wandering away, her sack is still empty. From a distance she stops and looks at the row of house-shops. Bread, yoghurt and biscuits jostle for space on their counters.

I close down my imagination. It would be too painful to know what she may be thinking. Instead, beyond the little girl, beyond the stalls, the monastery and the pass, the land opens up into an eternity of river and weaving grasslands.

Running slightly downhill from the monastery is a wild-west-style street, straddled by eating places, lodging houses, supply shops, hairdressers, a police station, a bank. On the mountainside above the street, the original community of small Tibetan homes lies in a clutter of odd shapes, separated by shoulder-width alleyways that seem to squirm in all directions at once. The houses look as if they may have been spaced out at one time, but have slowly slipped down the mountain and collected at the bottom.

After negotiating a dormitory bunk space in a lodging house, I follow an invitation to visit an elderly grandfather somewhere among the muddle of old houses. With his granddaughter leading, we climb a track that branches from the main street. Due to the torrent of water that can flow down the mountain, it is no more than a rubble of tarmac, stones and clay.

We turn into a narrow alley and pick our way down steps, into an enclosed courtyard known only to the searching eyes of the sun. In the deep shadow of the wide eves, on a hard, straight-backed chair, an elderly man sits out the day, and perhaps most days. He emerges from the dark as the the soft, reflected light from the stone and brick courtyard falls lightly on his grey hair and deeply-etched face and hands; a close-to-perfect study of a man who has lived at peace with the frozen wilds of Tibet. His features are distinct, but the shadow retains his mystery, and that is how it should be.

He has been a herdsman all his life on the mountain slopes and the high plateaux, a natural horseman, his family born and raised in a yurt. In his sixties he sold his herd and moved into this small home. The worn fingers of his right hand hold a rosary of beads, the size and colour of chestnuts. He moves them one by one along a looped cord. His lips move slightly to the murmur of a prayer. I am impressed by the quiet strength and dignity his presence gives to the courtyard. He brings identity to his house, and perhaps to the surrounding homes. It explains the loving respect his grand-daughter has for him.

It all makes me acutely aware of my foreign awkwardness, and I begin to question my right to enter his space. I need not worry. I point to my grey hair, and then to his. His weather-browned face creases into a smile and his laughing eyes speed a welcome, as they have done a thousand times to lone individuals on the Tibetan plain.

We trade simple conversation, translated by his granddaughter who stands lovingly behind his chair. He has three grandchildren. The two boys are in the Chinese army, and the young girl looks after him and his wife. The father has deserted the family, so the patriarch's daughter, the mother of his grandchildren, still works out in the grassland, coming home occasionally.

I feel that the deep silence within him has absorbed this sadness. He has gladly taken the pain so that his family can be free. The grandmother, a small, smiling lady who seems bent over by the weight of traditional Tibetan clothes, has a simple job: for a few hours each day she sweeps up the traders' waste from the long street.

Their home is simply built in the shape of a nomadic yurt, its only room divided by a cooking and heating yak-dung stove. Its heat flows through the base of a large bed in which all the family sleep side by side. A monk's room is attached, furnished and kept ready for use. Many Tibetan homes have one, often the best in the house.

We are comfortable in each other's company, and stretch out our conversation until the sun begins to dip behind the peaks and signals my time to leave. His adoring granddaughter, who shares his firm spirit, smiles and leads me back to the stone steps. The old herdsman has not moved from his seat, nor stopped shuffling the beads through his fingers during my stay. He watches me cross the courtyard, his eyes smile goodbye ... but his lips form the shape of the ancient Sanskrit mantra: *Om mani padme hum.* Hail the jewel in the lotus, Amen.

It has been a happy visit. I have enjoyed the welcome of his hospitality, but I am also aware that the ten steps across the courtyard are a ten thousand mile journey back to my world. On the crude lane down to the road I look up at the sentinels towering above the pass. The orange flame of the sinking sun plays on their sheer upper slopes. Clinging among the rocks are clusters of white dust specks, tinted by the evening: they are the large Tibetan sheep or goats. My admiration for the old herder grows as I imagine his lifestyle among them. Did he sleep in a cave, or under a rock overhang? I shiver and pull my thick coat around me, and wonder.

When the sunlight dies before the advancing night, and the cold air sweeps down the mountain slope when there is no cloud to retain the heat, the temperature in the pass takes a dramatic plunge. This is one part of the world where I dress, sometimes in all that I have, before lying down on a hard, narrow bunk in an unheated room under a thin quilt. Amid the snores and grunts of tired men's dreams, I attempt to slip into the rhythm of the night.

I am approaching the edge of sleep's wide grassland when the dormitory door opens enough for a slim body to wriggle through. I follow his outline in the dark. He makes for an empty bunk, takes off his cap and boots, and lies with his feet on the pillow, his head overhanging the bottom of the bunk. He suppresses a cough and, from a heavy tar cigarette, breathes smoke into the air. He chain-smokes through the night, and his lungs gurgle in complaint. By the morning he has disappeared, and the bed looks undisturbed. The sleepers wonder at the thick blanket of smoke that lies in the room.

Days pass quickly. I have come with the hope of being able to stay in the monastery, perhaps sharing a dormitory room, but possibilities are receding as I have failed to gain permission. The desire for a time alone in reflective prayer is growing within me. Thoughts of mountain solitude are always appealing ... and I am spoilt for choice.

I follow a trail which leads upward from the monastery. It lies in a ravine gouged out of the rock by a river that has, for centuries, forced its own route. Stepped barriers have been built to reduce the strong flow, but these have filled with clay and boulders. A number of yak lumber towards me. I am always amazed at the bulk of these long-horned animals yet, at the sight of a stranger, some baulk, balancing on their back legs and turning in the air. I step to the side of the track and they gallop past, eyes bulging with fear ... or aggression.

A scree path worn into the curve of the mountainside looks attractive. Breathless in the rarefied air, I follow it. The beating of powerful bird wings startles me. It settles on a large boulder and watches my movements. A number of others are circling overhead and losing height. Scenes from Africa jump from my memory. These are not kites, but perhaps the most repulsive of all birds – vultures; not the scrawny, black-feathered, common African variety, but with tan colouring and heavy. There is no mistaking the vicious beak. The higher crags are alive with vultures and some, with open wings and outstretched necks, are defending their roosting areas from the ravens and each other.

The path leads into a clearing outlined by prayer flags. Two small fires spiral smoke into the air, one freshly lit and burning furiously. Blackened human bones mingled with fresh body parts lie scattered on the bare earth. I have walked into a Sky Burial site. At dawn the corpse would have have been laid out, the vultures called, and a specially licensed monk would have crushed the remaining bones and stacked them into this fire. Yesterday another took place, the families sitting and watching the ceremonies.

At this site, earth and sky meet with inescapable finality. I recall that in the most ancient of biblical writings there is a stark, poetic line which describes life without purpose. Suddenly it has new relevance: *He wanders about, food for vultures.*

I continue upward to a ridge that forms the horizon. It is cool, although a blaze of sun is burning my skin. Drifting islands of pure white cloud fall behind the rim of the ridge, and the mountain drops sharply to the monastery, and the village with the wild-west road.

The lanes between the rows of monks' cells are filled with shadow. I can see the large gathering-rooms where time seems to be on hold as hundreds sit cross-legged on their mats. Stunted trees shade a garden of low stone tables, where others are making notes from texts. On a broad flight of steps a small group is hotly involved in their unique style of debate, a vermilion blur of arm-swinging and feet-stamping in rhythm with their voices.

Almost all the buildings and walls are the red colour of earth, except for the temples. The architecture of these symbols of Bon and Buddhism stand apart. The gold leaf worked into the elaborate design of the roofs, the towers, the eternal wheels and the animals, powerfully reflects the sunlight.

Behind the closed doors yak-butter lamps with floating wicks burn holes in the dark, and diffuse light onto the shaven bowed heads of rows of sitting monks. They clasp their hands and the low moan of their mantras rises and falls like the wind among the rocks. Overhead, the fixed smiles of huge idols look down over their pot-bellies or from behind hideous masks of fang-like teeth and bulging eyes. Their gold-painted skin attracts light from the flickering butter lamps and creates an illusion of movement. They stare out of a darkness inhabited by hierarchies of demons. They represent thousands of years of collective thought in the pursuit of life beyond the cycle of reincarnation.

In the deeper vaults of my memory are images I am reluctant to raise: the sound of the long horns blown in the temple courtyards, a deep earthy melancholic sound that reverberates through the mountains calling for an echo of its own kind; the strutting, ugly wild-eyed dance of the monks; the parade of the devil masks and of the imps of hell; the ferocity with which the small boys slam shut the doors against prying eyes – though they admit that they don't know why.

The ceremonial language of idol worship tastes bad. Eastern idolatry has its disincentives, as does the West. We are simply more familiar with our own terms which float easily in our vocabulary. The worship of any god who will give us what we want frames our religious thinking. As greed by biblical interpretation is idolatry, so by our culture, if not by our nature, we too are drawn by the worship of this idol.

The return journey down the scree slope is uneventful. The vultures do not stir; their meals are always served by the figures that ascend from the valley. On the far side of the ravine a Tibetan runs down the steep slopes with ease. I am not tempted to try the same.

The Third Step

In the main street I climb a stone stairway to a Muslim noodle eating-place. The solitude of the mountain has worked. I have slowed down. The fragments of my inner silence have come together again. I have a strong sense that my next hours will be crucial to my beginnings in Tibet. A leisurely meal costs thirty pence; I pay the waiter and begin to descend the steps.

Someone is hurrying behind me. I reach the third step, the roadway is in sight, so I squeeze aside. A lady passes, turns, smiles and is gone. I walk the forty paces to the lodging house and realise that I no longer have my small wallet. Both my credit card and money have been stolen.

I have been robbed before, many times before, and in different countries. It is just the style that makes each occasion unique. The loss of money is usually the easiest to manage, the loss of reputation the most difficult. Right now my immediate concern is my loss of pride at having to tell the young Tibetan manager that I have no money to pay my bill.

I find the courage when the reception desk is free. I lean across and whisper to the manager that I have no money. I think that I am confiding a secret, until a voice behind me booms out, "Lost your money, eh? Pickpockets, eh? Come and see me if you need some."

By the time that I can break eye contact with the manager, the stranger has disappeared on to the busy street, and everyone knows my plight. Sympathetic looks greet me and a European couple say, "Best of luck!"

The manager accompanies me back to the eating house, and to the local police station. Both shake their heads.

"Come back in ten days," says the policeman as I explain that I don't want to pursue a prosecution but just need written confirmation that I have reported the loss.

"Now come for a meal with me, Rowland," says the young manager, who introduces himself as Goba, and his girlfriend as Dechen. Over another bowl of noodles and a mug of yak milk tea, infinitely better than rancid horse milk, a friendship begins to form.

"Why are you doing this?" I ask Goba, noticing what little money he has in his wallet.

"You are very brave being such a long way from your country," he replies, "and if we do not help each other, what other meaning is there to life? Please let me know if there is something more I can do for you, Rowland," he says as we part company.

In spite of my loss, I begin to feel a warm glow of satisfaction. By being able to do nothing to help myself, I have made my first Tibetan friendships.

During the night an explosion splits the sky. I cross to the window to see the mountain I climbed earlier backlit by a sheet of intense, white light. It looks about to topple into the pass. Rain as thick as a breaking wave crashes into the window, walls and roof. As sheet water cascades off the mountain I wonder about the torrent building up in the ravine, and the huddle of Tibetan homes. And what of the specks of white near the summit, and their shepherd?

Another horrendous crack and the pass, like nature's sound box, thunders its echo. Lightning sears the sky, and with a terrifying crash drives into the earth, smashing rocks. The village plunges into blackness as the electricity supply fails, and water rushes through the lanes and streets. The anger of the river grows by the moment and hurls the boulders that stand in its way. It washes across the fields, and mudslides cover the roads. I think of the friendships made in the day and the fury of the storm at night, all part of the dramatic music of this wilderness.

I lie awake, my scattered thoughts gathering like tributaries to a mountain stream. The strength of my inner conviction has increased. I have the distinct sense that destiny is searching for me, drawing me into a divine wilderness – where all things are possible. Wilderness is not barrenness, but land without boundaries. Journeys without endings are the most exciting journeys of all.

Through the sky burial, nature took responsibility for the body that was no longer of use to the person who lived in it. The hand that robbed me brought to an end an unproductive lifestyle. I have crossed an invisible line, and immediately found friends. In my helplessness they have begun to demonstrate to me a love that I thought I had come to show them.

A memory from long past filters into my mind, and with inner eyes I watch while it replays. My wife and I had sought a future in missionary work that we believed to be ours. Slowly we began to understand that the key to it lay in the loss of our self-dependence and to place ourselves into destiny's hands. The answer for us was to give away our income and all that we possessed, from Anne's engagement ring to my army medals. We won the battle that raged within us and found the peaceful assurance that, although we would be among the poorest of people, we would never need to compete for finance in the religious market place because our key fitted the divine treasury. Neither of us realised at that time that we were personally laying the foundations for the birth and growth of *World Horizons*, an international missionary movement which would in its lifetime require multiplied millions of pounds.

The storm subsides, electricity is restored to the village, and I know that I have crossed my personal Jordan. I have recovered my poverty and am no longer a middle-class mission leader, the product of a middle-class church.

Providentially, at this moment the dormitory door opens and Goba smiles into the room.

"You okay, Rowland?" he asks.

Perhaps one day I will be able to tell him that, just as he opened the dormitory door, symbolically he has helped open the door to a future I have already grown to love.

It is now the next morning. There is a freshness in the air that mirrors the calm within myself. I ask Goba for a bunk in the cheapest dormitory accommodation he has. Reluctantly, contrary to his generous nature, he agrees to let me have it.

As I throw my rucksack onto the one free bunk, he says, "The lodging house owners would like to meet you."

I join them and their staff for breakfast. The bread and yak milk are like some holy sacrament.

"From now on you are part of my family," the wife says. "You may join us for meals whenever you want."

From a wallet she takes out a hundred yuan note.

"Here is some money for you to spend. I do not want it back."

There is a tear in my eye as I receive it.

Later in the morning Goba and Dechen accompany me to the bus garage to arrange transport for tomorrow. He returns from the ticket hatch with my ticket. He has paid for it.

"It's time for lunch," he says as he pushes open the door of another eating place, and our conversation begins to take on the quality of intimate friends.

"Now Dechen will take you to the horse fair in the grasslands," he says, pressing more money into her hand from an already-thin wallet.

Where Grasslands Swirl to the Sky

Beyond the pass, an ocean of green trembles in the mystery of the breeze that sweeps its whispers into the sky. This living landscape, high above China's polluted air, has a transparent crystal quality and a luxurious sweetness to its taste. Dechen melts into the surroundings. Her weathered Tibetan complexion, her long plaited hair, her colourful dress and shoulder scarf, rival the blaze of the *sangke* flower. The tune she continually hums to herself captures the quality of the wide open space. The flying horsemen, the animal herds, and the lone yurts all have a home in her melody.

At the beckoning welcome of a nomadic family, more yak-milk tea, yoghurt and *tsampa* flow, and I sit transfixed by the scene. To the south, low on the horizon, is the ragged saw-edge of distant peaks. Alluring, frightening, layered in snow-white cloud, they rise into an intense blue sky.

Reluctantly, with the sun about to bow off the stage in a pageantry of changing colour, we make our way back to the village. The pass has begun to close in and the chilled air falls from the peaks. I commit to the care of providence the fact that I have not been able to meet up again with the stranger who offered to help me with money. Even more sadly, I have not spent time with at least one monk near my own age with whom I might build a friendship. In other ways it has been a perfect day, and in Goba and Dechen I may even have found an adopted Tibetan son and daughter. After yet another meal of yak-meat dumplings where Dechen has gathered some of her friends together, I return to my rucksack and bunk.

The dormitory is filling up as sleep searches for tired men, until just two bunks, one either side of me, remain empty. Perhaps I should not be surprised that the next person to slide around the door is a lama who makes his way to one of the empty bunks. I judge that he is an older man, perhaps near my age. His name is

Kunchen.

The last man enters and sits on the other empty bunk, greeting me with the words, "Now, how about this money you need?"

He is Michael, a German national working for *Greenpeace*, and the final man I want to meet. I set my alarm clock for six the following morning, and discover that both men have planned to leave at exactly the same time, from the same bus garage, but to different destinations.

Goba is already waiting for me when I reach the lobby. He picks up my rucksack and walks into the dark. From somewhere a car appears. After a hug he pushes me into a seat. Michael and Kunchen follow. Finally he leans through the window and pays the driver.

Later, when I return to Wales, I will find a surprise email waiting for me from Goba, signed: *Goba and Dechen, your Tibetan best friends.*

The bus yawns and I climb aboard. The driver, in Chinese fashion, is clearing his throat onto the floor amid his passengers' passing feet. The big diesel engine is doing something similar into the air. They are both preparing for the downhill slalom that lies ahead. There are treacherous swinging bends, and if one is taken too wide the snapping fury of the river, boiling with ill-temper, will be satisfied.

My ticket number does not correspond with an empty space. The passengers take over and point me to a seat alongside a stern-looking European lady. She is Swiss. She has an interest in birds and also, as I find out later, very heavy luggage. She complains bitterly about being moved from a front seat by people who don't realise that she has long legs. A Tibetan family of four now occupy the seat meant for two and, although their ticket corresponds to its number, her eyes remain glued to it. Above the rumbling sounds of travel, she commands the driver to turn down the Tibetan music he is playing. Her voice stings his ears, but he is unable to interpret what she has asked. I begin to understand that it may have been fear rather than courtesy that moved the passengers to offer me the seat. I am tempted to induce her into a state of shock by telling her a vulture story I have invented ... but I don't.

Back at the frontier town it is decidedly warmer, but the mists still curl around corners and lie flat along the roofs. With the heavy cases and the Swiss traveller safely into a taxi, I make my way across the river into the university area, where I have borrowed an apartment in which to drop my rucksack. In Chinese cities my brain needs time to reconfigure itself, and to find the silence that is not easily there among such a breadth of contrasting audio and visual demands.

I pass a point where snorting traffic dives into an underpass. A man in his late thirties is edging his way along a two-foot wide pavement. He has a heavy coat and a rolled-up rush mat over his shoulder, from which his possessions hang in a sack.

"Many people live down here," he says. "We sleep along this narrow ledge. I have been robbed," he complains; "this is why I am here."

I am immediately sympathetic. He was a contract workman on a building site, but when the contract was completed they were paid off with one tenth of their promised wage, just enough to get back to where they had come from. Have they protested? No, they are frightened of police or army involvement.

I know he has passed the glitzy shops where I am heading. The sterile smiles and poses of luxury-dripping, polystyrene manne-quins would have mocked him from behind the windows. Not unlike the idols, these invite entry into crystal temples with heavenly rewards for those with money. His poverty has saved him this time.

I don't want to be alone, so I make my way to where students meet, talk and eat. Doors bang and chairs scrape on the hard-tiled floor, but I don't mind. I sit by a wide window, painted with dragons but still giving me a view of the street. I live in my strange world where polarities have been reversed. I have gained what I hoped for by losing all I had. My future now seems clearly defined but lies somewhere beyond my power to help myself. My internal mirror has fractured, and reflects many images. I would like to piece them together to make a whole, so I take out my pad and write.

What Lama Kunchen knew
In the grassland, wandering unmilked yak had raised concern

among a nomadic family for a neighbour some ten miles to the north. News of circling vultures brought urgency to an immediate visit. The yurt stood deserted, except for a tethered horse that nodded weakly, and the vultures which at a safe distance hopped, spread their wings, and squawked.

Inside, a seven-year old daughter sat between the lifeless forms of her mother and father. The *tsampa* she had served them was untouched, the yak-milk tea cold. The child's stained face and red eyes asked the question: *Why?*

Kunchen followed the bodies up the hill to the mountain slope, the little girl holding his hand and weeping into his robe. She was the history of a tragedy she could not share. Now she struggled and screamed at the sight of the vultures tearing from her the remains of the only life she knew.

Weeping in his spirit, Kunchen took her to the edge of the village to the room where her elderly grandmother lived. On a small table he put all the money that he had. They had nothing more, but they had each other. She was the small girl I had seen holding open an empty sack in the market, who bore the mark of a terrible loneliness, her eyes haunted by the horror of a bad dream. Another time, she collected the discarded cabbage leaves and bad fruit saved for her by the gentle, smiling street-cleaning lady whose husband I had visited with his granddaughter.

During the evening in the dormitory, Kunchen had listened intently to the tale of my lost wallet, his eyes not leaving mine for a moment as I mentioned the staircase and the third step. He nodded and murmured something I had not understood.

"Ah, Hariti."

Instinctively I felt that I had said nothing that he had not already known.

I thought no more of this until our breath smoked the early morning chilled air as we waited to load onto our buses. I looked across at Kunchen, who always stood apart. I wanted to put my hand on his shoulder as a parting gesture, but he was already engaged. I followed the line of his gaze. It led to a little girl who also stood at the edge of the feeble light. She wore a long, thick dress and a shawl around her shoulders, her hair brushed back in the customary plaits. There was something familiar about her nomadic features.

Kunchen's smile and gesture of his hand were signalling her to step forward, not towards him, but to me. Both her small hands were holding a crumpled, coloured page from a popular Chinese magazine. On it was a picture of a singer. It was probably the only possession she had that was of value to her. As I looked into her upturned face, her eyes were asking me to accept it. That moment a shout from the driver who was pointing at my rucksack meant I had to carry it to the luggage hold and wedge it into what space I could find. When I turned back to my place the lama was no longer there. Neither was the small girl, and I had not accepted the treasure of her torn-out page.

I boarded the bus and took my place alongside the Swiss lady, my mind filled with thoughts of the little girl I had disappointed. It was well into my journey before I became convinced that the child with the begging sack I had first seen on my arrival, and the sweet girl who had offered me her torn-out page, were the same.

Why had she come in the early morning? And why her interest in me? And what had happened to change her appearance?

Return to the The Third Step

It was then that a memory returned which I had thought to be the imagination of a troubled mind. At the top of the steps, at the time I had been robbed, I thought that I had heard the tinkling sound of a child's voice and a hint of someone small and poorly dressed. At the same time a glimpse of the bolder presence of a lady dressed in a flowing black skirt, a thin, black, sleeveless top and long loose black hair.

It was she who had passed me on the third step, who had turned with a laughing smile that had altogether disarmed me. It was her half-turned, friendly acknowledgement that had shown me that both her hands were empty.

As the third step was halfway around the bend on the stairs, the one way she could have had empty hands was to pass the wallet back to someone who had been out of sight ... possibly the child. In fact, the child may never have seen her take the wallet. Yet on my

190

return to the eating house with Goba, the other contents of the pocket in which I carried my wallet were still lying on the third step.

Ah, Kunchen had said as I spoke to him of the steps, *Hariti!*

Is this where my two and a half thousand yuan had gone? To the child and her grandmother? Is this why her appearance had changed so dramatically? Is this why Kunchen had asked her to come? Was her picture of the singer meant to be her way of saying thank you?

This is speculation, of course, but the hint of possibility it holds is as bright as a longed-for sunrise.

While I have been musing, I have also been staring into the street and unconsciously registering the visits to the waste bin that stands under the street light. First an old man in green country dress, with the features of a villager, searches but finds nothing for his sack. Then a similarly-aged town man, who is also disappointed. Following is a lady who has tied a plastic carrier bag around the hand and arm that reaches into the bin. Then a younger man whose energy has paid off, for some plastic bottles already shape his sack – but he finds no more.

There is a disturbance further along the pavement. Three well-dressed men are kneeling over a fourth, who is lying motionless. His clothes bear the signs of the homeless.

"They have caught a thief," says someone in the crowd; "they are waiting for the police to collect him."

The man, already broken into submission, is about to pay dearly for what he hoped to be today's bowl of noodles.

Later that night another walked out into the traffic stream, and lay down. He was a lame man. Carefully he arranged his crutches. Metal clashed and agonized tyres smoked the road with melting rubber, except for the wheel that struck his shoulder with the velocity of hurtling steel. From his chest he felt the involuntary rush of breath and the taste of blood, slightly warm. No longer the pain of freezing hungry days and nights on slabs of pavement. He turned his last moments of freedom into a statement: *I, too, am a human being!* – His poem ended, written in the ink of courage on pages of suffering. Pages that no one will read. No one will own the guilt.

China looks the other way.

I walk back to my apartment and hear someone behind me ask for money. Just as he says, "It doesn't really matter," I turn around, but he is already hobbling away. He, too, is an old man, bent over. Somehow he carries his sack. His left arm and hand are crudely bandaged. Blood has been soaking through. I share with him what money I have. Now there is a tear in his eye. Perhaps I am home 'at last' ... a long, painful 'at last'!

The writing on my pad looks like a letter, but I have no one to send it to. So I use it to relieve my stored-up feelings of gratitude to so many who have helped me find myself, and have reintroduced me into the family of the poor to which I am proud to belong. I know that a new eloquence will accompany me through the change.

Thank you little girl, so small as to occupy almost no space in our world, who got in my way and taught me about myself.

Thank you Hariti. I am sure that you, too, have a story waiting to be heard. We met on the third step, and I admire your compassion for the small girl who got in your way also. I had no right to the money I had called my own. You fed and clothed the hungry, and did what I should have done.

Thank you Lama Kunchen, who watched and saw everything, but who told no one, yet served everybody.

Thank you, Goba and Dechen. You helped me back into the world I'd lost, and where I need to grow up for the second time. You met me with the love I thought I had come to show you.

It was when I returned to my apartment that I found, tucked into the folds of my rucksack, a leaf torn out of Lama Kunchen's small notebook. It simply said:

> *Name: Jalus*
> *Age: Seven years*
> *Status: Orphan*
> *Schooling: None*
> *Income: None*

Home: Cares for Sangmu, her grandmother
Jalus means 'Rainbow'
In Peace,
Kunchen

I hope that my lost yuan have been enough to buy Jalus a sheepskin coat that she can fold around herself when the freezing winds of the Tibetan plain snarl and bite with cold.

WHERE ONLY CAGED BIRDS SING
- Last Train Home -

To the Eagle
Wander wild, my friend,
do not easily return.
Fly higher than any eagle has flown before.
The wind is kind to the sweep of your wing,
the sweetness of freedom the sky will not tame.
Rise, rise on earth's gentle breath,
an elixir to your soaring spirit.
Rise beyond height
until you pale into the morning
of your new creative day.

(A poem dedicated to Ripple Foster,
a companion on the Great China Odyssey)

It was when her daughter, Coralee, applied to join the missionary movement we were building, that Ripple Foster first walked into our lives. My personal world expanded and, in one sense at least, she never left. It was not that we were ever close. Sometimes years would pass without as much as a chance meeting. News of her interests in China would filter through to us, though it was the passion with which she pursued those interests that always gripped us.

Then, in the unravelling mystery of providence, I discovered that an event I had never dreamed of was waiting to happen. Along with a companion, I was able to enter her world by accompanying her team to East China, where I worked for some days among one of the least known minority groups – its Jewish

194

people. What brought with this invitation an added sense of awe was not only the way she managed her hours, so that she had time to give 'to everyone who asked', but she was also in the control of a severe illness that hungrily fed on her energy.

Apart from instantaneous acts like swatting flies, most events of value are like ships at sea; from over the horizon they arrive at their full size slowly. In this way my personal interest in China's Jewish community has matured over several years. So this is one man's account of how slender threads of purpose entwine to become a cord.

I have a picture embroidered in silk. I can see it as I leave and enter my home in Wales. It is both the inspiration for a journey and a welcome return. As I enter my living room, my eyes naturally rest on it. When night enfolds day, it is the image I take with me.

It is dusk; a robed and turbaned old man is quietly contemplating a blaze of stars in a middle-eastern sky. His hands are slightly raised, enough to make his robe droop from his wrists. My imagination tells me that I can also see grains of sand, alive with starlight, fall from between the thumb and fingers of one hand. There is a lonesome hush about this scene. The wind is no longer crying in the dunes. The silent sky alone is speaking, confirming him in the journey he has begun.

Yes, but every journey we take is a road to our own finale.

True, but he regards the stars and sand as powerful symbols of hope in a promise he feels has come from beyond them. It is his faith in that promise that waits at the door of his tent and guides his sandalled feet. It assures him that he will drink each day from streams that have no name until he discovers a land of mountains, valleys and rivers described by the promise, where the symbols of stars and sand will match the number of his descendants. His search for this land has about it the urgency of his search for God.

"It is from the eastern city," said my colleague who, knowing where my interests lie, had bought me the picture. "It is embroidered by the descendants of a caravan of Jewish people who, in the early centuries, travelled the Silk Road eastward."

Ever since, I have especially treasured the picture, as the story of Abraham brings together the history of both Chinese and Hebrew cultures. Ancient Chinese characters record the faith of Abraham, as do the Hebrew writings recorded in the Bible.

These were the elements of a drama replaying in my mind as I shared a hard bench seat with the colleague who had bought me that picture. We were on a train that rumbled westwards, a journey of days and nights the width of China. The boredom of a long slow journey had set in, and hundreds of pairs of eyes found interest by watching us. Each gaze asked the question: *Why?* – Why are you making this journey? Why do you sit here, when the more luxurious carriages for foreigners are maybe a third of a kilometre away, nearer the sweating diesel engines?

My mind explained to them that I liked the soft seats, the uncrowded space and the clean air, to say nothing of the bunk beds in the forward carriages, but I preferred being among *them* – the people. My lips, however, only grumbled at the number of bodies and sacks I needed to negotiate to reach the hot water tap and make some Chinese tea.

This was the last trans-China train westwards that would stop at our location for who knows how many days. It had already started its journey from a city on the east coast by the time we joined. At larger towns, empty carriages filled up with migrant workers. Throwing their sacks of belongings into the carriage through open windows, they either fought for the door or climbed through the window after them.

Uncut, dishevelled hair crowded the faces of the workmen travelling back to villages and families, perhaps after a year around-the-clock, building the glassy show palaces of China's modernised cities. Their clothes, ragged and blackened, covered unwashed bodies. Hardened, some broken by injury, they tiredly slumped into any position space would allow.

The carriage windows were permanently open. The rolling dinosaur clattered on, scattering the ambush of night, sometimes hiding in shadows of sidings while faster trains thundered their importance at the dark. Those who lost interest watching us made up small groups, clacking in their card-playing language. Others looked on; some slept. I at least shared a cramped seat, where I could sit and muse over the last few days.

We were returning to Central China from a distant eastern province. The ancient city where our small group of five, by Ripple's arrangement, had met up and made home is still defined by the walls and gates that once defended it. These are slowly being reclaimed by the earth. It is set in a horizon of patchwork fields and sprinkled villages. Here, mothers and daughters squat in their baggy blue under the shade of shoulder-width conical straw hats, and through sun-long days empty the earth of weeds, one by one.

It is a refreshing, undeveloped city, with dark lanes, an armada of cycles and comparatively few cars. During the Northern Song dynasty it held great prominence, and some claim it was the largest city in the world. From this point, the mighty Silk Road reached Rome. Among the Silk Road traders a caravan of Jews was welcomed by the emperor, and they settled there in the security of the city. Later a decline in the economy began with the silting of the Yellow River, and their synagogue was destroyed by the flooding of the shallow river bed. Their Torahs were passed to interested collectors and can be found in the British Museum. Without identity, the Jews were slowly assimilated into the Chinese community ... or so it had seemed.

On the streets I watched while the busy owner of a one-room open-fronted noodle eating-house emptied a soup of washing water over the slabs of the stone pavement. Fragments of yellowed cabbage leaves and chicken bones fixed themselves among the rusting table and chair legs. The homeless poor sat and watched the noisy eaters in the hope of a clawed foot or chicken head, sucked clean, being tossed their way.

Further back in the hierarchy of the street was a seven- or eight-year old boy. Dirty, unwanted, perhaps a second child and so illegal and abandoned, he knew no one with love to spare. Bullied and condemned by the street to nowhere, his arms were clasped around his knees, hunger and hopelessness meeting together in his eyes. My old feelings returned. In different circumstances, I have been here, too. Perhaps here lies the painful root of my affinity with Old China's streets.

I turned towards the ruins of the flood-swept synagogue. A few standing stones carrying inscriptions were all that remained. In its place, a soot-encrusted once-white building of jarring design had opened its doors to me. Somewhere in the bat-black darkness a coal-fired boiler wheezed its way towards inevitable disaster. It looked Russian-inspired, with flaking insulation and rusting water pipes. It served a small hospital which, in a lighter shade of sooty white, stood on the other side of the yard. Nurses in stained uniforms bothered between doorways of finger-marked walls. I have been told that some of China's poor dread hospital more than police interrogation.

"Birds do not sing in this city," said a friend. "Depending on wind direction, it can receive the air pollution of Beijing or Shanghai. Besides this, insecticides sprayed over the fields have killed the insect population. "

The soul of song has died, except from a number of caged birds which sing from the walls and windows where they hang, or when old men carry their cages to the empty spaces where old men meet and, like the birds, sit and wait.

In a cramped apartment, the home of a Jewish family whose living-room also doubled as a Hebrew teaching school, a two-year-old bundle of fun tumbled and toddled around the floor. She was playing to her audience and, like children, we responded. She exuded a charm that captured us, and we loved it.

It was then that I particularly noticed the eyes of my colleague, Ripple Foster. They were radiantly alive with the enjoyment of the moment, but her expression told me that her spirit was engaged ... somewhere else. Her lips were moving, but she breathed no words, even though by right she had the most to say among all of us.

More than two years before, Ripple had visited this town as the news spread that the mother of the little girl had been hijacked off the street by her neighbourhood communist officials. Her crime? The baby in her womb was a second child. Unless an exhorbitant fine was paid, in spite of her protests, the baby would be forcibly aborted. I did not ask how the fine had been met, and Ripple had said nothing, but I strongly suspected that she was involved.

Since then the baby's elder sister, just sixteen, had followed her inner urge to return to Israel, her ancestral homeland and, with her parents' consent, had successfully joined the number of younger people who have dribbled through the tight control of China's emigration service.

"We receive no favours," said a Jewish friend who had spent seventeen years in prison. "We are a minority group. Few things have really changed; the pains of China fall easily on us."

The song of the caged birds was perhaps a lament for Israel and freedom.

Chairman Mao is said to have been responsible for the deaths of seventy million of his own people. I wonder if this record is being challenged by the one-child policy. I have read that the official statistics for a large city can account for three hundred thousand deaths by abortion each year.

That evening, I found myself watching Ripple closely. She looked tired, paled by the exhaustion of her journey to the city, but there was something else; something very powerful that I did not understand, that made me want to be in her company. She carried an air of quiet assurance, of someone who knew ... like a prophet in no doubt. I remembered her lips moving when there were no words. It was as if she were offering a benediction to the final stage of a private journey.

There was an intense moment when she stood by the window and looked out over the China which had gladly received her over many years, and to which she belonged. Feeling like an intruder into her holy space, I left her to the close friendship of her two travelling companions and returned to the dark lanes. Walking alone, I knew that I could visit Wisdom's deep source and find answers to questions that I did not know how to ask.

The next morning, plans for departure came together. If we could buy tickets, my colleague and I would leave for central China on the last available train west.

Soon the smile of a willing Jewish friend greeted us, holding up two tickets. We decided, together with Ripple and her friends, that they would take the early morning flight straight into Hong Kong, which would save a tedious overland trek and place her within reach of professional medical help should she need it. The plan gave us the satisfaction of knowing that there was nothing better that we could do ... It was as if we had discovered a purpose, already designed, that held no room for argument. It needed only the nod of our approval.

The thunder of a passing train and the pressure of the shockwave through our open windows wrenched my mind away from the memories of the city, and of Ripple and her small team, to our present reality: the crowded carriage, the hessian sacks, and the stale scent of several hundred crumpled bodies in various stages of sleep.

The rhythmic clatter of our carriage wheels would soon be entering Central China. In the early morning we would leave the train to continue its journey westward. At about the same time, Ripple would be leaving the airport and soaring, soaring, soaring into China's morning skies. We had separated to go our individual ways, which our different geographical journeys seemed to symbolise; I to the conviction that I could safely add a few more years to my present total of seventy, Ripple to her understanding of the point in time she had reached within her personal journey.

What broke into my thoughts and caught my interest was the figure of a middle-aged Chinese lady, stepping towards us through the tangle of sacks and unwashed bodies. Balancing herself and smiling, she stood in front of us, her hands held together in a gesture of prayer – the signal from someone who is eager to let you know that they have faith..

She bowed and quietly said, "*Shang di bao you ni.*"

Her words penetrated my shuttered mind: "May *Shang Di*, the Lord of Heaven and Earth, bless you."

She had used the most ancient name for the one God of China, perhaps the nearest equivalent of the Hebrew, *El Shaddai.*

"A mad woman," commented the lady squeezed alongside my colleague.

A blessing upon our journey and that of Ripple's group, argued my inner feelings. As it was given in the sincerity and strength I was accustomed to hearing in Ripple, I was inclined to believe them.

Later that day came another unexpected event. A Chinese publisher asked me if I could write a book that would pass government censorship, meaning that it would need to present truth, and promote a hunger for vision and reality, without religious terminology. Such books, he said, would be welcomed in the secular market, where an appetite for reading was growing among the younger generation.

The publisher could not have known how deeply that desire was rooted in me. Perhaps, with help, I could cultivate the skills and make a small but valid contribution to China's future. Then maybe I would even discover the reason for which I was born.

Later I began to believe that both events, which I could not have engineered, would prove to be directly related.

The following day, a phone call from Ripple's friends in Hong Kong told us of their flight. Ripple, tired from the early start, slept during the flight and did not wake again, at least not to this life ...

In death, as in life, she carried a profound dignity. She knew her word, her place, her hour. As a missionary figure she has won the highest acclaim. She died among the people she had chosen to serve. She has found her new creative day in a fuller measure than I have found mine. A pioneer to the last, she has gone ahead ... alone.

I am left with just one question. When I saw her lips move, yet could hear no words, was she praying over the little Jewish girl, that bundle of fun whose radiant confidence won us all? I don't know, but if she was, I am going to guess what she may have said; but without her passion for the Jewish people, my few words can only point to the many more that, in my ignorance, I will have to leave unsaid.

> *Fly, fly little caged bird.*
> *There is a land and a freedom waiting to receive you*
> *and a Father's love to care for you.*

I think that in that little bundle of life, so miraculously preserved, she saw beyond to a new hope for the Jewish community.

Ripple, having done all that she could, quietly left the stage ... for the new production to begin. And in a way I would not have conceived, she had taught me how to die.

Shalom Proved

HEALING TIME'S WOUNDS
- Eastern Memories -

Wales welcomes my return, surrounding me with the sea that stimulates my inner warmth of belonging. There is a timelessness about the sea. The sounds of the ocean soothe wounds made by the tick of the clock and the urgency of the mobile phone. I am restored from computer-generated flight schedules and rail timetables to nature's measure of time; the falling leaf, the movement of cloud on the water, where moments become a year, and slowness has its spiritual quality restored.

The mood of the sea fits perfectly into nature's plan. Perhaps we find harmony in the sea's sound because it has no mood that does not accurately depict the play of passion within the human breast. Above all else, its unchangeable nature inspires security. It lives and moves yet – like divine intention – it is always there, bridging the span of time. It is there when the sky is hidden behind dark cloud restraining the sun's crimson afterglow; when there are no stars nor moon; when the black sea is reflecting the sky's serious mood, and when the breakers that expire at my feet have only a subdued phosphorescent glow. It is then that the voice of the waves speaks in its clearest tones. Tonight the waves help my memory navigate between time's tides. The dark ambience of the night and the luminescent glow also have their place.

I remember standing in the bows of a ship and looking down on another sea, or more accurately a river that runs into a sea. It was with a similar soft sound that the bow wave curled beneath my feet. I had left Hong Kong and started my journey along the Pearl River into inland China. In the morning I was to be in Canton, and I awaited the fulfilment of a childhood dream. That journey represented the end of a beginning and I wished to savour every moment of it.

I sense that I have completed another of life's stages, and recognize that I have been here before. The waves at my feet seem to be telling me that once again I am at the end of a beginning. My borrowed earth is not due to be returned yet. In fact, in my proving months, roots have been growing strongly, and perhaps by the morning the first green shoot may break the surface. Then the evening and the morning *will* begin a new creative day.

That night journey to old Canton, although my first, happened in the wake of so many hundreds of old-time missionaries whose faith and presence had hallowed this route. Faith brings a unity of purpose, yet at the same time each knew that they were pioneering a personal voyage towards a particular destiny. For many, hardship and death were the silent unseen passengers accompanying them.

I felt no different. I was only doing what others have done. It is my personal belief which encourages me to abandon the restrictive definition of who I am and what I should do. I simply believe that my borrowed earth can raise new growth beyond my expectation.

When I think I am alone it is seldom the case, for behind my pleasant moments lie ugly realities. I may wipe them from my landscape, but the realities remain. My hallowed journey navigated one of the East's most prolific smuggling routes, to say nothing of the rampant piracy in the South China Sea. The rusting Chinese tug boats that plied the river were possibly towing bundles of contraband. I have read that the Hong Kong water police boarded a Chinese vessel towing three expensive cars. Each was plastic-wrapped and floating just below the surface. Stolen to order, they were likely destined for China's bourgeois hierarchy.

At Canton, when my feet touched the ground the hand that reached out to me was that of a rip-off driver of an ex-Hong Kong taxi. He delivered me to an hotel where I could afford nothing more than to breathe the free air.

I had no money. At that time foreigners were issued certificates which could be used at designated outlets. Street touts offered better exchange rates, but they cleverly folded their banknotes around their finger and counted out the same notes twice.

I quickly learnt my first Chinese word, 'mayo', which has a staggeringly wide application. It could mean: *I cannot help you.* In a government Friendship Store, behind windows whose insides had never been cleaned, where the persistently bad-tempered assistant had her head on the counter attempting to sleep away the long day, it could mean: *Whatever it is you want, I don't have it ... even when I am holding the goods in my hand!* Or, in a worse scenario, it could mean: *Clear off, you foreign idiot, I'm trying to sleep!*

On the shore I speak back to the dark sea and the waves, and tell them of my decision. I will defy the supposed wisdom of the many words that tell me what I cannot do. I will reject the rule of 'what if?'. I will apprentice myself to faith, and walk the path of purpose. I will accept the challenge of the ugliness that will accompany me. I will choose the act of greatest freedom and allow death, which was born on the day of my birth, to come upon all that is unpromising. I will choose to dream, and watch fulfilment grow larger on the horizon. Some of the threads that will complete the tapestry are mine to weave into place.

On the steps of the Potala Palace – historically the winter home of the Dalai Lama in Lhasa, capital of Tibet – and breathless because of the altitude, I watched while off-duty Chinese occupation troops pushed their way to the head of a small queue at the entrance gate. The local people fell back in fear. This was an ugly scene, but typical of the reality of conditions in Lhasa.

My indignation flared, and I shouted something in the tone of an army command which was as unintelligible to me as it was to them. There was an instantaneous reaction. The offending soldiers jerked back and stood to attention. The others, wondering what had happened, joined them.

An officer appeared, looking puzzled. He held the platoon to attention until everyone passed through.

Even the ugly responds to courage in the most unlikely way.

My home is five minutes from where curling waves are unrolling quietly at my feet. When the sea is angry I can lie awake at night and listen to it thrash the shore.

Tonight I am restless, for upon the soft breeze I seem to hear a low groan accompanied by the shuffle of padded feet. Perhaps I have an over-active mind; perhaps not, for there is only one region of the world where I have heard that sound. It is in the very high mountains south of China's Gansu Corridor.

It is made by the turning of prayer wheels, hundreds of them, the smallest about a metre high, the largest three times that size. They follow the outside walls of a large monastery holding perhaps more than two thousand men and boys. The punishing glacial wind makes me shiver. I see them draw their vermilion cloaks tighter, raise their hoods and keep walking clockwise around the walls, turning each heavy prayer wheel as they go.

Against the incessant low chanting and the smell of yak butter lamps burning in the dark temples, I once heard a transcendent sound that gave me hope.

I had wandered the earth lanes of the monastery with a crude bamboo flute in my rucksack. Some little boys, in monk's habit and sandals, asked me to allow them to play it. Each made sounds that caused the others to laugh. This drew the attention of older monks. They did little better. By this time a crowd had gathered, and some had begun to sit down.

Another monk pushed his way forward to take his turn. He sat on a low wall, and immediately the flute began to call the surrounding wildness to join us in celebration.

It was at that moment that my Asian colleague, who had not joined me in the monastery but had climbed the mountainside which surrounded us in a natural amphitheatre, began to sing a melody of praise in his own language. His voice filled the air, and with it the sound of the flute found its completion. For just a few minutes it seemed that the surrounding creation echoed its harmony with the Creator and, in a way my words are unable to express, so did I. This was the sound that inspired hope.

Sometimes I have searched among those temples for men of my

own age with whom I could share my experience. I once asked a monk if his work attending the temple idols was his full-time occupation, or part-time.

"Oh no," he said, "this is not my full-time work. I am simply giving ... twenty-two years to it!"

The ambience of the dark night and the faint glow of the waves that wash out onto the beach are alive with welcoming sound and movement and places ... calling, calling. The Pearl River of purpose waits to carry my vessel. I think that my inner soil has experienced some preparation, and nature bears timeless record that miracles of growth always follow the plough.

BEYOND THE WELSH REVIVAL
- The Black Mountain -

A hundred years have draped over Wales since revival flames licked our mining communities and its warm afterglow healed our valleys, savaged by industrial greed.

Earth has claimed personal memory of these events. What remains are books based on letters and articles, sometimes by authors who may not have understood or visited the scenes.

Sadly we watch as a significant monument, weathered by time, slowly disappears under a sea of history ... or do we? There has to be a consequence to every event. Are we living in the day of that consequence now? Could the Welsh revivals themselves be a parable pointing to something even greater ... something waiting to be understood?

A Portrait of Chen
Chen's presence precedes his smile and outstretched welcoming hand. His words are few, as they often are in a man who is sure of what he believes. He can break silence without disturbing it. He speaks slowly and deliberately, as if each word is carefully selected. They seem to rise from a well within himself. He has the ability to hear wisdom in the voices of the very least of those who talk to him. Experience has taught him that divinity has many disguises.

His life, lived straight from the heart, gives him an enjoyable freedom that is quite infectious. Its simplicity is appealing, yet it hides the profound. With captivating style he is able to glide through troublesome issues. By the same token, he intuitively knows the direction of progress. It is often the language he *doesn't* use that is quite surprising.

He values the present moment and does not squander it on clichés. He has a transparency that does not use words to cover a hidden agenda. His language is crafted by his faith. 'Impossible' is not in his vocabulary, nor is 'hard 'or 'difficult' or 'problem' or 'can't do it because'. His descriptions of circumstances never crush his hearers, but enlighten and uplift and, like a stream full of stars, bring all things within reach.

He is in demand, but gives no sense of busy-ness. In fact his presence seems to create space. He has the ability to define the precise 'now' for which there is always adequate time. He unconsciously guides others away from the lairs of time's thieves.

He lives in unaffected innocence of his qualities. He has a generous capacity to receive other people which, I think, is a sign of true greatness. He speaks passionately of becoming a servant to forgotten people for whom he could live and die, yet he is altogether free from a self-righteous spirit. He considers his commitment to people to be his reasoned choice, and death to be the ultimate expression of his personal freedom. He carries no sense of brash loudness and control. His quiet strength accentuates 'differentness', which is neither aggressive nor condemning but is what others love. Young and old alike gladly apprentice themselves to him as he walks with them as a friend in the dignity of a person who has truly come home to himself.

He views heaven and earth as coming together in a man, and his spiritual perception has insight I have learned never to take for granted. It was this way now as we alighted from my car, which I had parked at the head of a valley among the Welsh mountains, within sight of the peak that we intended to climb.

By Way of the Hills

The valley greeted us with the pleasant sound of loneliness, broken only by the bleating of small mountain sheep. These had, for forgotten centuries, thrived on the wind-chiselled rock and the damp scantily-grassed slopes. They appeared like abandoned mariners in a sea of mist.

Ahead lay my most favoured of all south Wales's mountain peaks. Its sombre outline had earned it the name 'Black Mountain'.

The forbidding dark escarpment held for me a sense of mystery which had always invited me to explore further. On many occasions, over many years, it has become a personal sanctuary. Sheltering in the solitude of its summit, I have thought and prayed.

We pulled on our boots, gathered our rucksacks, and prepared to turn away from our last touch of modern convenience. Chen lovingly running his thumb over an age-yellowed book, slipped it into his rucksack pocket, and pulled the last zip.

I had seen him caress the pages of this book many times as he sat with it open, sometimes reading, sometimes staring at the sky. This much-loved biography is a reflection on Rees Howells, the master of the practice of intercessory prayer. Chen valued intercession, not as what he did but as what he was. I had noticed that the book had been open in his hands as we had wound our way along the narrow country roads, for we were now on the ground and under the sky where Rees Howells had learned his history-making prayer skills.

On the journey it was as if Chen was searching his heart for something from the distant past, perhaps visiting memories where his past days waited to be relived. I had no doubt he had made the connection, for now, among the songs of the mountain streams under the valley's own sky, he was speaking his thoughts to the wind so that they would scatter to where they were blown.

A valley always seems to have an intimate sky framed by the mountain's slash of dark paint. This ceiling, as it arches across the mountain rims, protects the valley's secrets – and this valley has many.

The sight of a small, dashing river barring our way brought Chen to silence as his eyes scanned the tumbling white water for a safe crossing point. He walked quickly to the bank and tested a boulder with his foot. To the wind he said, "We may be able to cross here."

His natural affinity with the land made me wonder if it may have been more of a request to the water: *May we cross here?*... He chose a route over the algae-covered rock slabs above a swirling pool of small mountain trout. I followed, and scrambled up the far peat bank.

The trail rose steeply. To our left another deep gully of cascading water thrashed its way to join the river we had just crossed. Its source lay somewhere in the mountain ahead.

Chen turned and, looking directly at me, his Chinese eyes almost closed in the strong sunlight said, "Rowland, do you think that, like this stream which flows from deep within the mountain, our vision flows directly from the mountain of the Welsh Revival?"

He took me by surprise, as he so often did. While I was still pondering whether he had asked me a question or had made a statement, he moved away and peered over a rock down into the gully. For a moment he listened to the wild energy of the water, and then continued up the hill with the confident stride of one who already knew the answer.

Unlike his abruptness, Chen's thought didn't surprise me. He was no one's man. He was well read, with a sensitivity finely honed by the stirring growth in the underground church in China's Hunan Province. He had come to our community in Wales, like so many others, in the understanding that new non-Western missionary movements are in the process of growing in countries that have had no experience of training and sending their own missionaries.

Chen is on a journey back to his roots. He is searching for an expression of the continuity of eternal purpose and, in particular, a point where he could pick up a baton laid down – for who knows how long – and begin to run his own race.

To be honest, I was very familiar with Chen's analogy of the mountain and the stream. I had listened to many from other nationalities whose thinking had evolved this way, and who had been drawn to Wales.

I realised how easy it would be to devalue his thoughts by an ill-judged response, so as I drew abreast of him I asked him if he would like to continue. He had no ready reply, but quietly pulled together the threads of the idea he was exploring. It was not a neat package, for he held many threads and they all led somewhere ... perhaps into the future.

With a soft voice and his distinctive Chinese accent framing the wisdom of one of earth's most ancient civilisations, Chen began.

"The 1904 Revival was a major historical event when perhaps a hundred thousand embraced faith. In keeping with previous

211

revivals, it lasted just a short time. But ... ," he hesitated; "all this is well known. Just for a moment, think. Could you imagine an event as powerful as the Welsh Revival that was not designed to produce a long-term consequence?"

"What should have happened?"

Surprised at my naivety, he replied, "The Revival was meant to have been followed by a missionary force travelling out of Wales and into a waiting world."

"Why didn't this happen?" I asked.

His reply, when it came, was hardly audible, and choked with emotion. "For many of them, their missionary dreams were shattered in the trenches of France. Twice in a century the world plunged into a war that was fought out in Europe. Two generations of young men flung themselves onto each other's steel. This was their inheritance ..."

His voice trailed off. These thoughts were not new to me. Hearing them voiced so passionately from mainland China, was.

At this point we were both glad to break off conversation and to direct our energy into the steady plod upward. The steep terrain was not the only reason that made me grateful for this lull, though I felt sure that Chen had more to say. My mind was swimming over years of events that had led me to form thoughts that were so close to what I was now hearing Chen say with such clarity.

For as long as I can remember I had believed in a God, but in a childish way. It had taken me nineteen years, and a baptism into a man's world of the flesh, blood and steel of a war in Asia, to realise that I had found faith in that God. For three years I had lived among Chinese, fought Chinese, been prayed for by Chinese. My resignation from the full-time Forces and release into the army reserve would, I thought, be a doorway out of Wales, to live in the Far East as a serving missionary rather than a serving soldier. My goal was clear, but painfully I learned that my route to it was not. In my naivety I had not realised that I needed to make an ascent of an inner Everest before engaging in the physical reality of the mountain called Mission.

During the following sixteen years the driving force of my

passion motivated me to a rigorous routine of work, study and evangelisation over an area that spread from the northern Shetland Isles to southern Italy. This helped to consolidate in me a prayer which consumed the final five years of this period. It was a simple one-line request: "Lord, give me your work to do!" – but one which had profound implications.

Over the next years, the unpretentious West Wales rugby town of Llanelli saw the fragments of my personal dream transfigure into young men and women who burned with the same passion. The flame had divided; I was no longer on my own. A new missionary movement had begun to grow. I struggled to come to terms with the implications of this.

Soon, not only were young men and women transplanting themselves among the Chinese, but also to the north, south, east and west where they were involved in aiding some of the most difficult areas of the world. During the ensuing years, hundreds more followed them. I had named the movement *Horizons* and within three years it had reached Australia, where it was nick-named *World Horizons* – the name by which it is known today.

My advancing years meant that the time frame in which I had to work was seriously decreasing, and the final stage of my personal dream still evaded me. I had mentally wrestled with the idea that very possibly the full value of humanity lay in the measure of how valuable we are to God, and that this can only be expressed as nations find their place in his purpose – and together we become that one great offering acceptable to him.

Having experienced an apprenticeship through founding one world movement, I now asked myself whether it would be possible for a Welshman to help found a new, non-Western indigenous movement, perhaps within a developing nation? Or even more than one movement simultaneously?

In moments when my faith was high, my feelings said, *Yes!*

So, in order to provide identity and structure to faith, a parenting organisation was born, and named ... *Nations*. This would at least attempt to provide a sympathetic climate in which the continuity of divine purpose could be explored, and hopefully experienced, through new peace-loving mission movements from Africa and Asia – perhaps fulfilling the dream and intercession of those who understood the Welsh Revival's intended purpose.

Through Ancient Wisdom

Lost in our thoughts, our time retreated like mist before a breeze. We found ourselves on the plateau above the the first rise, with the small lake Llyn y Fan Fawr gradually coming into view. Radiant in the sunlight, its wavelets danced to the embrace of the wind, and our spirits seemed to rise to meet its beauty.

Chen whispered, "Few eyes ever see this example of the Creator's art. Even though it is out of sight, he has not failed to complete each detail. It is perfect."

With reluctance I drew myself away, and led around the stony shore to the trail that went steeply up the wild escarpment towering over us.

Two hours later, and we were astride the summit ridge. We sat, our backs resting against the stone survival shelter, sandwiches and a water bottle passing between us. We listened to the silence, broken only by the low moan of the wind among the rocks. Our eyes drank in the grandeur of miles of green rolling hills, forests and lakes. Even the scar of the tarmac road was hidden by leaf-blooming hedges. The afternoon sun reflected dully from the sprinkled quarried-stone village communities. Way below our feet Llyn y Fan Fawr, in its deep jade setting, sped arrows of light back at the sun.

"The far horizon is like a future certainty," said Chen, thinking out loud. "It brings together sky and earth in token of the promise that heaven and earth will meet in divine harmony. Though for now," he continued slowly, "that ideal, like the horizon, retreats away from us at exactly the pace we reach out to it. This is hallowed ground, isn't it?" he continued, his eyes searching mine for confirmation.

I weighed the feeling behind his words.

"I used to come here often during the period of my five-year intensive prayer," I replied. "I felt my tears could fall where, before me, others' tears had already wet the ground. I have sometimes wondered if there was need for human eyes to weep for the sons of the Revival."

Often, over many years, I have walked alone among the trenches of Vimy Ridge and gazed across the fields of the Somme. The rows of crosses run out to the horizon in all directions, tortured earth blasted by shell and mine, the inheritance of every fallen soldier. *What of their dreams?* I wondered. *Where does dream go when life takes its flight?*

It was that then Chen said quietly, "Rowland, dreams are not lost. The One who gave them gathers them and allows a following generation to dream them again. Perhaps you will find that it is through people like myself, and hundreds of others from different nations, that their dreams will finally be realised and his purpose for the Revival will be fulfilled!"

I was right to believe that Chen had not fully unburdened himself, for he continued: "What if the ultimate purpose of the Revival is far greater than the event? Could it be for the sake of that purpose that he gave revival? What if the purpose, delayed for some generations, has begun to surface in time again? I know that we speak longingly of the event, but we need not let this mist the reality of now. Perhaps the opportunity to fulfil its purpose is with us again. Could the ancient wisdom of prophetic words also have some bearing on our time? – *The vision is for an appointed time. If it is delayed, wait for it, it will surely come.*

"When we think of the scale of the devastation of the wars, we can begin to judge the scale of the purpose which the ambitions of pride sought to defeat. What is more," holding back his words as if they were not meant to fall on wrong ears, "if we live out the purpose of the Revival, could its energy in a different form continue supporting this purpose?"

As I listened to Chen's words, some seemed to lodge in a deep recess within me. They were warm and friendly, but frightening. Most of all they were what I needed to hear. I had begun the day as the trainer, but was ending it as the trainee.

My silent prayer said, *O God, allow me to pick up the baton from where it has dropped. The cold earth did not swallow up the dreams of the fallen, for many had dreamed your dream, divided and shared between them. Now you are sharing your dream again among your Revival's grandchildren. Please, let us succeed!*

Time and eternity are separated by a thin veil, and when this becomes translucent, time's significance changes. The sun was now well past its zenith and eager to warm the far side of the western horizon. With playful artistic touch, it had begun its evening pageant. The bare rocks of the Black Mountain summit were now clothed in a red glow, and in constantly changing deep shadows. It was that magical moment of sunset when the stones take on comical shapes and seem to come alive. This was another of the mountain's secrets which it had held for a finale.

Meanwhile, Chen was nowhere to be seen. It was the sound of singing that eventually led me to where I could see his outline at the highest point of the summit. His head and hands were raised to the air, enjoying the evening sky. He was quietly singing a hymn of praise in Mandarin, his own heart language.

Then, with an outstretched arm pointing directly to the west, I heard him say: "Hundreds and hundreds."

He then turned north, east, and finally south, making the same pronouncement: "Hundreds and hundreds."

With his head bowed, he stood motionless for some moments before making his way towards me. As we walked back to the shelter to collect our rucksacks he said, "There are more than one billion people in every direction I faced, and I have commissioned hundreds of missionaries to go there." He paused, and then continued: "All of them grandchildren of the Welsh Revival."

He shouldered his rucksack and, before beginning the descent, took a last look over the escarpment at the valley and rolling hills. The dark hand of the summit's shadow was now pointing to where sky and earth met.

He turned to me and said, "Before our sun sets, we too will reach the horizon farthest out."

On our journey back I could not help but notice the air of confidence about his gait, the signature of one who had completed what he had set out to do.

The warm closeness of the summer's evening made our descent a delight, and we were soon back at the river crossing and the car. Instinctively we both glanced up at the mountain, now fully living up to its name, black and forbidding, but with the last rays of daylight still playing softly along its summit ridge.

Without him realising it, Chen's intimate conversation had confirmed in me a growing belief. Within the reality of eternal purpose there are no new things, just the continuation of the original perfect plan that re-emerges into time in different ages and places. This purpose is not the sole possession of the West, but for all nation-families. It is as if by this means God receives the full return on his investment into people. Had the short event of the Welsh Revival fulfilled its purpose, it may have been the wind in the sail that could have carried thousands from many nations to the final frontiers. However, this dream has died with passing generations and, like a faded photograph, can no longer be easily interpreted.

But this is not the end of the story. Eternal purpose cannot die – it can only be suspended – and is still the highway and inheritance it is meant to be, though the event of the Revival is beyond living memory.

Our evenings and nights in Creation's order guarantee that we awake to a morning of new creative activity. Sunrise has already begun in the east. Perhaps purpose is once again surfacing in time, and many thousands from developing nations are beginning to find their place within its flow. Many of these are passing through our little town in West Wales, almost back at the point where the Revival visibly began. Could it be that a door stands open, and the dream for hundreds of new missionaries from every conceivable ethnic background is being dreamed again?

"I love the mountains," said Chen. "The sky is so wide up there. From there I could see the horizon furthest out."

I reversed the car onto the road, and headed in the direction of Llanelli.

To the Horizon Furthest Out
My thoughts were aligning in a comfortable flow and I was fully

enjoying giving my lecture, when a shiver of irritation disturbed me. A thin, distant voice was calling my name.

"Rowland," said the insistent voice; then, in softer tones: "Where is Chen now, can we meet him?"

Two worlds collided, and for moments I stood trapped between them. I fumbled helplessly for the words to respond, but my mind was reluctant to cooperate.

"Chen?" I stammered, my confusion obvious to the group of young men and women who were seated around me. "Chen ... er ... I think he is in China now, perhaps in the north-west province of Xinjiang among the towns along the ancient Silk Road."

"When did you see him last?"

I now realised the source of the questions, as the group turned to me as one, waiting for my answer.

"I met him first about twenty years ago, I think, but I have worked with him ever since then. Maybe ... even today."

That prompted an immediate response from a girl student who looked more Chinese than Korean, which was the nationality of the group.

"Rowland, I don't understand. Why can't we meet him then?"

"Because ... er . . ." I struggled.

Two realities were confused. I was unsure how to unscramble them.

"Chen is a figment of my imagination. Within my dream he symbolises my ideal missionary."

The expression of puzzlement in the looks of my hearers relaxed, and the smiles that began to play around their eyes register the beginning of understanding.

"This afternoon," I continued, "I had planned a talk on anthropology. Instead, you entered my personal dream, and met Chen. When my mind pieces together what my heart understands about the continuation of divine purpose through Wales and its Celtic people, I create Chen in the mystery of my imagination. So he is in Xinjiang Province, perhaps disguised as a Korean. He is also in many other parts of the world, and with a different nationality. He represents those who have dreams, and are determined to see them fulfilled. We must never damage another's dream, for dream holds the future – for them, and for us.

"Dream and vision are how the inner eyes view a promise. Action adds flesh and bone. Divine promise has eternal significance; dream guides to the point where it is realised. I think that the flow of divine purpose in Wales has always been destined for the rest of the world. Our many revivals have been the means of reaching this ultimate goal. Some of the sparks escaped the devastation of the wars and were fanned into flame, at least in Korea, North-east India, the USA, North-east China, Europe, South Africa and, through these countries, who knows where else?

"You are the grandchildren of Wales. You come from many nations. You are in the process of finding your place in this continuity of purpose. Behind you is the heritage of revival. Waiting ahead of you, the greater purpose for which the Revival was given – a destiny on the far frontiers of our world.

"So, dream on. It is a holy dream. Run as far as your dream takes you ... but be prepared to make the most surprising discovery of all.

"Our personal dreams are intricately woven into the dreams of others, so it is by enabling the dreams of others to be fulfilled that our own dreams are realised.

"So the parable of Chen opens a window to where the hidden truth of dream waits to be explored."

With one voice my Korean colleagues said, "Yes!" – and began to sing softly. Within the sound I think I overheard Chen saying, *Hundreds and hundreds, from the ancient land of Shen Zhou to the horizon furthest out.*

> *In the realm of eternal purpose*
> *there are no new things*
> *For the original perfect intention continues*
> *and re-emerges into time in different ages*
> *and at different places.*

ECHOES FROM A WIDE SEA
- Aelwyd -

Though their words hover silently in my space,
Wil and Dan
are no longer with me,
but then they are!
In some way that I do not understand, out of their essential lives
they have both passed some transfigured elements into me.
So too has it been with Don from the Hebrides,
Christian from Zimbabwe,
George from America and Jérima from Central Africa's rainforest.
All men I have greatly admired.

As age begins to settle its accounts
some friendships end in the finality of silence.
We will never crew together again
but they will always be part
of who I am.
When flames divide there is always more,
nothing diminishes.
Few things really die.
They are sown and left in trust to grow in another's soil.

I long to be able to craft words that carry the sounds
that unveil truth and lead to where it can be found.
Yet if this already lies within another's work,
I trust that faithfulness will clothe my interpretation
of their dreams.
I have a passion to be no more than who I am,

true to my life alone.
Though I have to admit
that person may be a stranger to me.

For there are few frontiers to life and I am in a state of change,
like the cloud that drifts across the sinking sun
constantly changing its form through a hundred different images,
yet just one in substance.
If I, or another, am able to describe myself,
or if my behaviour can be predicted
then I have failed.
I am no more than a passenger on my own ship,
looking back at the wake and living again the story
of what has been.

Life at its core has a beautiful thought.
From whatever race we trace our ancestry,
from the dawn of birth we accompany each other
on a journey into sunset.
The pace at which we travel does not alter.
Age simply refers to our position in the cavalcade.
I am near the front, a position I am beginning to enjoy.
Mature years no longer hold the nightmare of the unknown,
rather my interest in the purpose of life's pageant increases daily.

The prospect of just being here
at the dawn
and day of each new moment of time
fills me with expectation of joy.
This has nothing to do with status,
nor what I own,
nor where I happen to be.
Whether dreaming on the wooden bench at the shore
of Llanelli's seagulled sea
or in the empty remoteness of a Chinese village
with a dog called 'Mouth',
the joy of being can over-arch the pain of birth and death.

The ancient Chinese character, *Tun,*
that represents
a new beginning,
has its tiny shoot above the surface stemming from the
mighty root below the soil.
Life is endless, whether embodied or disembodied
or even, as Christian doctrine implies, in resurrection form.

Nothing is lost.
Even the sacred, where it has been profaned, is restored.
I am excited; the world is small and life is everywhere.

I see a veil of uncertainty drift across your eyes.
I wonder, you say, if you could be prey to a subtle self-deception
by shaping an identity by which you choose to be known,
yet you may have no intention of fulfilling these ideals,
so will never need to pay the price of succeeding.
You raise your eyes and look for my response.

I know that you have proved that saintly wisdom
may not be the companion of silver hair.
Self-gratifying passion can deceive into believing
that all ideas are good,
like Stalin's rotting factories that tombstone Central Asia's plains.
My ideas too, like a celebration of what was not born of wisdom,
have sounded among the worst,
tarnished mirrors that have reflected so little light.

So now I have no wish to be a servant to the power of good idea.
I would prefer to risk my life to the cloud of unknowing,
where the enquiry of faith alone can be heard.

Are you thinking seriously about those unpredictable moments, you ask,
when sadness invades your day?
For the power which provides the future with a key
lies hidden in our difficulties.

I turn my eyes away.
I know, I say, but often fail to fully understand.
I know the pain of disappointment's ugly wound
when expectations lie in ruins;
of friends I have lost in smoking fiery trails;
of those whose lives have ebbed away too soon,
for whom I have not ceased to grieve;
another whose murderers are yet to be found;
yet another for whom prison has leached away four years of life,
while his most bitter drink he has yet to taste.
For the hundred friends, who would have welcomed his release,
now sleep in burnt and tortured earth,
while many more who fled their village flames
are lost among Darfur's refugees.
I too have shared their sufferings,
in fever's grip and with weakening breath.
"Not yet," I said to death, "not yet."
I know, but still I find it hard to understand.

The dancing figure relentlessly marches against
the broken flowers,
and the machete and gun make the news.
The Poet shares the grief of this troubled house
and the embattled star of promise waits ...
yet strangely, my thoughts begin to warm
as I reflect on those whose days have ended so savagely.
For from their darkest hours, life is rising.
Their shadows bring their finest features into boldest relief
and their bravery adds its quality to the life I am proud to live.
With them I will take my place
so that my clay might bear the imprint of their seal.

For I will walk the poem's lines
with those whose lives have seeded earth with trees of life
and let faith overcome my need to understand.
Then, unveiled, my eyes will see the greatest miracle of all,
that I, a mere man of clay,

a broken echo of all that could be,
have found that ...
my sea is wide.

EPILOGUE
- That Final Place -

What I have written has only the accuracy of one man's perspective, so where detail is blurred I trust that the underlying truth these events are meant to convey will be more clearly seen. Remember the images that emerge from the dark among old China's streets. Seeing less is sometimes more, when less means the loss of confusing detail. Progress is made by each one receiving what we need to know, and not by everything that there is to know.

The greatest teacher of all time taught by turning the ordinary into parable. His words were the signposts to where truth could be found. He also said that the wind blows without us knowing its source or destination but, as it passes, it offers a world of sensation that is ours to explore. But the sail hangs slack when there is no wind. When the sail fills, it is the wind that drives the ship.

So it could be that the height of spiritual development is to be ordinary, and perhaps the ordinary self is the extra-ordinary self. Living in the value of the ordinary is the axis around which life is meant to revolve.

I know now where my life will continue to find its meaning. For though time has eaten away my seventy years, my new career has begun. I have no project orientation, no detailed plan as to how it will work out, just the deep assurance that it will. For I can weigh all this against the unfathomable deep silence within myself, a silence that is undisturbed by the presence of my dream. I too, like yourself, am among those to whom he said, *Old men shall dream dreams.* Dreams, and the words that accompany them, are not the future, but the core around which our personal futures can be built.

I am standing at a border post between Morocco and Algeria. It is well south into the Sahara region of north Africa. Working in North African countries has taught me that, as a Westerner, I am sometimes out of favour. The level of aggression is high, this is an extremely remote place and, by their reckoning, I am 'fair game.'

I have a Land Rover and a small team, and we have already been asked to wait some days. I think it is for the guards' amusement that we have been made to line up, our rucksacks emptied and our possessions searched piece by piece. Tensions have been heightened between Morocco and Algeria over the Western Sahara, so there is no traffic passing. The soldiers are bored. They decide that we can take no Moroccan currency into Algeria, on pain of arrest. We suspected this, so we have little. Still, eager hands reach out for it.

Their officer paces back and forth, barking orders. He points at the small book among my possessions. He snatches it from my hands, opens it at random and stares at a page. For the first time he looks at me squarely and speaks in immaculate English. We realise that from the beginning he has understood the conversation between ourselves. Closing the book and handing it back, he surprises us by giving the order to allow us through.

So from this barren crossing, amid a burial ground of rusting oil drums, barbed wire, wooden shacks and hope; from the dispirited soldiers and the flies; from a landscape of deceptive realities, of burning, shifting endless Sahara dunes, from lakes that do not exist; from a romance of desolation with beauty, I let the army officer speak again the quotation he read from my ragged Bible – which brought about his change of heart.

And the glory of the Lord shall fill the earth
as the waters cover the sea.

For in the final place
is God.
During this year of proving His shalom,
and through the
many people who have
shared this journey with me,
I have walked and talked with Him.

Sir Francis Drake's Prayer

Francis Drake was England's most famous sailor and explorer. He sailed around the world in 'The Golden Hind' in 1580 and led the outnumbered British Navy to defeat the Spanish Armada in 1588. This prayer was found in his ship's diary, written on the eve of one of his great adventures:

Disturb us, Lord, when
We are too well pleased with ourselves,
When our dreams have come true
Because we have dreamed too little,
When we arrived safely
Because we sailed too close to the shore.

Disturb us, Lord, when
With the abundance of things we possess
We have lost our thirst
For the waters of life;
Having fallen in love with life,
We have ceased to dream of eternity
And in our efforts to build a new earth,
We have allowed our vision
Of the new Heaven to dim.

Disturb us, Lord, to dare more boldly,
To venture on wider seas
Where storms will show your mastery;
Where losing sight of land,
We shall find the stars.
We ask You to push back
The horizons of our hopes;
And to push into the future
In strength, courage, hope, and love.

This we ask in the Name of our Captain
Who is Jesus Christ.

GLOSSARY

a bydd eich hynafgwyr yn gweld breuddwydion	and your old men shall dream dreams
a city that descends ...	Revelation 21:2
aelwyd	the centre or heart of home, the place where you belong, the hearth
agreement	Hebrew for this is covenant, a strong word implying lifelong commitment and the complete giving of oneself to another.
Alopen	First recorded Christian missionary to reach China during the Tang Dynasty. He was an envoy of the Assyrian church of the East, commonly known as the Nestorian church.
And the glory of the Lord ... waters cover the sea	Habakkuk 2:14
As greed by biblical interpretation is idolatry	Colossians 3:5
bach	little one (term of endearment)
Berber	Ethnic group indigenous to Northwest Africa
Black Mountain	A wild mountain in South Wales
Bon	Himalayan religion pre-dating Buddhism
Bride on the Threshold of Time	Two brides appear in the Bible. One is in Genesis in the Garden of Eden on the threshold of the beginning of time, the other in Revelation at the close of time on the threshold of eternity.
bychan	boy (term of endearment)
Chang-an	An ancient Chinese capital of many dynasties meaning 'Perpetual Peace'. Now known as Xi'an meaning 'Western Peace'.
Clasemont	Suburb of Swansea, now covered by the DVLA offices
Cofia	remember

Come my darling ...	Song of Songs 2:10
Confucian	Confucian belief focuses primarily on non-religious ethics
Desert Fathers	Christian Hermits who lived mainly in the Egyptian desert from the beginning of the third century.
Dewch mewn	come in
Disgwylfan	High place, viewpoint, where vision is unrestricted and a place of waiting expectantly
Dreamtime	Aboriginal explanation of the origins of the culture, the land and its people
dy freuddwyd di yw hi	it is your dream
El Shaddai	Almighty God (Hebrew)
fan hyn	here or this place
Feng Shui	Ancient Chinese practice of placement and arrangement of space to achieve harmony with the environment.
food for vultures	Job 15:23
Gansu Corridor	Sometimes known Hexi Corridor. Part of the Silk Road running northwest from the bank of the Yellow River.
Great Wall	Series of stone and earthen fortifications in China built, rebuilt, and maintained between the 5th century BC and the 16th century to protect the northern borders of the Chinese Empire during the rule of successive dynasties. Several walls, referred to as the Great Wall of China, were built. The current wall was built during the Ming Dynasty.
Gwir dy eiriau	your words are true
Hawdd cynnau tân ar hen aelwyd	lighting a fire in an old hearth is easy (Welsh proverb, literal translation)
he now called very good	Genesis 1:31

Hell money	An afterlife monetary paper offering used in traditional Chinese ancestor worship, that can be printed in the style of western or Chinese paper bank notes.
hiraeth	Longing for home
Hui	Islamic Chinese minority group
imprint of their seal	Job 38:14
in her preparation	Revelation 19:7
"It is finished"	Last words of Jesus on the Cross – John 19:30
Last Adam	Jesus Christ
Lazarus	Luke 6:20
Llangyfelach	Village outside Swansea
Loughor	River Loughor located between the Gower Peninsular and Carmarthenshire, South Wales
Lu Xun	Major Chinese writer of the 20ᵗʰ century
'machgen annwyl i	my dear boy (term of endearment)
'machgen i	my boy (term of endearment)
Mahayana	Mahayana Buddhism is not a single group but a collection of Buddhist traditions: Zen Buddhism, Pure Land Buddhism, and Tibetan Buddhism are all forms of Mahayana Buddhism.
Mao Tse-Tung	Leader of the People's Republic of China from its establishment in 1949 until his death in 1976.
oed yr addewid	Age of promise
Old men shall dream dreams	Joel 2:28 & Acts2:17
pa boen?	what pain?
Poem	A creation, a product, workmanship: For we are God's workmanship (Greek 'poiema' = poem) Ephesians 2:10
Poet	Maker, Creator

PSB	Public Security Bureau: refers to government offices that handle such things as policing, public security and social order
Rees Howells	Founded the Bible College of Wales in Swansea, a centre of nearly a century of intercessory prayer
Rho eiriau iddynt	put words to them
Salaam Alaikum	Peace to you. A traditional greeting among Muslims
Sangke	bright yellow flower found in the Tibetan grasslands
Sanskrit	Indo-European classical language of the Indian sub-continent . A liturgical language of Hinduism, Buddhism, Sikhism and Jainism and one of the 23 official languages of India.
SARS	Severe, acute respiratory syndrome: outbreak in Asia and other parts of the world in April 2003
Shalom	The full good intention of God towards people
Shang Di	Lord of Heaven, Supreme God in the original religious system of the Han Chinese people
Shang di bao you ni	May Shang Di, the Lord of Heaven and Earth bless you.
Shen Zhou	Land of God. For five thousand years the Chinese have called their native land Shen Zhou. Strong traditional and archaeological evidence suggests the early Chinese were devoted to one heavenly God.
Silk Road	The Silk Road is a phrase coined in the late 19th century to cover a network of trading routes through which two great empires – the Roman and the Chinese – were able to trade with each other. The Chinese knew of a country called Li Kun, which historians believe was Rome, while the Romans knew of Seres, the Kingdom of Silk.
Smokey Mountain	A large inhabited rubbish dump in Manila

stone ... field	Job 5:23
Syrian General	Naaman who was cured of his leprosy by dipping himself seven times in the River Jordan according to the instructions of the word of Elisha, the Prophet. 2 Kings 5
Taklamakan	World's largest sand-only desert in Western China. Its meaning: 'If you go in, you won't come out'
The vision is for an appointed time ...	Habakkuk 2:3
Tienshan	Mountain range in Western China
Tinopolis	Llanelli's nickname in the 19th Century because of a thriving tinplate industry
To the place from where the streams come, they will return.	Ecclesiastes 1:7
Tsampa	Tibetan staple food consisting roasted flour, usually barley.
tun	Chinese character for "new beginnings"
Uyghur	Minority group in Western China and Central Asia
Warring States	Covers the period from some time in the 5th century BC to the unification of China by the Qin Dynasty in 221BC
Wild Goose	In Celtic tradition the Holy Spirit is represented as a wild goose
with trees of life	Genesis 2 & Revelation 22
Yn y dechreuad roedd y ... Freuddwyd	In the beginning was the ... Dream
Yurt	Tibetan tent

The Author, Rowland Evans
Photograph courtesy of Maria Jin, *New Wine Magazine*

45 Minutes in China, by Rowland Evans
Available directly from Nations Trust, International Centre,
Glanmor Road, Llanelli, Carmarthenshire, SA15 2LU, UK.
£4.00 per copy, including post and packing, to UK addresses.

Produced by

SUNPENNY PUBLISHING
www.sunpenny.com
A Christian-based publishing house

IMPRINTS OF SUNPENNY PUBLISHING INCLUDE:

ROSE & CROWN BOOKS
Inspirational Romance
www.roseandcrownbooks.com

SUNBERRY BOOKS
Author Services
www.sunberrybooks.com

BOATHOOKS BOOKS
Sailing and Boating
www.boathooksbooks.co.uk